Studies in the Legal History of the South

EDITED BY PAUL FINKELMAN AND TIMOTHY S. HUEBNER

This series explores the ways in which law has affected the development of the southern United States and in turn the ways the history of the South has affected the development of American law. Volumes in the series focus on a specific aspect of the law, such as slave law or civil rights legislation, or on a broader topic of historical significance to the development of the legal system in the region, such as issues of constitutional history and of law and society, comparative analyses with other legal systems, and biographical studies of influential southern jurists and lawyers.

Gender and the Jubilee

Gender and the Jubilee

Black Freedom and the
Reconstruction of Citizenship
in Civil War Missouri

SHARON ROMEO

The University of Georgia Press
Athens

© 2016 by the University of Georgia Press
Athens, Georgia 30602
www.ugapress.org
All rights reserved
Set in Minion Pro by Graphic Composition, Inc.
Printed and bound by Thomson-Shore
The paper in this book meets the guidelines for
permanence and durability of the Committee on
Production Guidelines for Book Longevity of the
Council on Library Resources.
Most University of Georgia Press titles are
available from popular e-book vendors.

Printed in the United States of America
19 18 17 16 15 C 5 4 3 2 1

Library of Congress Cataloging-in-Publication Data

Romeo, Sharon.
    Gender and the Jubilee : Black freedom and the reconstruction of citizenship in Civil War
Missouri / Sharon Romeo.
        pages cm. — (Studies in the legal history of the South)
        Includes bibliographical references and index.
    ISBN 978-0-8203-4801-8 (hardcover : alkaline paper) — ISBN 978-0-8203-4804-9 (ebook)
    1. African American women—Civil rights—Missouri—History—19th century. 2. Slaves—Civil
rights—Missouri—History—19th century. 3. Citizenship—Missouri—History—19th century.
4. African American women—Legal status, laws, etc.—Missouri—History—19th century.
5. United States Army—History—Civil War, 1861–1865. 6. Civil-military relations—Missouri—
History—19th century. 7. Missouri—History—Civil War, 1861–1865—African Americans.
8. United States—History—Civil War, 1861–1865—African Americans. 9. Missouri—History—
Civil War, 1861–1865—Law and legislation. 10. United States—History—Civil War, 1861–1865—
Law and legislation. I. Title.
    E185.93.M7R65 2016
    305.48'896073077809034—dc23

                                                                          2015008712

For Brian, for everything

"It must be now that the Kingdom's coming, the year of Jubilee."
—James Thomas, *From Tennessee Slave to St. Louis
Entrepreneur: The Autobiography of James Thomas*

Contents

Acknowledgments

FEW TASKS ARE MORE overwhelming than acknowledging my debts to the many people who contributed to the completion of this project. At the University of Iowa, where this project began, I had the great luck to be taught by extraordinary scholars. The invaluable mentoring of Leslie Schwalm and Linda Kerber deeply influenced my scholarly interests. I thank them for their continued guidance and support. Catherine Komisaruk, Laura Rigal, Allen Steinberg, and Deborah Whalen all read various incarnations of this work and provided valuable feedback and insights. Other faculty who were generous with their time and support included Jane Desmond, Virginia Dominguez, Johanna Schoen, Isaac West, and the late Ken Cmiel. I thank Isaac for some timely discussions about the nature of citizenship and for his generosity in allowing me early access to his recent monograph. During one lovely Iowa summer, Ken Cmiel volunteered to run a fascinating tutorial session on cultural studies with Russ Peterson and me. The fact that Ken would go out of his way during his time off to review cultural theory with two graduate students reflects on his dedication as a scholar and a teacher.

My friends and colleagues at Iowa created a warm and invigorating atmosphere. I am particularly thankful for Michelle Armstrong-Partida, Caroline Campbell, Christy Clark-Pujara, Karissa Haugeberg, Mike Innis-Jiménez, Angela Miller Keysor, Junko Kobayashi, Heather Kopelson, Sharon Lake, Jennifer McGovern, Megan Kate Nelson, Aminta Perez, Russ Peterson, Yvonne Pitts, Sara Shreve, Sue Stanfield, Charissa Threat, Meagan Threlkeld, George Toth, and Matt Weiss. Our community has continued in our postgraduate years, and I fondly remember our writing groups and meetings at coffee shops. The late Jacob Hall was a wonderful colleague and writing companion in Iowa City. Kristen Anderson took the time to host me in St. Louis, and John McKerley, who has been generous with his time and insight over the years, deserves extra gratitude for reading the complete manuscript and for kindly sharing valuable primary research.

Similarly, my time and work in Edmonton have been buoyed by warm friends in a cold environment. Donica Belisle, Siobhan Byrne, Jonathan Cohn, Bob Cole, Liz Czach, Deborah Eerkes, Ashley Esary, Jaymie Heileman, Jocelyn Hendrickson, Adam Kemezis, Ken Mah, Ken Mouré, James Muir, Sara Norquay, Dennis Sweeney, and many others have made adjusting to a new city, a new country, and a new institution much easier than it could have been. Jaimie Baron provided invaluable friendship and advice about the manuscript. Susan Smith welcomed me, gave me invaluable advice, and enriched my experience at the University of Alberta. Finally, I also thank Jennifer Vining, who has listened to me and helped me without fail for the past two years.

Over the years, I have had the good fortune to cultivate a wonderful group of colleagues, and each of them provided input into the final form of this manuscript. In particular, I acknowledge Diane Mutti Burke and especially Laurie Mercier, who read revisions of the first chapter and provided cheer and encouragement in the last stages of writing this book. The following scholars also provided generous and thoughtful commentary at conferences and other venues: Nancy Bercaw, Diane Mutti Burke, Nikki Taylor, and LeeAnn Whites. Other fellow panelists and conference companions include Brandi Brimmer, Christy Clark-Pujara, Amrita Chakrabarti Myers, Yvonne Pitts, Sue Stanfield, and Charissa Threat.

The Civil War Cities conference, held in the unlikely locations of Calgary and Banff, Canada, provided me with another chance to expose this material to an amazing collection of scholars who offered critiques from many different angles. In particular, I thank the organizers, Frank Towers and Andrew Slap, for providing not only such an opportunity but also timely, patient, and incisive feedback. The comments and suggestions of Mary DeCredico, J. Matthew Gallman, William A. Link, and Richard Reid were exceptional and much appreciated.

This project has also benefited from assistance from a multitude of institutions. I am grateful to the American Historical Association for the Littleton-Griswold research grant, which provided support for one of my many trips to St. Louis. The Missouri History Museum, at the time known as the Missouri Historical Society, also provided a research grant that allowed me to make extensive use of their collections. The University of Iowa provided the Seashore-Ballard dissertation fellowship year and vital research and conference travel assistance. The University of Alberta and the now-closed Alberta Institute for American Studies granted additional conference and research travel support. In addition, the University of Alberta has purchased crucial microfilm resources from archives in Missouri. And finally, Robert Cole at the University of Alberta Libraries has provided superior support by acquiring many books and helping me find additional resources. His time and generosity—and his warmth as a human being—enabled me to survive my first year in Edmonton.

This project also required many hours in archives in both Missouri and Washington, D.C., where I received support from more archivists than I can mention. I must, however, highlight the extraordinary generosity of Mike Everman and his wife, Diane, which included showing my husband and me where to get the best frozen custard in St. Louis. Mike and the archivists at the St. Louis Circuit Court Historical Records Project are a tremendous resource for scholars, students, and lay researchers. The documents from the St. Louis Freedom Suits, preserved and digitized by this amazing team, promise to keep historians busy for many decades. I must also thank Steven F. Miller and Leslie S. Rowland at the Freedmen and Southern Society Project, who provided me with assistance navigating their own impressive document collection. I also thank John McKerley for pointing me to specific items that he found during his time at the project.

Finally, my immense thanks go to Noralee Finkel and Mary Farmer-Kaiser for their early reading of my chapters and for their invaluable suggestions. I similarly thank the two anonymous readers of the manuscript, whose insights and suggestions have made this a far better book. At the University of Georgia Press, Nancy Grayson encouraged me to submit my proposal and suggested it for a legal history series. Walter Biggins has been reassuring, gracious, and supportive as he has ushered this manuscript through the various stages of publication. Beth Snead and Mick Gusinde-Duffy answered the many questions of the novice author and helped propel the project forward. I thank Paul Finkelman and Timothy Huebner for their support and advice and for accepting the manuscript in the Studies in the Legal History of the South series.

I could not have researched and written this book without the unending love and support of my family, close and extended. My parents, Nick and Mary Romeo, enthusiastically supported my education and liberally purchased the books that fed my voracious reading appetite. My late father helped me develop a love for history at a young age, and he indulged me as a child with a gift of the complete series of history books by Will Durant. His broad love of the past, commitment to social justice, critiques of inequalities, and optimistic futurism shaped my outlook in ways I am still realizing. My mother and my sister, Elisa, have supported me in all stages of this project, particularly during the final push. Bob and Marcia Almquist also gave me great emotional support. My deepest gratitude goes to Brian Almquist, who has been with me every step of the way since we met as undergraduates at The Evergreen State College, including journeys to archives and to our new home in Canada. He has read every word of the manuscript, and I could not have completed this book without him. I am very lucky to be the beneficiary of his love, time, and companionship.

Gender and Jubilee

Introduction

IN 1862, CATHERINE MCNEIL, a twelve-year-old African American girl, was kidnapped by a St. Louis couple who wanted her for their own use. The St. Louis couple sought to re-create labor conditions similar to slavery, while Catherine's mother, Charlotte McNeil, struggled to claim custody of her child. This kidnapping and its resolution demonstrate a struggle for different visions of the nation and citizenship. This struggle was fought literally over the body of Catherine McNeil. The transition from slavery to freedom was, most of all, a process of enslaved people reclaiming their own bodies.

Both Catherine and her mother had lived as slaves in Dent County, Missouri. Their journey to freedom began when they fled to a Union encampment at the town of Rolla. Charlotte McNeil found work as a laundress for Union soldiers, while Catherine labored as a nurse for the infant child of the Robbins family.[1]

After two months, Dr. and Mrs. Robbins prepared to travel home to St. Louis. The couple wished to retain Catherine's services and convinced the military commander of the post at Rolla to prevail on Charlotte McNeil to release her child into their custody, who agreed after receiving assurances that Catherine would be returned whenever her mother wished. Catherine left Rolla with the Robbinses, but when Charlotte sought to reclaim her child, Mrs. Robbins refused to release Catherine.[2]

In Union-occupied St. Louis, Charlotte McNeil sought out the military police and described the circumstances of her daughter's capture.[3] After McNeil made her statement, an officer was dispatched to investigate the situation. The officer interviewed Catherine McNeil at the Robbins residence and asked the child where she would prefer to live. Catherine replied that

1

she feared she would never again see her mother and wished to be returned to her custody.[4]

By requesting military assistance, Charlotte McNeil inserted herself into a system of justice and redress that was organized and enforced by the U.S. Army. McNeil performed political work when she brought her complaint before a Union officer. The captivity of formerly enslaved children was not necessarily a military concern, but McNeil made it so. She and many other formerly enslaved women brought petitions and complaints before Union officials as part of their pursuit of justice.[5]

Enslaved women insisted that the abuses and inequalities perpetuated by the institution of slavery were not just a domestic or state concern. By transforming domestic and civil complaints into military matters, Charlotte McNeil and women like her justified the insertion of federal power into the administration of race relations. Their actions established a precedent for the federal government to protect the principle of equality under the law when the states would not. This early use of military power preceded the postwar adjudication of freedpeople's petitions in the Freedmen's Bureau.[6]

McNeil and other petitioners applied great creativity in their use of the military justice system for "civil" concerns. African American women entered this legal system as petitioners and claimed specific rights, including the right to paid labor, the right to state protection from bodily assault, and the right to custody of their children. Freedwomen such as McNeil who claimed custody of their own children threatened the political ideology of the slaveholding class. Men who possessed whiteness, manhood, and mastery held all political and civil rights in a slaveholding republic.[7] McNeil challenged this political ideology by asserting her own definition of citizenship informed by her experience as an enslaved woman.

*   *   *

In Missouri, Reconstruction arguably began in 1861. Under President Abraham Lincoln's authority, the U.S. Army received permission in April 1861 to establish martial law if necessary to restore order, and martial law was subsequently declared the following August.[8] After the secessionist governor fled the state capital in June 1861, a state constitutional convention, run by Unionists, elected loyalist Hamilton R. Gamble as provisional governor, a choice that Lincoln quickly recognized.[9] In Missouri and other border states, this process of employing military power to overrule state authority and to ensure the presence of a Union-friendly government served as a prelude to Reconstruction in the seceded states.[10]

St. Louis, a border city located in a slave state, provides a specific theater in which to analyze the wartime process of emancipation and the struggle for civic recognition.[11] As borderlands, both Missouri and St. Louis experienced a rupture in the nation-state as two national entities fought for control. The Confederates and the Federals fought this battle on multiple terrains, including the military, political, social, and cultural.

Geographically situated at a juncture between north and south, St. Louis was a significant port on the Mississippi River and was home to Confederates, immigrants, enslaved people, and Union soldiers. To be a slave owner in St. Louis was a signifier of cultural and social status, but the years leading up to the war had seen the arrival of many merchant-class New Englanders.[12]

Martial law meant that civilians suspected of secessionist activity faced arrest and trial, and Missouri had the greatest number of civilian arrests among all of the Union slave states.[13] African American women, enslaved and free, informed on disloyal white citizens, subjecting elite members of society to military justice and imprisonment. This turn of events allowed specific legal, social, and cultural work to take place around the identifier of "the citizen." Both enslaved and free women used patriotism as a strategy to undermine the institution of slavery. In an articulation of civic identity, black women asserted their loyalty to the United States and affinity with President Lincoln as evidence of their right to national inclusion.[14]

African Americans had been ill-treated by the legal system and the structures of white authority. Slave patrols, police, sheriffs, judges—all of these elements of state authority presented constant threats to the African American population. African Americans in Missouri were regularly arrested and imprisoned as suspected fugitive slaves. Slavery remained legal in the city of St. Louis until January 1865, and slave owners continued to recapture fugitive people throughout this period.

In light of their past treatment by the structures of state authority, it is noteworthy that African American women were willing to engage with precisely those structures. These women chose to use the apparatus of the Union Army and the strategy of claiming national inclusion to maneuver for a better life and to construct a civic existence.

* * *

The process of slave emancipation took a gendered path at a number of key points during the Civil War.[15] Enslaved people ran to Union lines in a bid for freedom, but the military responded differently to escapees based on their gender.[16] Union officers tended to view women as unfit for military labor and were more disposed to admit fugitive men into camps. Mothers with children were particularly unwelcome in camps and regiments on the march. Enslaved men were more likely to keep up with Union troops, and they were not as likely as women to be burdened with caring for children.

But African American women acquired another route to freedom with the July 1862 passage of the Second Confiscation Act.[17] This legislation allowed the Union military to confiscate the slave property of masters engaged in disloyal activities. When enslaved women reported disloyal behavior in the households where they labored, they transformed the domestic institution of slavery into a military concern.[18]

The gendered paths to freedom diverged further in 1863, when the Union military began enrolling male slaves as soldiers in Missouri. Enslaved men who enlisted received freedom in return for their service, but this bounty did not extend to their families. The female relatives and children of enslaved soldiers had to find their own routes out of slavery. Many escaped to St. Louis and remained there throughout the war, waiting for their male relatives to return home. Other women freed themselves under the Second Confiscation Act by reporting slave owners' Confederate sympathies.

This contact with the Union Army was not without risk. The inherent violence of war and military occupation meant that the process of emancipation carried its own dangers. The Union Army itself was filled with young men engaged in a violent enterprise, and women who had contact with Union troops risked rape, sexual exploitation, and physical attack.[19]

In addition, refugees, including the thousands of enslaved African Americans fleeing their homes, faced the elements, the stress of relocation and upheaval, crowded conditions, and disease. As Jim Downs has eloquently illustrated, many formerly enslaved people did not survive the process of emancipation to partake in the fruits of the jubilee.[20] Women who served as laundresses and cooks for the army experienced a continuation of the economic exploitation that they faced under slavery. Washerwomen were exposed to disease through handling dirty and bloody clothing, work that military men were reluctant to do. They offered their bodies to the Union Army just as much as African American men did.[21]

African American women used their access to the military police and courts to press a multitude of claims impossible under the Missouri legal system.[22] These demands for inclusion within the military judicial process constituted a critical step in emancipation. The complaints and petitions of African American women promoted a gendered conception of citizenship derived from their experiences in bondage and the wartime struggle to destroy slavery. Freedwomen developed their own visions of what freedom ought to be in response to living under the slave system.[23] Their demands for civic inclusion entailed legal, cultural, and physical claims. The Civil War then mobilized women as they fought to free themselves and their families from bondage.

Charlotte McNeil is just one example of the varied ways in which African American women engaged a sustained struggle for freedom and civil status during the era of slave emancipation. Popular conceptions of the Civil War have been dominated by histories that erase the political actions of the enslaved population.[24] But the actions of enslaved women illuminate their struggles for specific freedoms. This book analyzes political beliefs as expressed through everyday social practices. As Robin D. G. Kelley argues in *Race Rebels*, political motivations do not "exist separately from issues of economic well-being, safety, pleasure, cultural expression, sexuality, freedom of mobility, and other facets of daily life."[25] Enslaved and freedwomen's daily acts of resistance and survival had consequences for existing power relations. It is through the study of these actions that we can understand the specific ways in which power operated during the Civil War. Studying the processes used by African American women to remove the bonds of slavery to claim freedom, and even citizenship rights, is crucial to understanding not only the early history of civil rights but also the evolution of federal power during the Civil War.

Charlotte McNeil engaged in a struggle to claim her own definition of freedom; her actions underscore the role played by the everyday activities of ordinary people in the wartime destruction of slavery. As a new generation of scholarship has demonstrated, slave emancipation was accomplished not by a single event but by a process that occurred unevenly throughout the slave states.[26] These everyday, on-the-ground contestations played a significant role in "freeing the slaves" and should receive serious attention

alongside the analysis of political moments such as the Emancipation Proclamation.[27]

Citizenship forms its meaning through access to a variety of arenas,
including markets, social institutions, and public space. As an identity, citizenship is constructed through daily contests for greater control over one's
life.[28] The enactment of citizenship is not simply a juridical status but also
a performance of civic identity.[29] African American women articulated the
identity of "the patriot" as they worked to position themselves as members
of the nation. Performance can be found in everyday actions that circulate
these contested meanings of national belonging.[30] The crisis of the Civil War
allowed African American women to perform their claims for justice and
equality. These embodied performances occurred on the city streets, before
military courts, and within slave-owning homes. The actions of enslaved
and free black women contested the juridical meanings of citizenship and
offered an alternative meaning of civic identity in wartime Missouri.[31]

Definitions of U.S. citizenship have historically rested on raced and
gendered articulations of identity that specify who is included in and who
is excluded from the political process.[32] The legal status of the formerly
enslaved population was unclear until the ratification of the Fourteenth
Amendment overturned the Supreme Court's *Dred Scott v. Sandford* decision (1857), which explicitly excluded African Americans from the privi-
leged status of "citizen." *Dred Scott v. Sandford* had established a narrow
juridical definition of citizenship and framed African Americans as a stateless group, set apart from the nation.[33] But the meanings of U.S. citizenship
have never been stable or uncontested.[34]

The historical circumstances of the Civil War collapsed the pretended
boundaries between the civil, military, political, and domestic spheres. Feminist scholarship has demonstrated that these boundaries are suspect and to
a large degree rhetorical constructions.[35] This book builds on the work of
scholars who use gender analysis to criticize definitions of civic culture and
the role of the public sphere in modern democratic republics. I apply these
critiques to a body of scholarship that charts the process of slave emancipation during the Civil War.[36] African American women were historical
actors in the material, cultural, and rhetorical collapse of these boundaries,
which, in turn, granted them further ability to maneuver in their struggles
for power.

The wartime actions of African American women illustrate the
inseparable links between the realms of the domestic and the political. For

example, enslaved women used their positions as household workers to report Confederate activity to Union officers. Enslaved women had a vested interest in revealing that slavery, which had been rhetorically classified as a part of household operations, was in fact a critical component of the political realm. The personal was political for enslaved women, who worked to reclaim their productive and reproductive labor, especially as their actions inserted the military into the "domestic" struggles of slaves and slaveholders. Household politics were intimately connected to the question facing the nation during the Civil War—the fate of slavery.

Legal historians have produced a methodology that moves beyond the study of statutes and legal precedents to demonstrate the role of enslaved people as actors in legal realms.[37] The legal system's role in the lives of enslaved people is revealed through the examination of documents such as trial transcripts and case records.[38] Grappling with the question of why African Americans thought to make their claims in legal forums opens up further questions about the enslaved population's assumptions about the role of the law, the uses of citizenship, and concepts of nationhood.[39] The study of court records, particularly transcripts of proceedings at the lowest level of the justice system, reveals how law was understood by African Americans who watched and participated in court proceedings.[40]

Union Army records expose the nature of claims made by African American women and the process by which they petitioned military justice officials. In addition, the Civil War pension files of African American widows contain information about the daily lives of women as they moved from slavery to freedom. Military correspondence, newspaper clippings, slave narratives, and diaries round out the sources and add texture to this study.[41]

This book begins with a description of Civil War St. Louis, with special attention to its resident African American population and its savvy understanding of the court system. Chapter 1 explores the civil court cases brought by African Americans in antebellum St. Louis. The city's black residents imagined a capacious understanding of federal citizenship that was informed by their struggle with slavery and the legal disabilities imposed by local black codes.

While a broad vision of citizenship was common to the St. Louis black population, the assertion of bodily integrity was a particular concern for women. Sexual assault and the sale of children figured highly among the motives of women who filed freedom suits. Women particularly valued aspects of bodily integrity that were denied to enslaved people, such as the right to protect oneself from sexual and bodily assault and the right to assert custody rights over their children.

The chapter also discusses the continued legal disabilities encountered by St. Louis's free African American community during the Civil War. African American women challenged the institutions supporting the slave system following the militarization of the city and the subsequent proclamation of martial law by the U.S. Army. As the war progressed, circumstances and features unique to the city drew African American women there, and institutions, societies, and clubs offered the migrants a rich associational life.

Chapter 2 identifies the gendered strategies employed by enslaved women in the Missouri countryside to escape slavery under the First and Second Confiscation Acts, passed in August 1861 and July 1862, respectively. The Confiscation Acts defined the terms under which enslaved people could be seized by the Union military and for all practical purposes liberated from their former masters. Lincoln's Emancipation Proclamation did not apply to Missouri, a loyal Union state, and slavery remained legal in Missouri until January 1865.[42] But the institution of slavery began to crumble much earlier, as masses of enslaved Missourians ran to Union lines.

The thousands of freedpeople who fled to Union camps and forts encouraged the military bureaucracy to develop new practices and policies. Union commanders instructed provost marshals to accept slave and free black testimony regarding the disloyal acts of slave owners. Enslaved women used the military officers and the provost marshal system to attain a de facto freedom under the Confiscation Acts. The acceptance of black testimony by military officials was a critical moment in the federal recognition of enslaved people as potential citizens. These impromptu courts allowed for the practical application of the Second Confiscation Act in Missouri. The provost marshals ran a low-level military court system and possessed the power to charge, arrest, and incarcerate civilians. African American women deployed their claims on the physical space of Union camps and provost marshal offices as a part of the process of constructing a civic existence.

Chapter 3 turns to the question of the kin of slave men who enlisted in the Union Army. The enlistment of slave men in 1863 changed the grounds on which enslaved women could seek military support. Enslaved women were now the kin of soldiers, they had contributed to the cause of the Union military, and they sought their freedom as a matter of justice. The enslaved wives, mothers, and sisters of Union soldiers claimed a military citizenship based on the service of their male relatives. In 1863, thousands of formerly enslaved Missouri men joined the army to serve in the U.S. Colored Troops. But their enlistment did not free the families of black soldiers, and the Missouri legislature would not abolish slavery until January 1865. Nevertheless, the grounds on which enslaved women could seek military support shifted: as the kin of soldiers, these women argued that they had contributed to the Union military cause and that their freedom was a matter of justice. The enslaved wives, mothers, and sisters of Union soldiers played a critical role in the wartime collapse of Missouri slavery. They identified the enlistment of their male relatives as a revolutionary moment and an opportunity to win freedom.

Chapter 4 shows how African American women used St. Louis's military courts to perform acts associated with citizenship. Missouri's black codes forbade any African American, slave or free, from testifying against white persons. But even though African American women remained unable to testify against them in civil courts, they could use the military court system to charge white residents with a variety of offenses under martial law. By 1864, African American women routinely sought justice in the local military courts, accusing white citizens of assault, rape, kidnapping, and unfair labor practices. This phenomenon may have served as a precedent for the claims accepted in Freedmen's Bureau courts, suggesting that women's wartime activism shaped the civil rights battles of Reconstruction.

Chapter 5 turns to a discussion of marriage. As part of the process of emancipation, freedwomen asserted their right to make marital and romantic choices. The Union Army, federal pension law, and Missouri law all played a role in recognizing and defining slave marriage. Freedwomen, however, worked to redefine the meaning of marriage to suit their own purposes, making marital claims in dialogue with the army, the Federal Pension Bureau, divorce law, and the African American church and community. In so doing, freedwomen demanded the right to define marriage on their own terms, working to emancipate themselves not only from slaveholders but also from patriarchal, church, and state authority. Emancipated women asserted the right to redefine marriage as part of their Civil War struggle to manufacture a civic identity.

Gender and the Jubilee reexamines the legal legacy of the Civil War. As the United States transformed from a slaveholding republic into a modern-nation-state, citizenship was reconceptualized through diverse mechanisms.[43] Among the multiple and contested visions of citizenship circulated during the Civil War, how did enslaved people come to be recognized as potential citizens of the nation?[44] Their struggles to enact their own emancipations contributed to the process that produced modern citizenship in the nineteenth century.

African American women inserted themselves as members of the nation-state during the turbulent years of the Civil War crisis, positioning themselves, rhetorically, as patriots for the Union cause. As self-identified patriots, women fled to federal troops stationed in the city and sought a right to federal protection from abusive slave owners prior to the enactment of any emancipatory acts on the part of military policy or the federal government. This assumption of federal protection prior to the ratification of the Fourteenth Amendment, in a state outside the jurisdiction of the Emancipation Proclamation, suggests a deep investment in the ideal of an inclusive national citizenship that included the African American population.[45] The litigating slave women of antebellum St. Louis and the female activists of the Civil War period left a rich legal heritage for postwar civil rights activists and set the stage for African American women to continue to play a critical role in their own liberation.

CHAPTER 1

"I Told My Mistress That the Union Soldiers Were Coming"

Black Citizenship in Civil War St. Louis

ON THE EVE OF the Civil War, enslaved cook Ellen Turner Jackson clipped a photo of President Abraham Lincoln from a newspaper and hung it on the wall of her St. Louis room. With this act of resistance to the institution of slavery, Jackson expressed her loyalty to the Union cause. When her offended owner demanded to know why she had placed the president's picture on the wall, Jackson retorted that "it was there because she liked it." In response, William Lewis knocked her to the floor, using physical violence to reassert his power over a woman who was challenging both his Confederate sympathies and the institution of slavery that bound her to him.[1] Jackson's physical struggle with Lewis was not simply a reaction to the sharp rise of political tensions in the Civil War city. Enslaved women such as Jackson took advantage of the fractured polity to reimagine themselves as citizens of the republic.[2] Jackson and other African American women played a specific role in reshaping American citizenship as part of the process of the wartime destruction of slavery.

Jackson and Lewis were engaged in a struggle over the meanings of American citizenship. Citizenship is both a legal status and a cultural identity that forms its meanings through social practices in which people test the boundaries of their rights and obligations.[3] Embodied performance, such as hanging a picture of a head of state or flying a national flag, can play a part in establishing the cultural aspects of political identity.[4] Jackson enacted a patriotic performance when she clipped and hung the picture. Through the act of hanging the picture, Jackson articulated a relationship with the nation. The rhetorical image declared an emotional attachment to the president. Through her affiliation with the head of state, she identified herself as a member of the nation. With this act, Ellen Turner Jackson, a stateless person, portrayed herself as a woman in possession of a civic identity.[5]

Jackson attempted to politicize Lewis's slaveholding household.[6] As domestic household workers, enslaved women were well positioned to challenge the rhetorical separation of "private" domestic life from a larger public culture.[7] Slavery, the "domestic" institution, defined enslaved people as household dependents. Civilly dead, existing as legal property and subject to the authority of the head of household, enslaved people were deprived of citizenship in the republic. Slaves could not claim membership in any state or nation; they were a stateless people. The Civil War ultimately led to the deconstruction of the legal meaning of the household.[8]

Jackson's patriotic performance was an implicit critique of both the institution of slavery and Lewis's authority. She asserted that she was not a slave dependent, bereft of civil status, but the possessor of an emotional connection to the president of the republic unmediated by her slave master. Her denial of Lewis's political authority and her challenge to the narrow understanding of citizenship that arose from slaveholder ideology, angered her slave master. Jackson confronted William Lewis's limited conception of American citizenship with a democratic, capacious understanding of membership in the nation-state.[9]

A few years prior to the war, Lewis had purchased Ellen Turner Jackson and her two daughters, Sarah Ann and Mattie Jane, from slave trader Bernard T. Lynch. Lynch operated a "slave pen," where enslaved people were held in preparation for auction, on the corner of Fifth Street and Myrtle, four blocks from the St. Louis Courthouse.[10] Outside of Lynch's auction house, the St. Louis cityscape bustled with business conducted in storefronts, saloons, and dance halls and by merchants waiting for stevedores to unload their goods from steamboats at the levee. As a port city on the Mississippi River, St. Louis was a major hub for the slave trade, with several traffickers establishing bases of operations downtown.[11] Enslaved people were bought and sold both from major ports down the Mississippi River to New Orleans and along the Missouri River into the state's interior. The farms of small-scale slaveholders, many of whom raised crops such as hemp and tobacco, lined the fertile banks of the Missouri River through the region known as Little Dixie.[12]

Enslaved and free people of color comprised 18 percent of the St. Louis population in 1820 and almost 25 percent in 1830.[13] Between 1840 and 1850, St. Louis experienced rapid urbanization and immigration as a consequence of its advantageous location for steamboat traffic, and the city's population increased fivefold over that time. By the late 1840s, St. Louis had established itself as the hub for the flow of goods up and down the Mississippi, Missouri, and Ohio Rivers, and by 1860, it was the country's eighth-largest city.[14] The influx of white immigrants and commerce greatly reduced the relative influence of the institution of slavery, and although St. Louis remained a major port for the slave trade, enslaved African Americans and free people of color made up only 2 percent of the city's residents on the eve of the Civil War.[15]

By 1860, St. Louis's free African Americans constituted a comparatively small but well-organized and politically active community. As residents of a major steamboat port, the city's African Americans had access to currents of thought from around the country, particularly the national debate about citizenship and slavery. Free black steamboat workers traveled along the Mississippi and Ohio Rivers, importing news and political thought from other regions of the United States. The black community was enriched by the flows of people and ideas coming in and out of the city.[16]

The city's fifteen hundred or so free African Americans socialized and attended church with members of the enslaved population, and marriages between members of the two groups were common. Ellen Turner Jackson and her daughters could have come into contact with such prominent African Americans as Elizabeth Keckley, who bought her freedom in 1855 with money raised from her skills as a dressmaker and went on to become Mary Todd Lincoln's seamstress.[17] Following the Civil War members from this community would take up leadership roles working for civil rights such as black male suffrage and education for African American children.[18]

Despite the fact that African Americans, enslaved and free, were only 2 percent of the St. Louis population in 1860, slavery was fully integrated into the city's daily life. The enslaved population was a key element of the urban economic environment where they labored as stevedores, cooks, servants, and laundresses and in such skilled occupations as carpentry.[19] African American women outnumbered men both in the slave and free municipal population. Urban slavery in St. Louis consisted primarily of domestic work and was a predominantly female experience. In contrast, the gender imbalance leveled out in rural areas, as men were more in demand to work on farms in agricultural areas.[20]

The legal system, including the police, prison, and courts, was designed to protect slaveholders' interests and influenced the city's cultural, social, and legal life. St. Louis produced some of the most well-publicized incidents of pro-slavery atrocities. In 1836, Francis McIntosh, a free black man working as a cook on a steamboat, was tied to a tree and burned alive on the corner of Seventh and Chestnut Streets.[21] When the *St. Louis Observer* printed editorials protesting McIntosh's lynching, mobs attacked the paper's press and ran its publisher, Elijah Lovejoy, out of town. The following year, Lovejoy was murdered by another pro-slavery mob in nearby Alton, Illinois, an event that became a touchstone for abolitionists nationwide.[22] Lovejoy had previously hired the services of William Wells Brown, who later escaped slavery and went on to become a noted abolitionist as well as a novelist and playwright.[23]

"He Cannot Have Any Rite to Keep Me Any Longer": The Antebellum Roots of Black Citizenship

Perhaps St. Louis's most famous enslaved residents were Harriet and Dred Scott. The Scotts and their two children, Eliza and Jane, sued for their freedom in the St. Louis civil courts. In fact, Harriet Scott may have initiated the original April 1846 suits out of concern for the future of her two young daughters. In 1857, Dred Scott's freedom suit reached the U.S. Supreme Court, where Chief Justice Roger B. Taney wrote the decision that declared African Americans ineligible for citizenship. The court's ruling intensified factional conflict between the free and slave states.

Women filed the majority of freedom suits in St. Louis, perhaps as a consequence of the gender imbalance in the city's population. Another factor may have been women's interest in establishing legal custody over their children and thereby removing slave owners' ability to sell those children.[24] Since slave status transferred to children through their mother, if a woman won a freedom suit, all of her children were also freed. Legal activism on the part of African American women during the Civil War can be understood in the light of this antebellum legal heritage.[25]

Harriet and Dred Scott were just two of more than three hundred petitioners for freedom in the St. Louis courts between 1814 and 1860. As a result of these efforts the members of the African American community developed legal savvy as they learned to navigate the court system.[26] An 1807 territorial statute permitted suits for freedom, and an 1824 state law allowed any person held illegally as a slave "to sue as a poor person to establish his or her freedom." The court assigned lawyers to the plaintiffs.[27]

Pressing suit against the politically powerful Chouteau family to whom she had been hired out in 1826, a woman named Ellin wrote to her lawyer, future governor Hamilton Gamble, "He cannot have Any rite to keep me Any longer," claiming of Agnes Chouteau, "She Abuses us on purpose to please the old man." Ellin asked her lawyer to have her removed from the Chouteaus' custody, signing her letter, "your obedient Clien—Ellin."[28] Enslaved plaintiffs such as Ellin were held in St. Louis jail or hired out until their court date. Even while restricted and hired out as a slave, Ellin self-identified as a legal actor and represented herself as a political subject with the rights of a free woman. She urged her lawyer to press her rights with the jailor and before the court. Women were active in developing legal strategies with their lawyers. Dorinda, another of Gamble's clients, wrote to him the same year, "Sir I wish to inform that Mr. Felps is trying his best to keep me a slave."[29] Marguerite, the descendant of a Native American woman taken into slavery before the United States assumed control of the Louisiana Territory, also pressed a freedom suit against the Chouteaus in 1825.[30] St. Louis's slave-owning families constituted a social elite with an investment in a cultural identity as slave owners. When women pressed freedom suits, they threatened this identity.

In 1827, *Freedom's Journal*, the first newspaper owned and published by African Americans, watched the Missouri freedom suits with interest. A correspondent from Illinois responded to a favorable decision from the Missouri Supreme Court by writing, "The friends of man will have a new cause to felicitate themselves on the progress of corrupt principles, and on the restoration of his long lost rights. . . . There have been several suits instituted by the negroes to recover their liberty."[31] This and other publications performed intellectual work when they promoted and circulated these expansive definitions of liberty and human rights throughout the nation's black public culture.[32]

The meanings of freedom were gendered for women, and the goal of bodily integrity and custody of children figured strongly as a benefit of personal liberty. As domestic workers in the urban South, enslaved women tended to work hidden from public view and in close quarters with those who could subject them to physical and sexual assault. In addition, enslaved women underwent pregnancy and birth with the knowledge that their children would hold slave status and could be separated and sold away from their mothers.[33]

In Missouri as in other border slave states, proximity to free states provided an important context. St. Louis slave owners often brought enslaved people to reside for a time in Illinois, just across the Mississippi River, enabling some enslaved residents of the city to sue for freedom on the grounds that they had lived in free states or territories. In 1839, for example, Polly Wash "decided to sue for her freedom, and for that purpose employed a good lawyer"—Francis B. Murdoch, who later became well known as the man who filed the original suits for Harriet and Dred Scott. Wash won her 1839 freedom suit because she had lived in Illinois, a victory that meant that her daughter, Lucy Ann Berry, also was free.[34]

However, being declared free did not automatically bring about Lucy's release from bondage. Not until three years later, when she was threatened with whipping, did Lucy bring her own suit to establish that she was being held unlawfully as a slave.[35] Lucy's inexperience as a laundress had brought her into conflict with the expectations of her mistress. "You have no business to whip me, I don't belong to you," she exclaimed in a heated argument. Polly had frequently told Lucy that "she was a free woman," and Lucy consequently, as she put it, "always had a feeling of independence." When the owners attempted to sell Lucy, she escaped into the city and hid with her mother's friend until Polly was able to get Murdoch to file suit for Lucy's freedom. Lucy then spent twenty months in jail awaiting trial.[36]

Women were legal actors in these claims, often strategizing over how best to press their suits. Polly Wash, for example, sought advice on legal strategy, hired Murdoch to file suit for her and later for her daughter, and then recruited Judge Edward Bates, a prominent attorney and former congressman who later served as President Lincoln's attorney general during the Civil War, to argue her daughter's case at trial. Although we do not know whom Polly Wash went to for advice, given the number of black St. Louis residents who had pressed freedom suits, it is quite likely that legal strategies were circulating in the black community. Wash was not simply a legal actor, she possessed a legal sophistication nurtured by the St. Louis black social environment.[37]

Lucy won her case, married Zachariah Delaney, a free black man from Cincinnati, and became active in black women's club work, charity, and religious groups, winning election as president of the Female Union in 1855. After the Civil War, Lucy Delaney served as secretary to a St. Louis black veterans' group. Such activities were not unusual among the members of her politically and socially active St. Louis cohort before and after the war.[38]

As was the case for many of her peers, the Civil War itself was a key moment for Delaney, and she dedicated the published narrative of her freedom suit to the Grand Army of the Republic. Delaney viewed the Union Army's victories as part of a "tardy justice" that "came at last and avenged the woes of an oppressed race! Chickamauga, Shiloh, Atlanta and Gettysburg, spoke in thunder tones!" She continued, "John Brown's body had indeed marched on, and we, the ransomed ones, glorify God and dedicate ourselves to His service."[39]

Religious organizations and churches, much like fraternal organizations and service clubs, also provided a space for African American public culture to operate.[40] Harriet Scott was a member of the Second Colored Baptist Church, also known as the Eighth Street Church. A fixture of the African American community, the Eighth Street Church served a congregation of approximately one thousand members, about half of them enslaved.[41] The church played a prominent role as a meeting place for civil rights activists during and after the Civil War. On January 1, 1863, African Americans began their celebration of Lincoln's Emancipation Proclamation at the church before marching in the midst of a blizzard in a "great procession" to Turner's Hall in downtown St. Louis, where the church's minister, John Richard Anderson, presided over the "great thanksgiving and speaking service."[42] Members of the Eighth Street Church and the city's wider African American community would have been aware of the Scotts' and other freedom suits.

The U.S. Supreme Court's decision, written by Chief Justice Roger B. Taney, in Dred Scott's case held that African Americans were not citizens and thus had no standing to sue in federal court. Because the Scotts were noncitizens, the U.S. government would not entertain their claims for freedom. A narrow view of citizenship, Taney's decision represented a vision of slaveholder republican governance in which household dependents were excluded from full political membership in the nation-state. The legal category of "household dependent" included a wide variety of people, including white women, enslaved people, and children, all of whom were expected to obey the head of household—the only person entitled to the privileges and responsibilities of the political and economic master of the house. Proslavery politics and the southern political culture defined citizenship as a category exclusive to the white, male, head of household.[43] In a sharp contrast to Taney's exclusionary articulation of rights, the black population of

St. Louis promoted a democratic and inclusive understanding of American citizenship.[44]

Although Dred Scott lost his case at the U.S. Supreme Court, the owners granted the members of the Scott family their freedom in May 1857 as a result of the national attention to the court battle. Dred Scott died in September 1858, but Harriet, Eliza, and Jane Scott remained in St. Louis on the eve of the Civil War. After their 1857 emancipation, the Scott family lived in a wooden home on an alley off Carr Street in the city. Harriet Scott resided in the city during the war and would pass away at her St. Louis residence in 1876.[45]

Even free African American residents of Missouri found themselves constrained by legal disabilities. In 1835, the Missouri legislature required all free persons of color residing in the state to obtain licenses from their county courts. The law required applicants to post bonds or find white citizens to stand as security for the applicants' behavior.[46] Free African Americans caught without proper licensing were subject to arrest, fines of between ten dollars and one hundred dollars, whippings of between ten and twenty lashes, and immediate expulsion from the state. Consequently, people of color living in St. Louis before and during the Civil War were subject to arrest by the city police and white citizens; even walking the streets was not a liberty that African Americans could take for granted.

Furthermore, an 1847 law prohibited free African Americans from any other state or territory from relocating to Missouri.[47] Earlier, in 1843, the state legislature passed a law that banned any ship carrying black passengers from docking anywhere in the state and required captains to turn over any free African American ship workers "to be jailed within twenty-four hours of their arrival in the state."[48] Despite the fact that as many as one hundred steamboats visited St. Louis's harbor at any time, captains who failed to provide lists of such workers to local police could receive fines of two hundred dollars. In practice, this law does not appear to have been widely followed, but black steamboat laborers were targeted on city streets for detention.[49] As early as 1835, free people of color challenged the licensing law in St. Louis, combating the arbitrary arrests and threat of expulsion from the state with federal constitutional claims.[50]

Soon after the law's passage, Seaton Stoner was arrested in St. Louis for illegally migrating to the state and was ordered to leave Missouri.[51] Stoner's lawyer explicitly argued for federal citizenship, pointing to the Declaration of Independence and the Declaration of the Rights of Man to support the African American assertion that free black residents were also citizens of the United States. On appeal to the Missouri Supreme Court in 1837, Stoner's lawyer argued that because he had been born in the United States, he was "entitled to all the privileges and immunities of citizens in the several States."[52] In short, Stoner's lawyer argued that as a citizen of the United States, Stoner could not be punished for residing in St. Louis without a license. Although the court rejected this argument, the case exemplified the developing legal reasoning that African American claims were grounded in the federal constitution.

The Missouri licensing law drew the attention of African American newspapers in northern cities. In September 1840, after the mayor of St. Louis expelled fifteen free colored people, New York City's *Colored American* responded, "Let the Mayor have his day, and do what is in his heart, trampling on the U.S. Constitution, outraging humanity." Continued the paper, "Law will have its day, yet, in Missouri, and then free citizens of the United States will go to St. Louis in their lawful callings, unmolested by this vandalism."[53] *The Colored American* argued African Americans were citizens and that licensing laws infringed upon constitutional liberty. The African American black press asserted constitutional claims on federal citizenship in the antebellum era, far before the passage of the Thirteenth and Fourteenth Amendments would establish the citizenship of all people born in the United States. Black Americans envisioned the possibilities of a federal citizenship, which would eventually be realized and enshrined in the U.S. Constitution after the Civil War.[54]

Despite legal setbacks, African Americans continued to contest the licensing law. In 1846, Charles Lyons, the Kentucky-born son of a Native American Seneca woman and an African American man, was arrested without a warrant for residing in the city without a license. Like Stoner, Lyons asserted before the St. Louis Circuit Court that as a free-born U.S. citizen, he was entitled to the privileges and immunities of citizenship, including the right to live in the state of Missouri.[55] The presiding judge rejected Lyons's argument, opining that citizenship "is not a condition which flows from birth" and that "negroes and mulattoes, though born free, never have been, and are not now, citizens of any state of this Union." Bereft of citizenship rights, Lyons could be arrested without warrant.[56]

"O LIBERTY!—E. LEWIS, a free negro, was fined $10 in St. Louis recently, for being in the State without a license!" proclaimed *The North Star*, an African American newspaper published out of Rochester, New York, in July 1849. Free and enslaved African Americans were routinely stopped, searched, and apprehended on the suspicion of being fugitive slaves or free individuals residing illegally in the state. The state passed exclusionary residency laws with the goal of expelling free African Americans, but St. Louis went further and enacted city ordinances that restricted the movement of all African Americans. In 1835, the city banned slave residents from the streets after nine o'clock in the evening for the majority of the year and ten o'clock during the summer months.[57]

The arbitrary arrest of free African Americans was characteristic of urban southern cities in the antebellum United States.[58] Not only could city officials such as constables, watchmen, and police apprehend and imprison people of color, but ordinary citizens could capture African Americans and take them to the local jail on suspicion that they were fugitive slaves—the urban version of rural slave patrols.[59] In December 1842, Francis Johnson, a Philadelphia bandmaster and composer, was arrested along with other members of his band for residing in the city without a license. The band had rented suites at the Planters' House hotel, lodging in the same parlor that former president Martin Van Buren had occupied when he visited the city. This violation of the color line provoked a local "gentleman of the highest respectability" to visit a justice of the peace and insist on enforcement of the law. All of the musicians filed writs of habeas corpus to attain their release.[60] A dozen years later, two St. Louis police officers arrested John Rudd on suspicion of being a fugitive slave. Rudd, too, filed a writ of habeas corpus.[61] Free black women also found themselves targeted: Emily White was prosecuted for residing in the state without a license in 1851.[62]

The activities of free African Americans alarmed St. Louis slaveholders. In 1846, men assembled in the rotunda of the downtown courthouse to discuss their concerns about a free black population that was "tainted with the poison of abolitionist principles, and who are constantly instilling into the minds of our slaves the most pernicious opinions."[63] Attendees at the meeting subsequently formed the St. Louis Anti-Abolitionist Society, popularly called the Committee of One Hundred, to push for further restrictions on free people of color, including city ordinances that would ban the "evils" of "negro preaching" and "negro teaching," which were "dangerous to the happiness, quiet and safety of our slave population."[64] Many of the men involved in the society faced freedom suits pressed by enslaved people. Colonel Alexander Sanford, whose daughter was involved in Dred and Harriet Scott's lawsuit, served as one of the group's leaders. In February 1847, the Missouri

Legislature responded to the society's suggestions by criminalizing black education and prohibiting black religious services without the supervision of a "white government agent."[65]

Civil War St. Louis

On the eve of the Civil War, the state of Missouri was deeply invested in the institution of slavery despite the rise of free labor sentiment in St. Louis that developed as a consequence largely of the steamboat revolution and the growth in white immigration and commerce.[66] In particular, many of the new German arrivals held strong antislavery views, and with the start of the war, they became fiercely pro-Union.[67]

Although St. Louis voters supported Republicans for office in 1859 and 1860, the city's legal system remained strongly committed to upholding slavery through the systematic patrol of enslaved and free individuals.[68] Sheriffs and justices of the peace not only were accustomed to supporting the rights of slave owners but also had a legal mandate to support slaveholders' property rights. City police understood their duties to include the surveillance and arrest of African Americans who entered the city.

Missouri remained heavily invested in slavery as an industry.[69] The 1860 U.S. Census found 114,931 enslaved people resident in the state, and the following year, Governor Claiborne Jackson estimated their total value at one hundred million dollars.[70] Missouri's legal support of slavery seeped into the city's cultural and social life. St. Louis abolitionist minister Galusha Anderson noted that "in 1860 St. Louis had but few slaves, nevertheless pro-slavery sentiment largely prevailed." Jessie Benton Frémont, the wife of John C. Frémont, who served during the war as commander of the U.S. Army's Department of the West, claimed that "in the city of St. Louis, [it was] unfashionable, to be with the North and for Freedom."[71]

James Thomas, a free African American, recalled that, in 1861, St. Louis "had a secession feeling" and that the "old and wealthy families of St. Louis were all southern in sentiment with few exceptions."[72] Writing from St. Louis in April 1862, Judson Bemis, a businessman, claimed that St. Louis had "plenty" of secessionists: "Very pleasant ain't it to have a Secesh living on each side of you." He observed that many wealthy people were Confederate sympathizers, while the "poor folks" backed Lincoln.[73]

At the onset of the Civil War, Confederates attempted to gain control

of the city. Pro-slavery residents organized a paramilitary group, the Minute Men, a wing of the Southern Rights Democrats, in January 1861. Many
members were secessionists, and they raised the Confederate flag over their
headquarters, Berthold Mansion. Other members, however, were Conditional Unionists who advocated staying in the Union under a compromise
that would protect the expansion of slavery to the Pacific Ocean for all lati-
tudes south of Missouri's northern border.[74]

St. Louis's Unionists responded by organizing their own paramilitary
group, the Home Guards, and many of its members were German immigrants who also joined such radical Unionist groups as the Wide Awakes
and the Black Rifles.[75] The Unionists worried that secessionists would attack
the St. Louis Federal Arsenal to capture the gunpowder and arms stored
there.[76] To protect its St. Louis assets, the U.S. Department of War brought
in soldiers from barracks south of the city and from Kansas and put them
under the command of Captain Nathaniel Lyon, a fierce abolitionist.[77] By
March 1861, about five hundred federal troops guarded the arsenal and were
digging up the lawns to install howitzers, as Lyon had ordered; for their part,
the Minute Men and the Home Guards were practicing marching around
their respective headquarters.[78]

St. Louis residents were disconcerted by the city's militarization and
wary of radical Unionist sentiment. With unrest increasing, the April 1, 1861,
elections saw Republicans lose control of the municipal government for the
first time in four years. The newly elected mayor, Daniel G. Taylor, was a
Conditional Unionist, opposing both Lincoln and abolition.[79] In addition,
statewide elections the preceding August had handed the governorship to
Democrat Claiborne Fox Jackson. During his election campaign, Jackson
had portrayed himself as a moderate and a supporter of antislavery Democrat Stephen A. Douglas, but the governor later proved to be a Confederate
sympathizer.[80]

The pro-slavery state assembly removed control of the St. Louis Police
Force from the mayor and created a Board of Police Commissioners that
reported to the governor. Jackson then placed four pro-secessionists on the
board, including a leader of the Minute Men.[81] To blunt the perceived threat
that the free African American community posed to secessionist goals, the
Police Board in April 1861 forbade black churches from operating without
an "officer of the police" present and warned that any "free negroes" who
lacked the required licenses would be prosecuted.[82]

In response, free people of color thronged to the county court to apply for licenses.[83] The forty people who appeared before the St. Louis county commissioners on April 20 included Theodosia Ambrose, a thirty-nine-year-old woman employed as a cook, and Manette, a forty-five-year-old laundress who brought her children with her to court.[84] Three days later, Eliza Scott, the twenty-two-year-old daughter of Dred Scott, appeared in court to receive a license.[85]

County commissioner Peregrine Tippet complained that "free negroes and mulattoes crowded the room for several days" and formally protested the liberal manner in which the board was distributing licenses. Tippet was not only appalled that the affidavit of a woman born in Kentucky was accepted as a "certificate of citizenship" but also objected to the idea that a person of color could ever attain a "certificate of citizenship" in light of the *Dred Scott* decision.[86]

People of color living in St. Louis during the Civil War continued to be subject to arrest by the city police; simply walking on the streets of St. Louis was not a liberty that African Americans could take for granted. Free African Americans were vulnerable to arrest and lashings as late as August 1862 for the crime of living in Missouri without a license. In August 1861, two unlicensed African Americans, Linton Pinks and Martha Vincent, were arrested, jailed, and finally brought before the St. Louis County Court, which sentenced them to ten lashes each and banished them from Missouri.[87] In 1862, James Monroe, Ben Freeman, Tim Roberts, Henry Berrick, and Isaac Hopkins were arrested for failure to obtain licenses, and they, too, were sentenced to ten lashes each and expelled from the state.[88] For their own safety, free people of color continued to acquire free licenses during the Civil War. Harriet Hoggar, a previously enslaved woman then working as a chambermaid, went before the county court in May 1863 and received a license to reside in the city as a free woman.[89] In April 1864, Julia Collins, a twenty-four-year-old washerwoman, became the last African American to apply for and receive a license to live in the city of St. Louis.[90]

Martial Law and the Institution of Slavery

As Union forces began to organize in St. Louis at the start of the war, tensions with Confederate sympathizers culminated in the Camp Jackson Affair, a minor May 10, 1861, skirmish between Union troops and Confederate sympathizers belonging to the Missouri state militia. Governor Jack-

son called for state militiamen to gather in St. Louis, where they set up
Camp Jackson on the city's outskirts. Alarmed by this display of secessionist
strength, Union officers feared that the city would fall to the Confederacy,
giving the rebellious states control of the city and all of the traffic on the
Upper Mississippi River.[91]

As part of a plan to hold St. Louis and its federal arsenal for the Union,
Captain Lyon recruited four regiments of volunteer infantry—mostly German immigrants—from among the city residents. Lyon's forces then sur-
rounded and dismantled Camp Jackson, taking the men prisoner. Pro-
Union forces subsequently chased Governor Jackson out of Missouri to
Arkansas, established control over the state with a provisional governor,
declared martial law in St. Louis, and purged the city's police system of Confederate sympathizers.[92]

The morning after the Federals confronted the state militias at Camp
Jackson, crowds gathered to watch Union soldiers mopping up the secessionist camp.[93] As troops loaded the tents and other equipment used by the
defeated militias, a white woman announced her Confederate sympathies
"with an air of triumph, stretching out her arm and excitedly shaking her
hand, 'We'll whip you yet.'" Not willing to let this political gesture stand,
two enslaved girls pointed "to the loaded wagons, [and] gleefully cried out,
'They've got all your tents.'"[94] These children verbally positioned themselves
against the Confederate woman and by implication the Confederate cause
and its support of slavery. The Union men who took up posts in St. Louis
challenged the city's social geography, emerging as a symbol of change and
possible liberation of enslaved residents.

As U.S. soldiers filled camps in and around St. Louis, "camps and barracks were everywhere, and the drilling, departing and arrival of troops
were going on night and day."[95] Resident Anne E. Lane observed that while
the black population greeted the Union Army with enthusiasm, white
women who supported the Confederacy scorned Union military men.
According to Lane, "Ladies go their own way holding their skirts away from
laughing federal officers & making much of all the secesh who come in their
way. To console them the darkies are universally their friends."[96] St. Louis's
African American population viewed these new military troops as allies in
the struggle against slavery.

The Union occupation of the city provided the enslaved population with
new opportunities to contest slave owners' authority.[97] "I told my mistress
that the Union soldiers were coming to take" Camp Jackson, proclaimed

Ellen Turner Jackson's daughter, Mattie Jane.[98] Mattie Jane, her sister, and her brother were all enslaved domestic laborers in the household of William Lewis during the Camp Jackson incident.[99] The Jacksons challenged Lewis's authority by expressing their happiness more freely as Union forces strengthened their hold over the city: "The days of sadness for mistress were days of joy for us. We shouted and laughed to the top of our voices."[100]

In the midst of this domestic and political tension, the Lewis family household exploded into violence. One evening, Mrs. Lewis erupted "in a terrible rage" and declared that Mattie should be punished. The mistress cut down a switch and placed it out for her husband to use against Mattie. In response, Mattie "bent the switch in the shape of W," the first letter of William Lewis's name, and fled the house with a fellow enslaved "servant." The two teenage girls spent the night with Mattie's aunt, a free woman.[101] The next morning, the young women sought refuge at the St. Louis Arsenal. Jackson recalled, "There was so much excitement at that time, (1861), by the Union soldiers rendering the fugitives shelter and protection."[102] Unfortunately for Mattie, the girls were turned away by the troops and had to search around the city for another place to hide. With these actions, Mattie Jackson and her teenage friend, like many other women, took matters into their own hands, making claims on the U.S. government even in the absence of martial law or any other federal policy that would have interfered with the institution of slavery. In so doing, these young women attempted to make the "private" practices of slavery a military matter. Young women such as Mattie Jackson grew up in a city filled with a rich discourse concerning citizenship rights. St. Louis bestowed to its young black residents a rich legal heritage filled with petitioners who had pressed claims for freedom throughout the antebellum period. These activists imagined a broad understanding of citizenship, which we can speculate was discussed within black associational life in churches and between friends.

The escape attempt was aborted when her friend's father found them and convinced them to return to the Lewis household.[103] He most likely encouraged the girls to return because he was concerned that his daughter would face physical punishment or sale as a consequence of her rebellion. Slave owners, such as Thomas Grider, began to visit the U.S. Arsenal to recapture fleeing captives in September 1861.[104]

Three weeks after Mattie Jane Jackson's aborted escape, her mistress grew upset about some task she claimed Mattie had not performed and "flew into a rage and told [her husband] I was saucy." William Lewis hit

Mattie on the head with a piece of wood, and "the blood ran over my clothing, which gave me a frightful appearance." Lewis ordered her to change her clothing, but Mattie refused, and he continued to beat her until her mother intervened.[105] Jackson wore her bloodied clothing to express her disdain for her legal owner; her refusal to obey his orders demonstrated her rejection of his right to attack her.

Still in her bloody clothes, Mattie Jackson eventually left the Lewises' house and walked to the St. Louis Arsenal, where a Union officer gave her refuge. Jackson presented her bloody body and clothes as evidence that her abuse, inflicted by her enslaver, was a military matter that warranted federal protection. By giving her shelter, the Union officer disregarded both state slave law and city practices with respect to the institution of slavery. Mattie Jackson remained at the arsenal with a formerly enslaved woman who was serving the troops as a cook until another officer sent her to a local boardinghouse.[106] Three weeks later, the commanding officer at the arsenal told Lewis where Mattie Jackson could be found, though the officer pointed out that Lewis's cruelty had led the girl to "seek protection of him." Lewis then recaptured her.[107] Mattie Jackson not only sought illegal federal protection, she received it on a temporary basis. She brought her bloodied body and clothes to give witness of the abuse she received at the hands of her slave owner and was determined that her claims making on federal protection would lead to a response on her behalf.

The Jackson women and others in St. Louis attempted to insert themselves into the national imaginary as part of their struggle for freedom. Ellen Turner Jackson imagined herself as a patriot, while her daughter took the further step of asserting a claim on the U.S. Army. When she fled to the arsenal in search of federal protection, Mattie Jackson sought to transform the "domestic" institution of slavery into a military concern. Both women insisted that they had a relationship with the federal government, a critical aspect of the process of slave emancipation and reconception of citizenship in wartime America.

William Lewis punished Mattie by imprisoning her in a local slave trader's jail. Union troops may have occupied the city, but William Lewis still owned Mattie Jackson and her family, and their maltreatment continued. He employed the powers granted to him by the slave system to reassert his control over the Jackson family. He hired Mattie out of the city, isolating her in the countryside, but her mother and siblings continued to resist his authority. Ellen Turner Jackson and her children escaped and hid in the city, but Lewis found them and sold them to Captain Tirrell, who operated a civilian ship.[108]

As the sale of the Jackson family demonstrates, the mere presence of troops was not sufficient to impede the practice of slavery in St. Louis. The interwoven system of courts, prisons, and slave traders maintained slavery's economic and legal framework. The criminal justice system still operated under the Missouri slave code, and resident slave masters used the local jails and court system to recapture and punish enslaved people. Policemen were "in the habit of arresting negroes" as suspected runaways, even when the courts had not yet issued warrants for the arrest of specific escapees.[109] Under standard procedure, suspected escapees were placed in the city prison for three months; those who went unclaimed by masters were sold as slaves, with the money received used to cover jail costs.[110]

Despite the civil court system's continued support of Missouri's slave law, the Union occupation challenged the institution of slavery in critical ways. On August 14, 1861, Major General John C. Frémont established martial law in St. Louis and the surrounding county, thereby allowing the military to override the civil courts. The ultimate authority became the military, and state law was subject to bypass. In some situations, civil courts were shut down entirely.[111] Guerrilla warfare rocked the countryside, as rebel "bushwhackers" struggled to capture Missouri for the Confederacy. The insurgency strained the civil court systems, and Union Army officers increasingly relied on the military justice system to punish civilians who had not donned a uniform or officially enlisted in the Confederate Army.[112] Frémont extended martial law to the entire state on August 30 and decreed the emancipation of any enslaved people owned by citizens who had joined the rebel forces.[113] Under this policy, Hiram Reed and Frank Lewis were among the first slaves freed by federal power in the United States. Reed and Lewis were owned by Thomas Snead, a secessionist associate of Governor Jackson, and they escaped to St. Louis and applied for freedom.[114] However, President Lincoln subsequently overruled Frémont's emancipatory provision, which exceeded existing U.S. confiscation policies, and removed the general from his post as commander of the Department of the West in order to avoid alienating powerful but loyal slave owners in Missouri and Kentucky.[115] Nevertheless, the U.S. Congress eventually partially reinstated Frémont's confiscation policy, and martial law generally remained in effect in Union-occupied areas of Missouri. The military justice system consequently offered enslaved people new tools to resist slave law.[116]

The patrol and arrest of civilians helped insert the military into the everyday practice of slavery. Military arrests and military commissions were more prevalent in Missouri than in any other state.[117] The advent of martial law allowed Frémont to begin the courts-martial of Missouri civilians (known as military commissions) in September 1861, and they soon spread to other states. Even then, the number of military commissions in Missouri remained nine times greater than those held in the border states of Maryland or Kentucky.[118]

At the outset, martial law required an organizational hierarchy of provost marshals commanded by the provost marshal general.[119] Headquartered in St. Louis, the Office of the Provost Marshal governed the organizational apparatus responsible for operating the military police and upholding military code. Under the aegis of martial law, the provost marshals gained the power to investigate, patrol, arrest, and detain civilians. Assistant provost marshals in the District of St. Louis had U.S. police and U.S. detectives at their disposal. By the end of the war, provost marshals were established in every district and subdistrict in the state of Missouri, allowing the military systematically to override the state's civil court system.

While Frémont's emancipatory proclamation has gained much historical attention, this system of military justice had much more far-reaching effects on the enslaved population. Frémont's military justice system was designed to repress Confederate activity, but military law eventually presented a significant challenge to slavery. Even early in the war, the military's interference with the civil court and police system disrupted the enforcement of the slave code. At critical moments, the enslaved population co-opted this system of military justice to combat the institution of slavery.

But martial law was not a panacea for the enslaved population. Justus McKinstry, the provost marshal in charge of municipal St. Louis, did not replace the secessionists on the city Police Board. Although he arrested the board's chief commissioner for disloyalty, McKinstry replaced him with Basil Duke, who not only was a leader of the Minute Men but also had been responsible for flying the Confederate flag over the St. Louis courthouse prior to the Camp Jackson Affair.[120] The city police continued to enforce the black code and arrest suspected escaped slaves. African American residents of St. Louis would have to contend with a secessionist, antiblack leader of the city police.

The provost marshals held detained civilians in military prisons established in St. Louis. Myrtle Street Prison, opened in September 1861, was located in a facility confiscated from Bernard M. Lynch, the slave trader who had sold the Jacksons to William Lewis and who fled to the South at the beginning of the war. The transformation of Lynch's building into a military prison altered the St. Louis cityscape. Wrote one April 1865 visitor in a letter published in a black newspaper, "Today, as I was passing down Fifth Street, as far as the corner of Fifth and Myrtle, I noticed a high brick wall, and six soldiers, with their guns, walking about it." A city resident explained to the visitor, the building had been "Lynch's slave pen," "full of slaves for market. But now the thing is changed, and it is full of rebel prisoners."[121] Similarly, the McDowell Medical College was converted into the Gratiot Street Prison in December 1861 after its founder, Dr. Joseph McDowell, joined General Sterling Price's Confederate forces as a surgeon.[122]

The authority and power held by St. Louis's slaveholding class may have been the impetus behind the removal of Frémont, but these strengths were sharply challenged by martial law. The enslaved population used military authorities, such as U.S. policemen, to protect their own interests. For example, when Mattie Jackson's new owner, Captain Tirrell, decided to sell her and her family out of state, he had to smuggle them out of the city to avoid regulations on sales that the provost marshals had imposed. His plan was foiled after he loaded the Jacksons onto a covered wagon. Ellen Turner Jackson "sprang to her feet and gave [her captor] a desperate blow, and leaping to the ground she made an alarm." The wagon left her behind, but her calls alerted Union police officers, who stopped Tirrell and ordered him to surrender the children.[123]

Martial law politicized the Missouri household, especially when military regulations contradicted the authority of slave owners. Sectional conflict and disloyal activity gave military officers a reason to interfere in what had previously been considered private household matters. In August 1862, Union soldiers visited the McCutchen farm, located about eight miles outside of the city of St. Louis, to investigate suspected rebel activity. The soldiers found a freshly abandoned rebel camp and discovered that Margaret and Catherine McCutchen, two enslaved women owned by Rebekah McCutchen, had been cooking for fifty men, presumably rebels. The soldiers also discovered that Rebekah's husband not only had assisted the Confederate insurgents but was working to raise a company of Confederate soldiers. The soldiers confiscated Margaret, Catherine, and Margaret's son, Charlie, and turned them over to the provost marshal general, Bernard G. Farrar, who granted them emancipation certificates under the Second Confiscation Act of July 1862. With this legislation Congress declared that enslaved people owned by disloyal masters could be confiscated by the military as "contraband of war."[124] The formerly enslaved family established its own household in St. Louis.[125]

But the provost marshals were not reliable allies in the struggle against slavery. Personnel changes could lead to swings in policy. By September 1862, Colonel Thomas T. Gantt replaced Farrar as provost marshal general. Gantt considered the emancipation certificates issued by his predecessor "not worth anything." He took a much more conservative approach to using military power to override the Missouri slave code, proclaiming that only a federal court could decide the status of people confiscated by the military.[126]

Rebekah McCutchen's male relatives were among those who received Gantt's verbal approval to recapture and reenslave their former bondspersons. John McCutchen and his brother-in-law received an arrest warrant from a justice of the peace, "deputized" some men who had "heard of the matter," and forcibly removed Margaret, Catherine, and Charlie from their St. Louis home.[127] The matter was brought to the attention of the commander of the Department of the Missouri, Major General Samuel Curtis, who objected to the arrest and declared, "If as stated the negroes of the McCutchens have been taken by any person associated with their former servitude you will regard it as a contemp of Mil power for the [pur]pose of restoring them to slavery. Arrest offenders."[128] Martial law justified the forcible confiscation of enslaved domestic workers from disloyal households.[129] Slaveholding households risked offending military officers by using civil power to reenslave people who had been given military protection. Civil police might recapture suspected slaves, but military police could trump municipal law enforcement.

The assertion of military authority resulted, not necessarily intentionally, in the erosion of the slave system. The struggle between provost marshals and the city police provides one example of the institutional conflict between civil and military power. Archer Alexander, a fugitive slave, fled to St. Louis from St. Charles County in February 1863. William Eliot, a Unitarian minister and moderate antislavery Unionist, sheltered Alexander in exchange for his services in gardening and tending the animals. Alexander's enslaver discovered his location and recruited sympathetic local officials at the St. Louis city jail and, perhaps, a local policeman as his allies. Three men with "clubs in hand" and brandishing knives and pistols approached Alexander on the Eliot property, confirmed his identity, and "kicked him in the face," handcuffed him, and dragged him away to the city jail. "One of the men had a policeman's star on his coat, and the wagon was a numbered city wagon," reported a bystander. "The poor devil was mauled to death, and they drove off quick. I heard one of 'em say 'jail.'" The witness also reported that Union soldiers were afraid to interfere "because of the star."[130]

Eliot went to the provost marshal's office to report the attack. The duty officer, Captain Dwight, "was no friend of slavery." After reviewing the case and realizing that the office had authorized Alexander's residence in the city, Dwight proclaimed, "I'll show these fellows what it is to defy this office!" Dwight found two U.S. detectives, verified that their "six-shooters" were loaded, and charged them with finding Alexander and returning him to the Eliot household. One of the detectives, John Eagan, queried whether he was authorized to use lethal force if Alexander's captors refused to turn him over, and Dwight answered unequivocally, "Shoot them on the spot. . . . Shoot them dead if necessary."[131]

Eagan found the two kidnappers seated at a table, drinking, in the office of the city's Sixth Street Jail. They were celebrating their successful capture of Alexander from Eliot, who they described as "a little abolition preacher." Eagan declared that Alexander "was under military protection, and I want him." He then informed the captors that he had a provost marshal's warrant for their arrest, drew his gun, and took them to the Myrtle Street military prison, where they were incarcerated.[132]

Like Margaret and Catherine McCutchen, Archer Alexander was freed due to the disloyal activities of his owners.[133] Once Alexander was granted military protection by the Union Army, his family members escaped from bondage in the Missouri countryside and joined him in St. Louis. In November 1863, Alexander's wife, Louisa, was still living in the Missouri countryside with her master, James Naylor, when her husband offered to purchase her freedom. In response, Louisa wrote, Naylor "flew at me, and said I would never get free only at the point of the Bayonet, and there was no use in my ever speaking to him any more about it."[134] Louisa and their youngest daughter, Ellen, escaped to St. Louis when a local German American farmer hid them under cornstalks in his wagon and drove them out of the neighborhood. Louisa Alexander lodged with Archer at the Eliot household and was reunited with three of their other children who had also managed to reach St. Louis.[135] While martial law and the military justice system helped the Alexanders escape bondage, the personal courage of family members and the farmer were also critical in allowing the Alexander family to organize a new household free of the authority of slave masters in the city.

"Ah, Jane, Your Boots Cry Out of Freedom": Wartime Migration to St. Louis

Living in a room overlooking Chestnut Street in October 1864, Judge W. B. Napton wrote in his journal: "This city is now a great rendezvous of refugees of all parties and creeds from the interior. All men who do not join one army or the other are here. One would suppose from the crowd on streets that there are little short of 50,000 persons in the city, who have fled here for safety."[136] At least forty thousand formerly enslaved people first glimpsed freedom as the Union Army moved down the Mississippi River and occupied Confederate territory; the defeat of the Confederacy at Vicksburg opened the Missouri Valley to Union control.[137] According to Galusha Anderson, the refugees "came on government transports, came by boat-loads, sent by Union generals because they had become a serious impediment to military movements; they came also in wagons and cars of wonderful make, and in large numbers on foot. St. Louis was for them a city of refuge."[138]

Newly freed from the authority of slave owners, women escaped forced agricultural and domestic labor as well as sexual exploitation. For one such woman, Jane Dicks, the journey from Vicksburg to St. Louis brought about her personal emancipation from William Dicks's sexual oppression.[139] Prior to the war, William had promised to free Jane if she would "live with me as my wife in the state of Concubinage." But he reneged and refused to hand over her free papers: as William admitted, "She never had these papers in her possession; I kept them all the time." After Vicksburg fell to the Union Army in July 1863, Jane ceased sleeping in the same room as William, and she later stole the key to Dicks's trunk and retrieved the documents for herself.[140]

Dicks became acquainted with Aaron Brown, a Union man working on a steamboat, the *Jessie Belle*. Toward the end of August 1863, William Dicks learned that Brown and Jane would be leaving the city together. When Brown called at Dicks's home with a military permit to take Jane up the river, William not only ordered Brown to leave but threatened to shoot him.[141]

Brown reported this threat to the Union provost marshal, and military authorities arrested and jailed William Dicks. He remained in custody for about a week, during which time Brown, Jane Dicks, two other African American women, and several children left Vicksburg for St. Louis on the steamer *Jessie Belle*.[142]

After his release, William Dicks pursued Jane to St. Louis. Within a few weeks, he had found Jane and Aaron Brown living together.[143] William Dicks located a justice of the peace and testified that Jane and Brown had stolen money from him. Jane was arrested by a St. Louis constable and asked whether she had taken any money from her master. According to the policeman, Jane "hesitated for a while and said that she did not think she had done anything wrong." She admitted to taking "2 Silver Mexican dollars" but asserted that Dicks owed her that money.[144]

William Dicks's journey up the Mississippi demonstrates his investment in a woman he viewed as his property. He wanted to reclaim his money, his enslaved woman, and perhaps his social status as a slaveholder. When Jane Dicks left his home, multiple forms of capital escaped his possession. She was more than property to him. Dicks admitted to having sexual relations with Jane: "If Jane says that I have had connection with her, it is so. . . . That if she says, I have co-habited with her, it is so." He reportedly exclaimed to another man in reference to Jane, "How would you feel, if a man was to take your wife away from you?"[145] But Jane Dicks did not view their relationship as a marriage. She had been coerced into a sexual relationship, and when the opportunity presented itself, she asserted agency over her own body by escaping from Vicksburg. For many enslaved women, the escape from bondage and reclamation of their own bodies was a critical moment in the transition to free status.

St. Louis's African American population grew by 600 percent between the 1860 and 1870 Censuses.[146] "I dread to think of the coming winter, the Negro's are coming in by the hundred," wrote St. Louis resident Bethiah Pyatt McKowen in July 1864.[147] Some families migrating during the war stopped only temporarily in St. Louis on their way to free states such as Illinois and Wisconsin.[148] Others made St. Louis their permanent home.

St. Louis's wartime legal and social environment allowed those who fled slavery to live in risky but nominal freedom. Formerly enslaved people lived in constant danger of arrest by civil authorities. Alice, a woman who had received her free papers, was arrested and placed in the city jail after a local slave trader falsely identified her as his fugitive slave and used the city's civil court system to apprehend and incarcerate her. The Union military investigated and found that Alice had been freed as contraband in

Arkansas and sent to St. Louis by Samuel Sawyer, the superintendent of contrabands at Helena.[149]

Alice was one of a group of contrabands the Union military sent to the city from the contraband camp at Helena, Arkansas. Hundreds of contrabands traveled up the river to St. Louis, where they were housed at the Missouri Hotel.[150] The superintendent of contrabands noted that the refugees were "rather pleased with the idea of the negroes running a big Hotel in St. Louis."[151] By April 1863, more than eleven hundred people had received emancipation certificates through the Office of the Superintendent of Contrabands. The occupation of public and semipublic space by African Americans represented a shift in the city's cultural geography. The sight of freedpeople living in the Missouri Hotel, which had formerly been reserved for white guests, represented a startling change to the cityscape. Space itself was reconstructed during the Civil War, as African Americans increasingly walked the streets carrying emancipation papers. Yet despite this reconstruction of public space, residing in the Civil War city was not without physical risk.

Some migrants emigrated to nearby free states due to the danger of capture and reenslavement in St. Louis. This danger derived from two sources: the civil court system in St. Louis and illegal kidnappers. The superintendent of contrabands reported hearing of several other instances in which people were illegally kidnapped. On one occasion, he sent two freedpeople to the provost marshal's office and had sent along a guard for protection. The guard fended off an attack by either illegal slave catchers or persons attempting to execute a legal writ.[152]

The threat of kidnapping remained a danger for African Americans living in the city, although the St. Louis cityscape provided a degree of anonymity. Fugitive people "quickly scattered over the city," living in "pocket settlements."[153] Nevertheless, fear of recapture haunted refugee women, who, according to white women from the Ladies' Contraband Relief Society, "think more of their children being sold South than of their death."[154]

In November 1863, Missouri began to recruit black soldiers, and waves of recruits and their families arrived in St. Louis.[155] A few days after Christmas 1864, Nancy Edwards; her half-sister, Mary Ross; and Nancy's husband, James Edwards, determined to "run-off" from their owner's St. Charles County farm. The escapees made their way to St. Louis, where James Edwards immediately enlisted, while Nancy Edwards "worked out at different places."[156]

James Edwards and other African American soldiers trained at Benton Barracks, a military installation located just west of the city at the old county fairgrounds. In 1863, the Union military opened Benton Barracks as a contraband camp and hospital.[157]

Soldiers' wives formed new social networks after arriving in St. Louis. Rosette Hughes and her husband, Tom, ran away from their home in Howard County during the war. Claiborne Holiday, a local African American man from Rosette's old neighborhood, noted that when "a whole host of colored people" left their masters, "Ozette went along with them and she never came back any more."[158] Tom Hughes enlisted in the U.S. Colored Infantry, while Rosette remained in St. Louis and worked for wages. Rosette then became acquainted with Nancy Watts, a young woman who was also working for wages and whose husband was serving in the same unit. When the husbands received leave, they traveled together back to St. Louis to see their wives.[159]

Fugitive women often fled slavery with insufficient clothing, in inclement weather, and in fear of their lives. Lacking money and other options, they often traveled on foot. Large numbers of these migrants died from illness. Emily Elizabeth Parsons, the nursing superintendent at Benton Barracks hospital, noted in the winter of 1863–64, "There are a great number of frost-bites in the hospital. The negroes lay in the woods and fields in cold weather while escaping from their masters." According to the Ladies' Contraband Relief Society, "Especially the women and children . . . arrive here, they are utterly destitute," while the *Daily Missouri Democrat* described the new arrivals as "scantily clad in mere rags."[160] Elizabeth Brooks traveled to St. Louis with five children; during their time at Benton Barracks, her two youngest, Nancy and George, died of disease, and her husband succumbed to pneumonia while serving in the Union Army in July 1864.[161] In some cases, pregnancy further complicated the journey and posed additional health challenges. According to Parsons, so many births occurred at Benton Barracks that a doctor suggested that the military base be renamed the "Recruiting Infantry Station."[162]

The city's established black population provided institutional aid and social support to the new migrants. The city was home to six African American churches, each of which operated "a poor fund, for the relief of needy persons."[163] The city also possessed a black Masonic lodge and numerous aid societies, among them the Robert Small Benevolent Society and a Preachers' Aid Society associated with the African Methodist Episcopal faith. African

American women built and participated in these benevolent societies. Ara Moore was a founding member of the Preachers' Aid Society.[164]

St. Louis's African American women participated in the formation and operation of secular aid organizations such as the Colored Ladies' Soldiers' Aid Society, founded in 1863 to assist black soldiers and contraband refugees. Led by the group's president, Mary Meachum, and secretary Charlton H. Tandy, members of the society cared for African American soldiers stationed in St. Louis and taught them to read. The organization negotiated with the streetcar lines to allow members of the society to ride inside the cars on Saturdays so that they could visit the soldiers.[165] African American women also belonged to volunteer societies such as the Freedmen's Orphan Home Association, which operated an orphanage for African American children.[166]

The white-run Ladies' Contraband Relief Society ran a school for African American children, while another white group, the Western Sanitary Union, provided books. By December 1863, the city boasted four "pay schools" and one free school for the African American population.[167]

Once the refugees arrived in St. Louis, they searched for paid labor to sustain their newly independent households. African American women found work as laundresses, cooks, and maids.[168] Enslaved and free women often performed the same types of labor. However, status as a free person dramatically transformed the meaning of this labor. As a woman named Harriet put it, emancipation meant that "she belonged to herself and had a right to what she earned."[169]

But life in St. Louis remained difficult for many migrants. The available paid work often was not sufficient to meet refugees' needs, and they found themselves destitute. African Americans lacked access to the almshouses and parish relief that had traditionally aided indigent white residents, and the African American community's voluntary associations could not pick up the slack.[170] Furthermore, the wartime economy depressed wages in St. Louis.[171] Contrabands lived in crowded conditions, with several people packed into small apartments and houses. A combination of sickness, destitution, and exposure caused the deaths of many refugees. On January 6, 1863, a local newspaper reported that an eighteen-year-old contraband woman died of "destitution and sickness."[172] J. G. Forman, the secretary of the Western Sanitary Commission, was concerned that "the care of these people is not half provided for by the W. S. Commission, by the Government, or by voluntary Associations."[173]

Moreover, some white residents reacted hostilely to the influx of African American refugees. One St. Louis newspaper complained about "the throng of free negroes that daily and nightly infest our city. They are without work, and consequently are dependent upon charity or dishonest means for support."[174]

Nevertheless, formerly enslaved women built new households for themselves and their families. Minerva Moore and her husband, Alfred, left Mississippi County, Missouri, when Alfred enlisted in the Union Army. He sent Minerva on a steamboat to Cape Girardeau, Missouri, a port town where contrabands had gathered. After just two weeks there, Minerva Moore braved recapture to travel into the countryside to escort her mother and six siblings to St. Louis. The family lived at Benton Barracks for four months until Minerva rented a house and found a job as a laundress that enabled her to keep "my mother and her little children."[175] Moore accomplished not only her own freedom but also that of her close relatives. Enslaved women such as Minerva Moore performed political work when they fled their slave homes and established independent households in St. Louis. The escapees did not ultimately wish to live as fugitives subject to arrest on the streets by city police; rather, they aspired to live unencumbered by the legal disabilities of slavery or black codes. They were engaged in a struggle to rework their relationship with the nation-state.

In the winter of 1863, a government steamboat carried a group of formerly enslaved people along the Mississippi River. When one woman, Jane, strode across the boat with a pair of squeaky boots, another refugee remarked, "'Ah Jane, . . . your boots cry out of freedom.'"[176]

These aspirations for freedom included the ability to live without fear of arrest; the definition of liberty included the freedom to walk in public and claim a presence in the cityscape. The *Christian Recorder*, a national newspaper published by the African American Methodist Episcopal Church, published an account of that community's 1864 New Year's celebration, which began with a procession to Turner's Hall, where people of all ages enjoyed speeches and entertainment: "I tell you this is 1864, and not the days of yore, that we now live in. . . . Only think of such a procession in this city, when Claib. Jackson was pursuing the colored people in this city not but a couple years ago with grievous fines for being here; and now he is gone, and the black men, with muskets and banners, are marching to the music of 'John Brown's Soul is Marching On.'"[177]

As the war drew to a close, a black visitor observed that the St. Louis police no longer enforced the black code: "There is no more closing up of the colored people's churches, to keep them from Divine worship. No arresting colored people for coming into this State contrary to law." Praising the "Lord of battles" and the Union Army, he celebrated the surrender of Petersburg and Richmond and noted, "Citizens, here, both white and colored, are making preparations for a grand jubilee."[178]

The ability to safely occupy public space became a defining feature of freedom, an explicit contrast to life under slavery.[179] Mattie Jackson noted that as a slave, she was "not allowed to advance a rod from the house, or even out of call, without a severe punishment." But after the war, when she was walking along a street, she "met my old master, Lewis, who strove so hard to sell us away that he might avoid seeing us free, on the street. He was so surprised that before he was aware of it he dropped a bow."[180]

CHAPTER 2

"A Negro Woman Is Running at Large in Your City"

Contraband Women and the Transformation of Union Military Policy

"I HAVE A NEGRO WOMAN, who I am informed, is running at large in your city," wrote Luther T. Colbir to the St. Louis provost marshal general in February 1863. Colbir believed that his enslaved woman had escaped and traveled to St. Louis with the 27th Missouri Regiment. In fact, he blamed men in the regiment who had "enticed" her "to leave her home."[1]

Between 1861 and 1865, approximately two million women and girls who had been enslaved in the United States achieved freedom in what constituted a legal moment of great significance for African American women specifically and for the enlargement of U.S. citizenry generally.[2] Among the first of these to achieve practical freedom if not legal emancipation in Missouri were the thousands of other women who escaped their enslavers in the countryside and fled to Union lines. Two more of these women were Melissa Abernathy and her daughter, Betty, who fled to the Missouri port town of Cape Girardeau, "where they's sojers who'd protect us."[3] Some women who pursued this strategy received certificates that confirmed their status as military "contraband" and were consequently regarded as "freedom papers." In a novel legal development, the traditional definition of *contraband of war* was expanded to include enslaved people; the military was then entitled to confiscate those human beings.[4]

In the clearest examples of military emancipation, the military issued emancipation certificates and declared fugitives forever free under the Second Confiscation Act. The First Confiscation Act, passed by the federal government in the summer of 1861, had "nullified" the claims of owners who had directed enslaved people to labor for the Confederate war effort, allowing the Union military to appropriate those laborers.[5] In the summer of 1862, the Second Confiscation Act expanded on its predecessor by declaring that any person owned by disloyal masters could be confiscated—and freed from slavery—as "contraband of war."[6]

The Union military viewed enslaved men as the ideal contraband to confiscate from Confederates. Men who could dig trenches and build military fortifications had obvious military value. In contrast, women were less likely then enslaved men to be classified as "contrabands" under the First Confiscation Act; officers initially viewed the presence of enslaved women as a problem and routinely expelled fugitive women and children from military posts and encampments, failing to acknowledge the contributions they could and did make to the war effort.[7] But women made a space for themselves in the military camps and regiments, providing valuable, if frequently exploited, labor as laundresses, nurses, and cooks.[8] The army, looking for an expedient solution to sanitation problems, was willing to extend protection to the refugee women who offered to wash their laundry. Cleaning was an essential service for the army, but these arrangements also continued the economic exploitation that these women faced when in bondage.[9]

"We Shall Then Be Freed from These Vexatious Questions": Enslaved Women and Military Emancipation

In the early stages of the war, opportunities for enslaved women to escape slavery were constrained by the Union military policy of not disturbing the institution of slavery in Missouri. In May 1861, a man from Greene County asked Thomas T. Gantt, a prominent Unionist from St. Louis, if the government would "interfere with the institution of negro slavery in Missouri." Gantt, a conservative who opposed military emancipation and would later serve as provost marshal general, answered "most unqualifiedly and almost indignantly in the negative." Gantt "felt certain" that the Union military would return escapees to enslavers.[10] Gantt wrote to William S. Harney, commander of the Military Department of the West, requesting reassurance on this point, and Harney responded that he had "no doubt" that the U.S. government would respect "the protection of negro property." General Harney further explained that enslaved people who had escaped to Union lines "were carefully sent back to their owners."[11]

A brief but radical shift in policy occurred with John C. Frémont's appointment as Harney's successor in July 1861. Enslaved workers were building Confederate fortifications and creating a complex system of breastworks in southern Missouri. In August 1861, at New Madrid, Missouri, less than 170 miles from Frémont's St. Louis headquarters, Confederate general Gideon Pillow reported that he was "pushing up the defenses at this place having some 160 negroes at work."[12] A few months later, Confederate general J. Jeff Thompson reported that construction work was being "done by negroes" as it would be "impossible to make my men work" on the fortifications.[13] Sympathetic to the abolition of slavery and frustrated with the Confederate use of slave labor, Frémont declared martial law on August 30, 1861. In addition, he proclaimed, "The property . . . of all persons in the state of Missouri who shall take up arms against the United States, or who shall be directly proven to have taken an active part with their enemies in the field is declared to be confiscated to the public use, and their slaves, if any they have, are hereby declared freemen." This proclamation anticipated how martial law would later be used by the military to circumvent the state's slave code. But at the early stages of the war, Frémont's orders caused consternation and uproar among Missouri's conservative Unionists and alarmed the president. In September 1861 he ordered General Frémont to confine his concerns with slavery to the scope defined by the First Confiscation Act. Later that fall, Lincoln removed Frémont as the department's commander.[14]

The U.S. Congress and military leaders understood that the labor of enslaved men gave the Confederacy a military advantage. Not only did it provide construction manpower, but it improved morale as the Confederate army transferred heavy and menial work from white soldiers onto the enslaved population. In December 1861, Missouri saw a rise in insurgent and organized Confederate activity.[15] Union officers in St. Louis responded by ordering the impressment of enslaved men owned by Confederates.

Union anger was particularly provoked by guerrilla actions that destroyed the state's infrastructure. Major General Henry W. Halleck suppressed "an insurrection of some 12,000 or 15,000 armed men . . . organized north of the Missouri River," where he found the greatest burden to be the rebel forces' "burning of the railroad bridges and destruction of the telegraph lines."[16] He ordered "the commanding officer of the nearest post" to impress "the slaves of all secessionists in the vicinity" to repair damage to "railroads or telegraph lines."[17]

"We have got to fight the devil with fire," wrote General Samuel R. Curtis, lamenting the fact that "we are not likely to use one negro where the rebels have used a thousand."[18] As the war progressed and Confederate activity escalated in Missouri, Union officers became more likely to confiscate enslaved people and less likely to ask questions about the legalities of the situation.[19] In March 1862, Halleck ordered his commander in southern Missouri to "impress all the negroes you can find."[20] Members of the Union military tended not to distinguish between enslaved and free people with these involuntary impressments, forcibly confiscating many men who did not wish to leave their homes. But women in particular were reluctant to leave children and elderly family members to join Union soldiers on the march.[21]

Union officers confiscated enslaved women when their labor was deemed appropriate to the war effort, particularly laundering, which was seen as "women's work."[22] Cathy Williams recalled that in 1861, soldiers from the 8th Indiana Volunteer Infantry "came to Jefferson city [and] took me and other colored folks with them." While traveling with the army, Williams cooked and washed laundry for the troops.[23] Technically, Cathy Williams did not qualify as a legal contraband under the First Confiscation Act, as she had not been put to work on the Confederate war effort. But in the very early stages of the war, wartime confusion and military necessity aided women who ran to Union lines.

Some Union officers, however, persisted in believing that women were unfit for military labor. Major Henry S. Eggleston of the 1st Wisconsin Cavalry ordered that "no more women or children under fifteen years of age should be admitted within our lines" because they "could be of no use to us whatever."[24] Moreover, women, children, and the elderly were perceived as potential drains on camp rations and the speed of military travel. The young, fit, and childless were more likely to attach themselves successfully to a Union regiment and keep up with the speed of military travel. Mothers with children and elderly individuals were more likely to be excluded from army camps in these early escapes to Union lines.[25]

Yet women and children continued to seek refuge with Union troops. In November 1861, an enslaved man, woman, and "three small children" came into the Franklin County encampment of Captain J. W. Towner, prompting him to ask his commander, "What shall be done in such a case?"[26] Frustrated by a deluge of such inquiries, Halleck sought to "be freed from these vexatious questions" by ordering the expulsion of all fugitive slaves from federal camps, posts, and regiments on the march.[27] The matter could be resolved, he felt, by a complete separation of the military from the slave issue.

Halleck's Exclusion Orders of November 1861 codified a contraband policy that did not assist fugitive women in their pursuit of freedom. His orders specified that "unauthorized persons, black or white, free or slave, must be kept out of our camps."[28] Young children clearly fell into the category of "unauthorized persons"; thus mothers with children were excluded from Union camps and forts. But not all Union officials shared Halleck's views. One officer stationed in central Missouri defended the presence of African Americans in his camp on the grounds that all of them were employed "in accordance with the Army Regulations" except for "one little child," and he hoped that an exception could be made.[29]

Though Halleck wanted to "keep clear of all such questions," his order did not have its intended effect.[30] Fugitive men and women continued to arrive at military camps, desperate, hungry, and willing to perform the labor that Union soldiers preferred to avoid, a pattern of behavior that occurred throughout the South wherever enslaved people had the ability to flee to Union lines.[31] In December 1861, slave owners complained to Missouri governor Hamilton R. Gamble that their enslaved people were living at the military post at Rolla.[32] The post's commander, Colonel Grenville Dodge, ordered all of his subordinate officers to "immediately deliver to these Head Quarters, All Fugitive Slaves" and not to allow any new escapees to "enter and remain within the Lines."[33]

Despite these efforts, the problems persisted. A fugitive woman named Viney was recaptured by Missouri citizens and brought to Lieutenant Colonel John S. Phelps in the fall of 1861. Viney had escaped her slave home in Greene County when Union regiments marched through Southwest Missouri. Phelps, who was "personally acquainted with all of the owners," planned to return Viney and three other escapees.[34] Halleck had hoped that his exclusion orders would prohibit this sort of involvement with rendering individuals who fled their enslavers.

In some instances, officers were confused about contraband policy and their ability to employ formerly enslaved people. Major George E. Waring Jr., the commander of the Frémont Hussars, stationed in Central Missouri, employed a fugitive woman as a mess cook. In December 1861, Waring received a military circular reiterating Halleck's exclusion orders and noting that "a number of fugitive slaves" still resided with Union camps and regiments: the document directed commanders to banish "all fugitive slaves . . . either male or female." Waring concluded that he had to return the woman back to slavery, though, he wrote, his "private feelings revolt" at the idea of excluding African Americans from his camp "as they would be homeless and helpless." Union officers often confused the exclusion of fugitives from camp with rendering escapees back to enslavers.[35]

The confusion regarding his orders alarmed Halleck, who wrote a letter in which he specifically addressed the Waring incident. Having military employees act as "negro catchers" was "contrary to the intent of General Orders No. 3." It was not the "duty" of the military, declared Halleck, to "decide upon the rights of master & slave."[36]

Some Union officials understood that the work performed by formerly enslaved women was vital. In September 1862, J. G. Porter, the medical director at Springfield, Missouri, wrote that "Negro women are needed in the Hospital located here."[37] Since army regulations permitted freedpeople to be employed as "servants, teamsters, and hospital attendants" and in other official positions, some officers attempted to work around Halleck's exclusion orders by arguing that the African Americans working in their camps were not enslaved. "These negroes all claim and insist that they are *free*," reported Major Waring. He had "caused all negroes in my camp to be examined, and it was reported to me that they all stoutly asserted that they were free."[38]

As the federals marched through Missouri in 1861, enslaved women, men, and children attached themselves to regiments. Women and children were most likely to be welcomed by regiments that had been mustered from populations with fierce abolitionist sentiments, such as the Frémont Hussars or the Kansas troops. According to Union chaplain H. D. Fisher, it seemed as if the "whole negro population of Missouri" had followed Frémont's troops to Springfield, where the Union "camp was the center of attraction to multitudes of 'contrabands' and refugees."[39] After Frémont's troops were defeated in the August 1861 Battle of Wilson's Creek, loyalists evacuated Springfield, and the enslaved population sought refuge with the retreating army.[40] As Confederate sympathizer Willard Hall Mendenhall observed, "a great many negroes are leaving thare masters and following off the army."[41]

Many attached themselves to Kansas troops under the command of abolitionist General James H. Lane. Kansas soldiers led between five and six hundred formerly enslaved people, including women and children, out of Missouri to "Kansas and freedom," dismaying conservative Unionists. Officers armed thirty African American men to protect the escapees against Confederate insurgents. At the Kansas border, Chaplain Fisher halted the refugees and declared that "they were 'forever free.'" In response, the crowd "jumped, cried, sang and laughed for joy." An eighty-year-old woman announced that the year of jubilee had come.[42]

Kansas officers, hardened by the violence of the border wars with Missouri that had begun during the debate over whether Kansas should enter the Union as a slave or free state and that had intensified during the Civil War, were more likely to disregard the legal restrictions of the First Confiscation Act. Antagonistic to Missouri slaveholders, Kansas troops often assisted entire families of African Americans escape bondage, even using carriages and wagons to help women and children, who may have had difficulty keeping up with troops on foot.[43] In one case, Kansas soldiers appropriated a buggy belonging to Margaret Hays to assist enslaved people near Westport, Missouri, in reaching freedom across the Kansas border. According to Hays, "It was very aggreviationg [*sic*] to see it driving up to the door and to see negroes jump into it and drive off." In addition, Hays's uncle, Judge James Brunfield Yeager, lost "upwards of ten thousand dollars" in slave property, and Margaret herself lost eleven people.[44]

Kansas remained a site of refuge for the enslaved population of Missouri throughout the Civil War, and many men enlisted in Kansas regiments. Within the first six months of the war, Kansas troops enrolled an estimated two thousand formerly enslaved Missouri men, and by the end of 1861, there were enough to "fill two colored regiments." The 1st Kansas Colored Infantry was commissioned in January 1862.[45] These men, in turn, liberated more people to flee from western Missouri to freedom.

In the fall of 1861, several African American and white Kansas soldiers came to the household of James M. Hunter, a slaveholder in western Missouri, and informed his daughter, Elizabeth, that "they had come after the negroes." Although Elizabeth had been sewing a Union flag and despite her protestations that her father was not a secessionist, the Kansas soldiers liberated the enslaved family of four. "They put them in the wagon and drove away off from the house" reported Hunter's daughter. James Hunter complained to General Lane about the theft of his slave property, and Lane arranged to have Hunter taken to the "little cabin" near camp where the family was living. With several Kansas soldiers watching, Hunter asked whether Jane wanted to return home. She replied, "If these men will do as they have promised by me, I think not." She and her husband and children remained with the Kansas troops.[46]

In March 1862, Union reports accused Kansas Jayhawkers "organized under the auspices of Senator Lane" of "stealing" Missouri "negroes."[47] Eleven-year-old Andrew Williams, his mother, and his five siblings escaped slavery with the assistance of the 6th Kansas Regiment in September 1862. While foraging for supplies at a rebel slaveholder's house, Kansas soldiers approached Andrew's mother and asked, "Don't you want to go to Kans and Be free?" When she answered, "Yess Sir," the soldier told her, "Get your childern in this wagon." The soldiers brought the Williamses to a camp in Southwest Missouri; they remained there until September 30, when the troops "sent an escort with all of the colored people" to Fort Scott in Kansas.[48] After an August 1862 skirmish at Hickory Grove, Missouri, John Burris, a lieutenant colonel with the 10th Kansas Infantry, reported, "About 80 loyal colored persons accompanied and followed my command out of Missouri."[49] The following month, he claimed that "upward of 60 loyal colored persons, tired of the rule of rebel masters, furnished their own transportation and subsistence and accompanied my command to Kansas."[50] And again in November, he wrote, "A considerable number of contrabands accompany us to Kansas."[51]

The confusion of war and the ad hoc treatment of enslaved people assisted women in their pursuit of freedom but also left them in vulnerable positions. In August 1861, after three enslaved people had traveled from Palmyra, Missouri, to the arsenal at St. Louis with an Illinois regiment, their master, S. R. Glover, attempted to recapture them; however, they had reportedly left St. Louis with another regiment. Soldiers in the same regiment also allowed an enslaved person to travel with them from Cape Girardeau County to Washington, D.C.[52] Although these particular individuals managed to leverage their informal attachments to Union regiments into successful escapes, many of those who fled were vulnerable to recapture, as we can see by the way Glover gained military support to pursue his property.

Officers stationed in St. Louis were displeased with the city police who were "in the habit of arresting negroes" they found on the street as suspected "runaways."[53] These officers were disturbed when their "servants" were taken away from them and returned to slavery. Legal practices long instituted to defend slavery as an institution hindered the military's use of runaways as a labor pool. The removal of servants from army officers "[was] exceedingly annoying to officers under marching orders."[54]

"On the Mere Statement of Slaves": Fugitive Women, Slave Testimony, and the Enforcement of the Second Confiscation Act

The passage of the Second Confiscation Act in July 1862 brought new opportunities for enslaved Missouri women to achieve official recognition as contrabands.[55] This act transformed the relationship between the military and Missouri fugitive women by liberalizing the concept of "disloyalty." Any enslaved woman who could demonstrate her master's disloyalty could claim contraband status. The Second Confiscation Act provided a method of escape that was friendly to the needs of enslaved women. Rather than needing to prove that they could keep up with regiments on the march, women, especially those with young children, now faced the much easier task of providing valuable intelligence to the provost marshals.

But the Union military needed to enforce the Second Confiscation Act for enslaved women to reap its benefits in any large measure. General John Schofield, administrator of the District of the Missouri from June through September 1862, was sympathetic to the interests of slaveholders and promoted a narrow interpretation of the Second Confiscation Act.[56] Gantt, now serving as Schofield's provost marshal general, refused to enforce the act on the grounds that military officers could not confiscate enslaved people without a federal court order. Gantt also asserted that court orders had to be issued in each individual case.[57]

General Schofield's conservative contraband policy would soon fall away. Lincoln's preliminary announcement of the Emancipation Proclamation in September 1862, while not legally relevant to the loyal state of Missouri, indicated a change of attitude at the highest levels of the federal government.[58] The same month, Lincoln appointed General Curtis to replace Schofield as commander of the Department of the Missouri. General Curtis took a more liberal view of the Second Confiscation Act and issued orders with the clear goal of enforcement.

African American women acquired a powerful tool in their pursuit of freedom on December 24, 1862, when General Curtis distributed Order no. 35, which stated, "Whenever slaves seek protection . . . it shall be the duty of all Provost Marshals to take evidence as to the facts." The order also permitted the marshals, in their capacity as administrators of the lowest courts of military justice, to accept the testimony of enslaved people.[59]

Curtis ordered local provost marshals to hold impromptu courts, collect testimony from enslaved people, and judge their rights to emancipation under the Second Confiscation Act. Those who qualified for classification as contraband would receive emancipation certificates. In addition, Curtis instructed soldiers under his command to "protect the freedom" of "emancipated slaves" and reminded his troops that under an article of war passed in March 1862, they could not assist slave owners in recapturing runaways.[60]

Acceptance of black testimony constituted a significant departure from the treatment African Americans routinely received in Missouri civil courts, which barred them from testifying against white individuals.[61] The Union military, an arm of the state, provided enslaved people with the legal tools necessary to achieve recognition of their contraband status.

By allowing such testimony, Curtis brought enslaved women under the purview of military authority and allowed all formerly enslaved people to have hearings with provost marshals. As long as a woman could reach a place where a provost marshal was stationed, she had a chance to gain an emancipation certificate: as a result, "colonies of runaway slaves formed near army posts, railway depots, and the larger towns," with new arrivals promptly accusing their masters of treason.[62] Missouri's slave owners were horrified.

By early February 1863, almost one thousand enslaved people had obtained emancipation certificates from the provost marshal stationed in Chillicothe, in Linn County.[63] The physical ability to reach a marshal played a critical role in women's ability to pursue freedom under the Second Confiscation Act. A Franklin County slave woman named Hulda and her six children made "nightly journeys to neighboring towns and military stations in search of imaginary Pro Marshals," wrote a sympathetic neighbor.[64] Unless Hulda was able to locate a provost marshal, she would not be able to attain freedom for herself or her children. Another woman, Betsy, escaped in the night on her master's horse, bringing her infant and her daughter, Clarisa, to a nearby Union encampment in the town of Washington, Missouri.[65] Because Curtis's orders allowed local provost marshals to issue emancipation certificates, women with children could travel shorter distances in their bid for freedom. Shorter distances reduced the chances of women and children being caught in transit to Union lines. If recaptured, fugitive women and men encountered violent reactions from pro-slavery white residents. One concerned citizen reported that "Henry Hibbard . . . hung a woman in St. Clair a few days ago to make her tell who she belongs to."[66]

Enslaved women, aware of the powers of the provost marshals, showed great facility in using this knowledge to gain freedom. At her hearing, Edy, an enslaved woman who traveled to Hannibal, Missouri, asserted that the "family who claimed her labor" were "all rebels," and she claimed that she had left "owing to cruel treatment." The provost marshal who heard her testimony gave her a pass that enabled her to live freely in Hannibal.[67] In another instance, Harriet Meyer reported that her master, James Wood, had ordered her to cook for Confederate rebels.[68] Lucinda Turner of Ralls County swore that her master "hoped Jeff Davis would kill all the abolitionists and that the federals would be driven out of Missouri." Like Edy, Meyer and Turner received papers.[69]

The new regulations incensed slave owners, who found themselves accused of disloyalty and stripped of their property "on the mere statement of the slaves." Missouri slave master Samuel Glover complained, "The negroes say that they belong to secessionists, and the officers believe them." Loyal slave owners were particularly offended that "little subordinate Provost Marshals" were acting to "gravely confiscate the best Union man's servant." Loyalty to the Union reinforced slave owners' sense of entitlement to their dependent slave property, especially when they felt that their "loyalty is unquestioned."[70]

Curtis's enforcement of the Second Confiscation Act and his contraband-friendly administration encouraged women, men, and children to escape en masse. Entire families fled to military posts. The provost marshal at Jefferson City reported that in May 1863, "hundreds" of escapees had congregated in the state capital.[71] Questions about the refugees plagued headquarters. Reporting the nighttime arrival of 270 people, "mostly women and children suffering of some thing to eat," in Sedalia in July 1863, the commander of the District of Central Missouri, Egbert Brown, asked General Schofield, "What shall I do with them?"[72]

Slave owner Greer W. Davis complained to General Curtis that "hundreds have escaped and sought protection" at the Cape Girardeau military post, south of St. Louis on the Missouri River. By February 1863, the town and impromptu refugee camp became a place where escapees exchanged information, outfitted themselves, and ventured back out to rescue family and friends. According to Davis, "Whenever they wish to release a relative from bondage, they issue out from that place, as I understand, armed, and by menace take property." Davis's home was "visited by two negroes" who "demanded" the "delivery up of a small girl"—"the only one I have." On another occasion, "six negroes, four armed, about 12 oclock rescued some three or four" enslaved Missourians from his neighbor. "Surely," Davis argued, "the Act of Congress never contemplated or intended to sanction the abstracting of property in this way."[73]

In July 1863, a Farmington slave owner reported, "The Women & Children are preparing to go also: Indeed, it is expected that in a short time there will be an extensive stampede among them."[74] Two months later, various posts around the state reported that the fugitive population comprised "women of all ages, children of all ages and sexes."[75]

Colonel C. W. Parker of the Missouri militia declared the "absolute necessity of some immediate action on the part of the Military authorities in Missouri to stop the running away of negroes from their owners."[76] Parker, who had enlisted in the Missouri Militia, and many others sympathized with slaveholder interests: "If steps are not taken very soon to exclude negroes from the lines of military camps," he asserted, Missouri "will be deprived of slave labor in a great measure."[77] Colonel Parker had good reason to worry. In May 1863, reports told of "negroes are going off by scores to Marshall & other places" and of "hundreds" gathered at Jefferson City.[78] African Americans fled southeastern Missouri counties in large quantities through the summer: Cook's Settlement (St. Francois County) and Fredericktown (Madison County) were "stripped of negroes," and slave owners complained that crops were "rotting in the Fields for want of Harvest hands."[79]

Eleven mule teams pulled "wagons filled with Negro women & children" into the town of Miami in the north-central part of the state on August 31. Accompanied by Union soldiers, more than two hundred men, women, and children marched behind, some "playing the fiddle" and "dancing about the street as though they were possessed." Late into the night, slaveholder Elvira Scott watched the freedpeople "thronging the yard . . . cooking, preaching, praying, & dancing."[80]

Slave owners complained to Governor Gamble about the mass escapes: "Our servants have been induced to run away and come to the Post at Lexington. . . . We suppose that there are now or were on yesterday at least 150 negroes at the College and around it." The Lexington post commander turned away slave owners and gave escapees tents and food. Masters found their former property protected from recapture by military authority. By August 1863, the camp held an estimated 250–300 formerly enslaved men, women, and children, about a third of whom had successfully applied for emancipation certificates.[81]

Many of the escapees "gathered at the various posts on railroad lines in the State."[82] In the absence of military directives, transportation via rail-road or steamship was quite difficult, as Missouri law held common carriers such as railroads and steamships legally responsible when enslaved people escaped via those conveyances. In 1862, Malinda, an enslaved woman from Pettis County, escaped bondage by traveling on the Pacific Railroad from Sedalia to St. Louis. Malinda's legal owner, George W. McClure, filed suit against the railroad in the Pettis county court, seeking six hundred dollars in compensation.[83] By August 1863, irate slaveholders had taken the Pacific Rail-road to court ten times, and the company's president was receiving threaten-ing letters "daily."[84] Not until the state legislature eradicated Missouri's slave code in January 1865 were common carriers relieved of responsibility for the "illegal transportation of slaves," and until that time, common carriers were reluctant to transport the refugees without a direct military order.[85]

In response to the gathering of people at transportation centers throughout the state, General Curtis instructed Colonel Bernard G. Farrar, an assistant to the provost marshal general, to arrange transportation for stranded African Americans. Many refugees were sent to employment in Iowa, Wisconsin, and Illinois.[86]

Curtis, formerly an Iowa politician with antislavery instincts, had entered the Civil War much more predisposed to support emancipation than many Missouri officers.[87] Before his appointment as commander of the District of the Missouri, Curtis had freed hundreds of enslaved women during a campaign against Confederates wintering in southwestern Mis-souri. In February 1862, Curtis moved against the Confederate army led by General Sterling Price. As Curtis marched through southwestern Missouri and into northern Arkansas, hundreds of enslaved people followed. Officers observed that "immense numbers ... were flocking into our camp daily," "quite a proportion" of them women and children.[88] In March 1862, Curtis won the Battle at Pea Ridge and marched his army to the banks of the Mis-sissippi River, where he set up camp at Helena, Arkansas. The escapees who had followed set up an impromptu camp on the outskirts of the city. Curtis emancipated these people under the First Confiscation Act, even though many were "unsuitable for military labor," and assigned them certificates of freedom, creating "a general stampede" of enslaved people "in this region of cotton and contempt for Yankees."[89] Curtis's distribution of emancipation certificates placed the contrabands in a more secure legal position compared with that of the enslaved people who informally followed the army. Curtis assigned the certificates to men, women, and children. And unlike some other Union officers, Curtis admitted women, children, and elderly people into camp.

The Helena camp housed at least a "thousand contrabands," mostly "old men, women and children" living in poor conditions. Paid labor was scarce, overcrowding was rampant, and sickness spread easily.[90] Seeking to reduce the size of the camp, General Benjamin Prentiss, the commander of the Eastern Arkansas Military District, approved a March 1863 plan to have five hundred contrabands travel up the Mississippi River to St. Louis. But Prentiss neglected to discuss the plan with Curtis, now the commander of the Department of the Missouri, which was headquartered in St. Louis.

Upon learning of the steamboat's arrival, the general exclaimed, "Five hundred contrabands! What in the world shall I do with them?"[91] After declaring that "Missouri must not be made the depot for the paupers of Arkansas," Curtis quickly recovered his equilibrium and resolved to assist the new arrivals. He assigned them to the abandoned Missouri Hotel and resolved to demonstrate to the people of St. Louis "a precedent of shipping & unloading contrabands" into a city that had long protected the institution of slavery. Curtis assigned "an armed force to prevent disturbance" and made a show of disembarking the contrabands.[92] As the new residents walked off the wharf to their new downtown home, the officer who accompanied them through the streets noted that "the whole city" had come out to watch this parade of recently freed people.[93]

The Missouri Hotel became a center of contraband life in St. Louis. Curtis assigned men from the 37th Iowa Volunteers to protect the hotel's residents, and the American Missionary Association opened a school in the kitchen.[94]

To the chagrin of politically powerful slaveholders in Missouri, General Curtis encouraged the process of emancipation through his recognition of the Union's obligations to the contraband population. Slaveholders' complaints about Curtis spiked in the spring of 1863, when they petitioned Governor Gamble and President Lincoln to replace the general. In May, Lincoln replaced Curtis with Schofield, who had also been Curtis's predecessor and had a history of supporting slave owner interests.[95] As late as July 1863, Schofield had questioned Secretary of War Edwin M. Stanton about whether it was "the duty of the Military authorities" to provide emancipation certificates to those enslaved people who qualified as contrabands.[96] Within two months of reassuming command, Schofield had overturned Curtis's Order no. 35 and directed the district provost marshals to surrender all "slaves claiming freedom" and send names of witnesses to headquarters "so that the matter may be turned over to the civil authorities."[97] Under Schofield's policy, enslaved women no longer had the right to military hearings before provost marshals, seriously weakening the women's ability to achieve free status through the Second Confiscation Act.

"I Had Had Already Trouble Enough with Her": Fugitive Women and Loyal Slaveholders

Lucy Mack, a thirty-five-year-old woman, "went off in the night" with her husband, George, and their two children, Harriet and Zeno, in October 1862. Her master found her living at a military camp in St. Francois County but "did not try to get her" because he thought it "useless." But Lucy Mack, like many other fugitive women who lacked free papers, remained in a precarious position, vulnerable to recapture. Lucy moved on to St. Louis, where her former owner again found her. This time, he visited a justice of the peace to request a warrant for her arrest. Police imprisoned Lucy and her children in the St. Louis jail, and the owner reclaimed them and sold them into Kentucky. In August 1863, her husband returned to St. Louis and discovered that his family was gone.[98]

The Macks were not alone in this situation. In 1863, Missouri slave owners reacted to the persistent departures of enslaved people by looking for ways to recoup their capital investments. With access to other slave trade routes cut off, the sale of enslaved people into Kentucky increased, and military officers estimated that more than one thousand enslaved people were sold in Louisville in late 1863. Though Schofield banned the out-of-state sale of enslaved Missourians on November 10, 1863, he loosened the restrictions to allow the sale of women and militarily ineligible men. Not until March 1, 1864, when General William Rosecrans had replaced Schofield, did the trade to Kentucky come to an end.[99]

Official military policy allowed loyal masters to retrieve their slaves from the army through a civil process written into Missouri's slave code. Once an enslaver determined the county in which his slave was at large, he visited the local justice of the peace, who issued a legal warrant, or writ, for the retrieval of the escapee. The master could then enlist local constables or sheriffs to recapture his property. Violence often resulted when escapees struggled to elude slave catchers.

Charles Jones and other loyal enslavers became infuriated when soldiers blocked slave catchers from retrieving escapees, particularly when all of the requisite legal procedures had been completed. Jones seethed in a letter to President Lincoln that the military had instituted "Evil by Civil Process," so that all of his "house servants down to the nurse of [his] little children" had found sanctuary with the Union Army. He had chased his escapees to Washington, in Franklin County, where "they showed me what they call their free papers." Jones insisted, "*I am a Loyal American Citizen.*"[100]

Troops from the 23rd Missouri Regiment Volunteer Infantry had set up camp outside of Washington, and its officers liberally interpreted the congressional acts regarding contraband policy, particularly the March 1862 article of war forbidding military personnel from assisting slaveholders in retrieving fugitive slaves.[101] Franklin County's enslaved population fled en masse to the camp. Recalled two of those enslaved women, Susan Roberts and Julia Jones, "We had all run away from and left our masters, and . . . we were living in a state of freedom." Similarly, Samuel and Edith Jane Perkins later recounted that they took their young son and ran away to Washington, "where there was a camp of Federal Troops."[102]

In his letter to Lincoln, Jones complained, "Nearly all the slaves of Franklin County are now congregated at Washington." Jones lost all of his enslaved property when twelve people, including a twelve-year-old girl, fled his farm to the camp at Washington, "taking with them whatever they saw proper." Military officers not only refused to render any of these enslaved people to Jones but further asserted that the encampment "would resist any & every effort to retake them." Lamented Jones, "We were all getting along prosperously & unitedly until a few months ago, when by some construction of some order, the officers assigned us in our County came to the conclusion that all negroes who came into the camp then, & ever afterwards were free."[103]

Jones persisted and eventually recaptured most of his enslaved household—a man named Sam, a woman named Polly, and her five children, Alice, Evaline, Sarah, Martha, and Benjamin.[104] To avoid losing any more of his investment, Jones immediately sold them to a St. Louis slave trader, who in turn sold them into Kentucky. The provost marshal in St. Louis investigated the sale, reported that Jones was known as a loyal man, and declared the transaction legal.[105] The experience of these seven people reveals the risky and tenuous nature of the freedom achieved by escapees, particularly those who fled "loyal" enslavers.

Jones was not the only Franklin County master to lose his enslaved property to the troops stationed in Washington. After eighteen-year-old Lethe escaped from a Franklin County farm to the camp, her Unionist master, William North, enlisted the assistance of a business colleague, John B. Gray, serving as the adjutant general of Missouri.[106] Gray wrote to Major General Curtis, detailing the conflict between North and the camp's commander, Captain Crandall: "The sheriff is fearful from threats which have been made by this same Captain Crandall that if he attempts to execute a civil writ, violence will be offered him." Curtis responded that according to official military policy, officers should "especially avoid any interference with the negroes of Mr. North, who is a loyal man."[107]

In July 1863, the soldiers encamped near Washington marched to St. Louis and set up at Camp Edwards, about a mile from the headquarters of the Department of the Missouri. Thomas North, William's adult son and the manager of the Franklin County farm, pursued Lethe to St. Louis and obtained a warrant from a justice of the peace.[108]

Early the next morning, Thomas North and a constable arrived at Camp Edwards with the warrant in hand. After reading the warrant, the constable handed Colonel W. P. Robinson, the camp commander, a copy of the July 11, 1863, issue of the *Missouri Republican*, which contained the text of General Order no. 63 reiterating the command that the military not interfere with the state's civil process. Robinson nevertheless refused to turn over Lethe "on the ground that it interfered with a part of the order or act of Congress or the Presidents Proclamation." Col. Robinson denied Thomas North access to Lethe despite the prominent North family's recognition as loyal citizens. Robinson told his clerk that he did not think that General Order no. 63 applied to Lethe's case because of the "existing orders from the War Department."[109]

Military authorities responded inconsistently to the legal writs issued by local justices of the peace. Some military officers did not understand that military policy allowed loyal masters with legal writs to recapture fugitive slaves. The federal act that forbade the military from "rendering" enslaved people confused many officers as to their legal and military obligations toward slave masters. Other officers deliberately disobeyed military policy and refused to admit masters into military camps. Commanders had to instruct military officers stationed in Missouri to admit masters with warrants into their camps. For example, in October 1862, a colonel in Wellsville, Missouri, was chastised for harboring "runaway negroes" and preventing civil authorities from executing warrants for their arrest.[110]

About a week after Thomas North's visit to Camp Edwards, the 23rd Regiment left for Rolla, Missouri, presumably taking Lethe along. Shortly after the regiment reached Rolla, Robinson was arrested and charged with disobeying General Order no. 63. He was court-martialed in St. Louis and suspended from rank and pay for one month.[111] But as far as can be determined, the Norths never recaptured Lethe: at Robinson's trial, Thomas North testified that he did not know Lethe's whereabouts and "had had already trouble enough with her. I have not seen or heard of the negro since."[112]

In the summer of 1863, the abolitionist *St. Louis Westliche Post* criticized Schofield for transforming the Missouri jail into "a real 'slave pen.' Every day blacks and colored people of all shades—men, women and children—are thrown into it." Continued the *Post*, "In the past month hundreds of liberated slaves have been carried back into slavery," including escapees who worked for Union regiments. Missouri had become "Lincoln's slave hunting ground."[113]

*   *   *

At the start of the Civil War, the issue of women refugees presented a quandary to military officials vexed by the question of what to do with escapees.[114] The Confiscation Acts provided officers a tool for handling the enslaved women who sought out military regiments with the aim of bringing about their own practical emancipation.[115]

The enforcement of contraband policies marked a watershed moment in the destruction of slavery in Missouri. African Americans petitioned provost marshals for "free papers" which confirmed their contraband status under the Second Confiscation Act. In this process, enslaved women testified against slave owners. The acceptance of slave testimony against slave owners was a critical construction of enslaved women's civic existence, encouraging them to bring complaints and petitions to provost marshals throughout Missouri. But access to freedom through the Confiscation Acts depended on the disloyal speech and behavior of former masters. Women could also make positive claims for emancipation based on the activities of their kin.

Office Provost Marshal
St. Louis Mo Sept. 5th, 1864

Col,

I have the honor to acknowledge the receipt of Yours of this date and in answer have to state that John Conner was forwarded to your office on the 1st inst with affidavits as evidence in his case. He is charged with using grossly disloyal Language and of insulting an innocent & inoffensive colored ~~lady~~ Woman who on account of having no white Witness is by the Laws of the State, debarred from redress in civil Courts,

Very Respectfully
Your obt Servt,
Chas S. Hills Capt &
Provost Marshal,

Col Joseph Darr
1st Capt Pro. Mar. Genl.

Letter from the assistant provost marshal for St. Louis, Captain Charles S. Hills, to Colonel Joseph Darr, an assistant provost marshal general with the Department of the Missouri, documenting Hills's handling of the arrest of John Conner for assaulting an African American woman. Either Hills or his clerk drew a line through the word *lady* and replaced it with *woman* when discussing the target of Conner's behavior. Hills to Darr, September 5, 1864, Letters Sent, Entry 1733, Provost Marshal Office, St. Louis District, Department of the Missouri, Record Group 393, pt. 4, National Archives and Records Administration, Washington, D.C.

The interior of the St. Louis Provost Marshal's Office as sketched for *Harper's Weekly*. Sketch by Alexander Simplot, *Harper's Weekly*, January 18, 1862. From the Lincoln Financial Foundation Collection, courtesy of the Allen County Public Library and Indiana State Museum and Historic Sites, Fort Wayne.

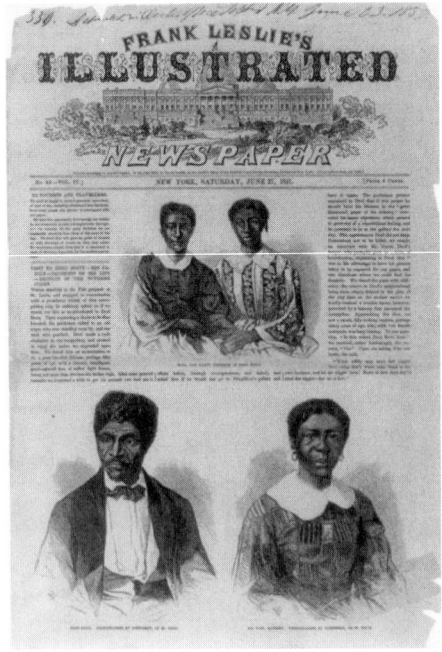

The infamous *Dred Scott v. Sandford* case involved the freedom claims of Dred Scott; his wife, Harriet; and his daughters, Eliza and Lizzie. From *Frank Leslie's Illustrated Newspaper*, June 27, 1857, courtesy of the Library of Congress, Washington, D.C.

A 1963 photograph of a basement cell in a building that had once served as enslaver Bernard T. Lynch's private jail until it was repurposed by Union officials for holding Confederate sympathizers during the Civil War. Courtesy of the *St. Louis Post-Dispatch*.

----- Rules -----

No charge less than One Dollar

All Negroes entrusted to my care for sale, or otherwise must be at the Risk of the Owners.

A charge of 37½ cents will be made per Day for board of Negroes, & 2½ per cent on all Sales of Slaves,

My usual care will be taken to avoid escapes, or accidents but will not be made Responsible should they occur

I only promise to give the same protection to other Negroes that I do to my own, I bar all pretexts to want of diligence,

These must be the acknowledged terms of all Negroes found in my care, as they will not be received on any other

As these Rules will be placed in a public place in my Office, That all can see, that will see, The pretence of ignorance shall not be a plea

5th January 1858.   B. M. Lynch.

N: 100 Locust St.

Handwritten notice from Bernard T. Lynch describing the terms under which he would hold enslaved people. Courtesy of the Missouri History Museum, St. Louis.

Gratiot Street Military Prison, a former medical school confiscated after its owner fled to Confederate lines that held both female and male prisoners. Courtesy of the Missouri History Museum, St. Louis.

The St. Louis city jail, located at Sixth and Chestnut Streets, 1870. Prior to and during the war, the jail's functions included holding recaptured escapees and African Americans arrested for walking on public streets without courthouse-issued licenses. Courtesy of the Missouri History Museum, St. Louis.

Thomas Satterwhite Noble, *The Last Sale of Slaves*, oil on canvas, 1871. This depiction of a disrupted 1861 slave auction on the St. Louis courthouse steps reflects an event that had entered popular history but may not have actually happened. Courthouse auctions continued to occur after the date of the event in the painting, and slavery was not abolished in Missouri until 1865. Courtesy of the Missouri History Museum, St. Louis.

Felix Octavius Carr Darley, *Fleeing from the Land of Bondage*, 1887. Courtesy of the Picture Collection, New York Public Library, Astor, Lenox, and Tilden Foundations.

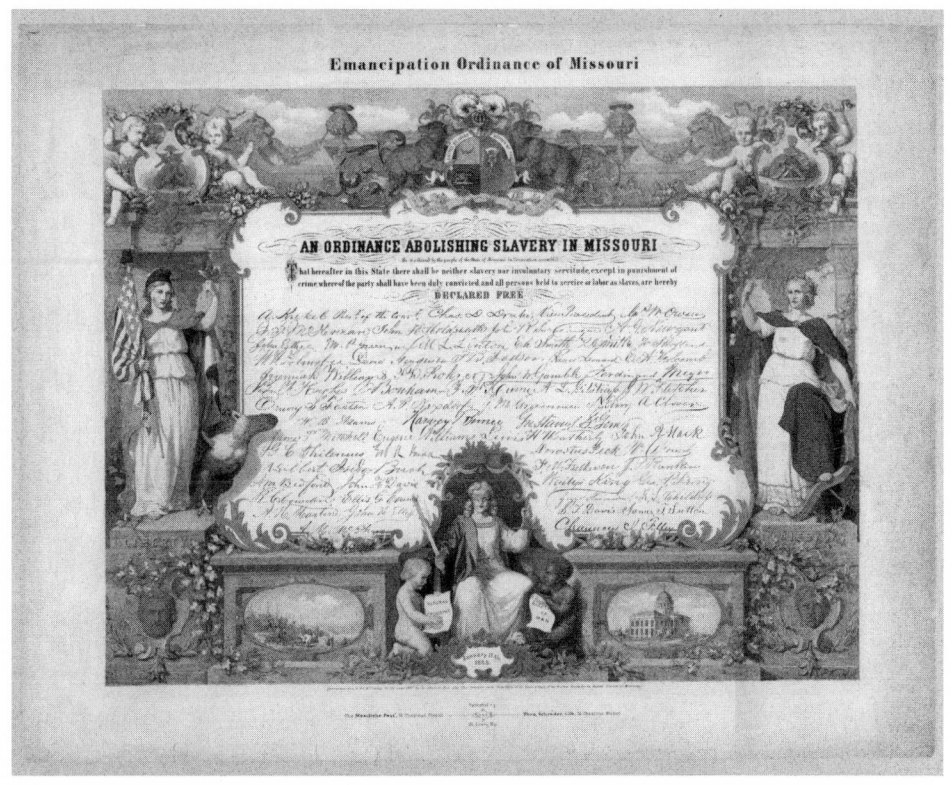

The state of Missouri issued an Emancipation Ordinance on January 11, 1865, before the passage of the Thirteenth Amendment. Courtesy of the Library of Congress, Washington, D.C.

EDWARD J. GAY

OUR CIT

(ST. LOUIS, MO.)

Published by Hagen & Pfau at the Anzeiger des Westens

Panoramic illustration of St. Louis, 1859. Lithograph by A. Janicke and Co., St. Louis. Courtesy of the Library of Congress, Washington, D.C.

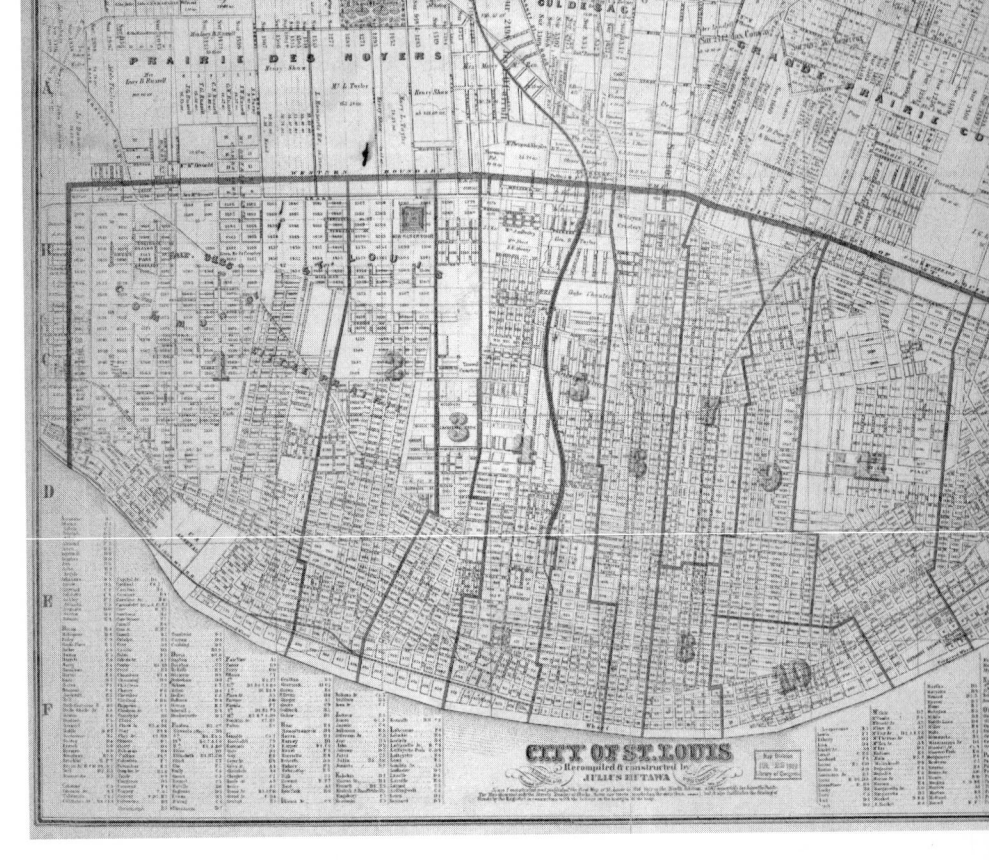

CITY OF ST. LOUIS
Recompiled & constructed by
JULIUS HUTAWA

Map of St. Louis, 1870. Courtesy of the Library of Congress, Washington, D.C.

Map of the Interior of Missouri, *Harper's Weekly*, July 6, 1861. From the Lincoln Financial Foundation Collection, courtesy of the Allen County Public Library and Indiana State Museum and Historic Sites, Fort Wayne.

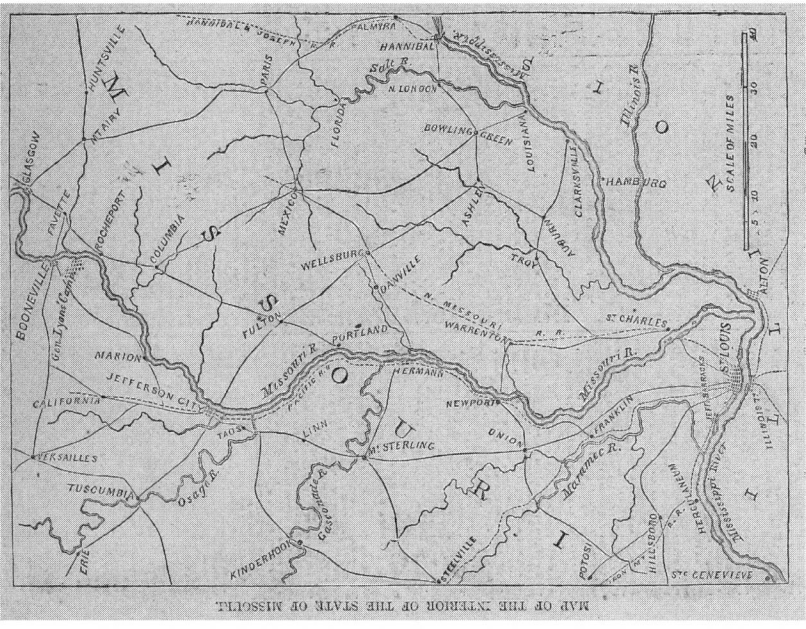

UNITED STATES VOLUNTEERS ATTACKED BY THE MOB, CORNER OF FIFTH AND WALNUT STREETS, ST. LOUIS, MISSOURI.—[SKETCHED BY M. HASTINGS, ESQ.]

On May 11, 1861, the day after the Camp Jackson Affair, the recently mustered Fifth Regiment of the U.S. Reserve Corps was attacked by a civilian mob while marching to headquarters. After the smoke cleared, two soldiers and six civilians were dead, adding to the twenty-eight civilians and one soldier killed the preceding day. From *Harper's Weekly*, June 1, 1861, courtesy of the Library of Congress, Washington, D.C.

Unknown African American woman. From the collection of Wilson's Creek National Battlefield, courtesy of the National Park Service (WICR-31936).

Rhoda, an enslaved woman living with the Ray family in the Wilson's Creek area at the time of the Civil War. Rhoda gained her freedom in 1865 and took the name of the Ray family until she married in 1868. From the collection of Wilson's Creek National Battlefield, courtesy of the National Park Service (WICR-01755).

Lucy A. Delaney. From Lucy A. Delaney, *From the Darkness Cometh the Light; or, Struggles for Freedom* (St. Louis: Smith, 189?), courtesy of the Missouri History Museum, St. Louis.

CHAPTER 3

"A Soldier's Wife Is Free"

African American Soldiers, Their Enslaved Kin, and Military Citizenship

"DO THE BEST YOU CAN and do not fret too much for me," wrote Ann Valentine to her soldier husband, Andrew, in January 1864. Andrew Valentine was an enslaved laborer before enlisting in the second regiment of black soldiers to be created in Missouri during the Civil War, organized at Benton Barracks in St. Louis. But Ann was still trapped in slavery deep in the countryside of Monroe County, part of the region known as Little Dixie, in the fertile lands along the Missouri and Mississippi Rivers.[1] As the Union Army began to enlist the enslaved men of Missouri, their families used the military status of their male relatives to deliver significant blows to the institution of slavery.

In November 1863, General John M. Schofield, the commander of the Department of the Missouri, ordered that enslaved men be permitted to enlist in the Union Army, though he forbade the use of traveling recruiting parties and required that would-be enlistees travel to the nearest provost marshal's office. Thousands of enslaved men were emancipated in return for their military service.[2] Five regiments totaling 8,344 men—almost 40 percent of Missouri's able-bodied African American men of military age—ultimately organized and trained at Benton Barracks in St. Louis, while thousands more escaped to Kansas, Illinois, and Iowa and enlisted in regiments there.[3] Thus, many if not most of Missouri's enslaved women had kinship ties to men who had enlisted.

"You know that a Soldiers wife is free," Sam Bowmen wrote to his wife in May 1864 from Benton Barracks Hospital. He urged her to escape her owner, contact military authorities, and join him in St. Louis.[4] But Bowmen's wife was not free. In May 1864, she was owned by a loyal Union man and was still legally enslaved under Missouri law. Indeed, the enlistment of slave men did not free the families of black soldiers in Missouri. Not until Missouri's constitutional convention abolished slavery in January 1865 did the relatives of enlisted men receive their freedom.[5]

Many wives, mothers, sisters, and children chose not to wait and instead found their own paths to freedom. Women identified the enlistment of their male relatives as a revolutionary moment, linking the service of their soldier-husbands with a transferable citizenship status. Ann Valentine and many others saw freedom as their right as a consequence of their loved ones' military service, closing her letter, "It wont be long before I will be free and then all we make will be ours."[6] Missouri's African Americans transformed the act of fighting in the Union Army into an act of liberation, part of the struggle to defeat slavery, even though many of the state's slaveholders cooperated with the Union under the assumption that their support would sustain the institution of slavery in Missouri.[7]

Enslaved African Americans discussed their political beliefs about the war with family, friends, and neighbors. Henry C. Bruce, enslaved in Chariton County during the war, recalled, "The Colored people could meet and talk over what they heard about the latest battle, and what Mr. Lincoln had said, and the chances of their freedom."[8] Enlistment decisions were made within slave communities. Eliza and Edy Jimmerson, two former slave women from Callaway County, recalled the communal experience of black enlistment. According to Eliza, when her husband left to enlist at Fulton, Missouri, "nearly all the Black men in this neighborhood joined the Union army."[9] Enlisted men were fighting not just for their own freedom but also for that of their wives and children.[10] Observed Edy Jimmerson, "I have often heard these men say they were free, and was going to join the army and fight to free their wives and children."[11]

Soldier Richard Morton proclaimed to his wife, Martha, "I must fight for my freedom & yours for I have as good a Right to do it as any person."[12] St. Louis slave owner Mrs. E. Stewart wrote to President Lincoln complaining, "I don't know what to do in present troubles but apply to your excellency for assistance." Two of the seven enslaved people left with the soldiers, while "two women & girls have left & gone to Chicago because they say that as the husband of one was in the army a year waiting on officers they are entitled to their freedom."[13] Even if their husbands may have been serving as impressed contrabands, these women shared the belief that a kinsman's military service entitled his wife to freedom.

Slave enlistment propelled mass escapes by enslaved women and children.[14] A former member of the community, Claiborne Holiday, recalled that when Ozette Hughes's husband, Tom, "went to the army, a whole host of colored people went to Boonville both women and men and Ozette went along with them."[15] According to Tom Hughes's sister, Charlotte Hicks, "When Tom went to the army Ozett went off, like a lot of other colored folks & she never came back to that neighborhood."[16] This group from Howard County traveled to Boonville because it was the nearest recruiting station in their area. After enlisting, the men traveled back home to assist community members who had remained there.

Men usually traveled on foot to recruiting stations, with mothers, sisters, wives, and children coming along when possible to escape as a family.[17] Enslaved women were familiar with the location of these recruiting stations, and they knew that these men were responsible for enlisting their relatives into the military.[18] The president of the University of Missouri in Columbia observed that with enlistment "opened to the Africans, . . . there was an exodus of the men of military age to the Missouri towns of Jefferson, Mexico, and other recruiting posts; and some women followed husbands and brothers."[19] In June 1864, slave owner G. W. Miller of Boonville requested that General Egbert B. Brown restrict the recruited men to quarters because they "are back here every few days in our kitchen," encouraging the "girls & women to run off from their masters."[20]

Not all escape attempts succeeded. Malvina, an enslaved woman living in Pike County, attempted to reach the recruiting station at Hannibal with three enslaved men, Alfred, Henry, and Aaron Mitchell, but four white men captured the group and forcibly returned them to their owners in Prairieville. The three men were whipped, and Alfred was later shot.[21] Confederate sympathizers, angry slave owners, and slave patrols made these escapes dangerous endeavors, especially considering the political implications that resulted when enslaved people enlisted in the Union Army.

Some women found a de facto freedom in Missouri's cities and towns, while other women "joined the army" and labored for their husbands' regiments as cooks, laundresses, and nurses, performing service in support of their regiment.[22] Sara Carter and her husband, George, enlisted at Columbia, and she stayed with his regiment for six months in Baton Rouge, Louisiana. Likewise, Edith Jane Perkins followed her husband's unit to Helena, Arkansas, and remained with them for five months.[23] Frassie Watkins migrated from St. Charles County with her husband, Frank, "at the time he enlisted in the Army, to St. Louis MO, and staid with him at Benton Barracks."[24]

"I went with him to the army," stated Sidney Castleman about her twenty-year-old husband, who served in the 65th Regiment of the U.S. Colored Troops. Sidney Castleman perceived herself to be an active participant in the Union cause. She did not remain at her slave home; she did not perceive herself as remaining on the home front while her husband went to war. She did not travel to a military post and wave farewell to her husband. Instead, she viewed herself as going with her husband "to the army," where she labored for the regiment and traveled with the troops. A woman who "joined the army" grew well acquainted with her husband's comrades. The Civil War experience cemented these ties, and in 1896, Sidney Castleman would testify in the Civil War pension claims of one of the soldiers who served with her husband.[25]

Sidney Castleman and other enslaved women directly contributed to the Union war effort. The memoirs of Susie King Taylor, whose husband enlisted in a South Carolina regiment, detail her active role in the unit's activities. Though she was officially employed as a laundress, her duties were far broader than this bureaucratic designation would indicate: "I assisted in cleaning the guns and used to fire them off, to see if the cartridges were dry, before cleaning and re-loading, each day. I thought this great fun." Taylor also taught "the comrades in Company E to read and write" and nursed the injured and ill soldiers. Taylor enthusiastically joined in the military mission, connecting it with the destruction of slavery.[26] Similarly, Martha Dickson, of Springfield, Missouri, ran away and "found refuge with some Illinois abolitionists, who managed to keep her out of harm's way until the outbreak of the war, when she followed a regiment as far south as Memphis as cook and laundress."[27] The fact that Dickson had already freed herself from slavery prior to deciding to follow a regiment shows the political significance some black women assigned to military labor itself.

For slave families, traveling with a regiment was also a strategy for the often pressing goal of keeping the family together. But Union commanders frequently did not allow families to continue to travel with soldiers once they reached a Union-occupied town. Jane Barker and her children were put off the troop transport boat at Cape Girardeau as her husband, Cain, urged her to "keep [the children] close to her."[28] John Poe recalled that Jane had remained with Cain "in the army as long as he could keep her there."[29]

Not all women supported the enlistment of their husbands. Robert Robinson traveled to Tipton, Missouri, "intending to enlist but my wife being opposed to my going from home I did not Enroll."[30] Female relatives who remained enslaved could suffer overwork, physical abuse, and even sale into the Kentucky slave market.[31] Some enslaved men chose to remain with their families and loved ones at home, while other men were conscripted against their will.[32] Henry Bruce hid from a recruiting party scouring the Chariton County countryside seeking African American enlistees for an Iowa regiment. A few months later, he escaped with his fiancée to Leavenworth, Kansas.[33] Women left behind in Missouri posted letters to their husbands concerning their opinions about military service. "I would not have you desert the Service dishonorably for any thing in the world," Sarah McBain wrote in a letter from Columbia, Missouri, to her husband serving after the war in Texas.[34]

Slave owners sold the families of men in service both as a punishment and to deter the enlistment of other enslaved men. Two months after her husband enlisted at the Warrenton, Missouri, recruiting station, Mary Jane Davis and her two children were "sent off to Kentucky with negro traders."[35] Masters also sold their slave property out of fear that they would lose their capital investments to escapes.[36] Mary T. Dyson recalled how Dr. Moore, a resident of St. Louis, sold both her husband and friend, Elizabeth Porter, to Kentucky because "when the Civil War came up, and people saw they were going to lose the slaves they sold them South."[37]

In November 1863, the month in which Schofield began to enlist enslaved men in Missouri regiments, Union officers reported a spike in slave sales, as about one thousand enslaved Missourians were sold into Kentucky.[38] Enlisted men feared not only that slave owners would sell their families out of state but that they would lose contact and be unable to track down their families on furloughs or after their release from military service. In February 1864, a man named Herbert P. Fromein warned the soldier, Henry, of a plot to capture a fugitive woman, Sallie, who was an acquaintance of the soldier. "Dear Henry!" wrote Fromein, "they will try to get Sallie to go to see her girl there and then they will take and chain her and sell her to Kentucky. She had better be on her guard before it is too late . . . better take my advise Sallie and leave the sooner the better."[39]

Women who were unable to escape slavery with their male relatives were vulnerable to abuse from slave owners.[40] In May 1864, Unionist J. F. Benjamin wrote to the provost marshal at Hannibal, Missouri, to express his concerns about the abuse suffered by Louisa, whose husband was serving in the Union Army. Louisa's owner, Jesse D. Gray of Selby County, had "subjected [her] to the most barbarous treatment." Louisa fled to Benjamin's household, and he reported, "Her condition was beyond description. Her clothing was nothing but a collection of rags not Sufficient to cover her body. She had been compelled to do the outdoor work during the whole winter and her feet had been frozen the toes and skin on them coming off. She had no shoes. Her feet were bound in rags. She has made two attempts to get off but each time apprehended and whipped most unmercifully. She is now kept locked nights up."[41] J. F. Benjamin most likely reported Louisa's condition to the local provost marshal because in addition to serving as the military police, the provost marshal had probably also recruited Louisa's husband. Provost marshals had an interest in the abuse of soldiers' families, especially because fear that their loved ones would be maltreated could slow the enlistment of African American men.

Enslaved Women's Complaints Travel up the Chain of Command

Enslaved women reported their abuse, and those reports made their way up through the Union military bureaucracy, where officials listened; the women quite clearly indicated that slave enlistment depended on an end to the abuse. In December 1863, Martha Glover wrote from Mexico, Missouri, to her husband, Richard, at Benton Barracks, "I have had nothing but trouble since you left. You recollect what I told you how they would do after you was gone. They abuse me because you went & say they will not take care of our children . . . and beat me scandalously the day before yesterday." Martha believed that Richard "ought not to left me in the fix I am in" and warned, "You need not tell me to beg any more married men to go. I see too much trouble to try and get any more into trouble too."[42]

Martha Glover's complaint, along with those of other women who described their abuse to their husbands, caused much consternation when it reached the highest level in the Department of the Missouri. General William A. Pile, the commander of black recruits in the state, directed his adjutant general to write to Martha Glover's owner, George W. Cardwell, condemning her treatment and threatening military interference unless it ceased.[43]

Not long after this letter was sent, Cardwell attempted to sell Martha and her six children into the Kentucky slave trade. When Pile learned that Cardwell had brought the family to St. Louis to sell them, he "went in person" and "took possession of the woman and children." Pile wrote to General William S. Rosecrans, commander of the Department of the Missouri, of the need to develop policies that would protect the "wives and children of colored Soldiers," in particular from sale into Kentucky.[44] General Pile also informed Congressman Henry T. Blow that the abuse the "families of colored soldiers are receiving at the hands of their masters in this State" has "almost suspended" black enlistment and asked him to provide assistance.[45]

Civilian media, in particular the *Daily Missouri Democrat*, a Republican paper that strongly supported the Union cause, also brought attention to the problem, proclaiming that such abuses "urgently demand attention from the military authorities." On January 20, 1864, the paper reported that the African American enlistees training at Benton Barracks "frequently receive intelligence that their wives and children, left behind, are subjected to severe maltreatment."[46]

When Simon Williamson and Richard Beasley enlisted in the army, their owner retaliated by whipping both of their wives. Lorinda Williamson recruited a sympathetic neighbor to send Simon a letter after she received "a severe whipping."[47] Williamson and Beasley reported the abuse to their captain, who forwarded the complaints to General Pile.[48]

After Martin Patterson enlisted, his wife, Almeda, was compelled to chop wood and do "out door work" customarily assigned to enslaved men. In addition, Patterson complained to his lieutenant, William P. Deming, "one of his children has been suffered to freeze, and has sinc died."[49] Deming reported to his superiors that Patterson's was not the only complaint "made to me by men in my company that their families are ill treated by their masters," including the sale of families to Kentucky.[50] According to General Pile, "Hundreds of able bodied men are deterred from enlistment by fears of their families being abused or sold to Kentucky." Pile added that "wives and children of these enlisted colored men are being smuggled across to Kentucky and sold,—and many others are suffering most brutal and inhuman treatment."[51]

African American Women Petition the Provost Marshals in the Missouri Interior

In response to this abuse and emboldened by the military emancipation of their male relatives, many women fled to Union lines. The provost marshal for Mexico, Missouri, reported in March 1864 that a group of enslaved women had fled to town after their owner made them perform the outdoor labor normally completed by their recently enlisted husbands. Lieutenant A. A. Rice, who did not "know what course to pursue," sought advice from the provost marshal general in St. Louis.[52] This migration of enslaved women to military posts and Union-occupied towns surprised army officials. General Brown estimated that two thousand women, children, and elderly men had gathered at military installations in the District of Central Missouri.[53] Sedalia's provost marshal wrote to Pile, "We have a large number, of Black women and Children, manny of them are the wives of soldiers, that have been enlisted in my District. . . . [W]hat can be done their benefit?"[54] Between two hundred and three hundred elderly men, women, and children had migrated to Independence by March 1864.[55] These refugees lived in crowded conditions; one officer in Warrensburg reported that around thirty families resided in ten houses in "the Negro quarters."[56]

"Several colored women have come to this Post," wrote Major A. C. March, the provost marshal stationed at Troy, in Lincoln County, in April 1864. The migrating women, many of them wives and mothers of soldiers, explained to the military officers that slave masters "do not want them about and are not willing to *feed them*." These reports alarmed the provost marshal, who asked for "some instructions on the subject" from his superiors in St. Louis. March believed that slave masters meted out such harsh treatment to discourage enlistment.[57]

These refugees traveled to railroad towns and military posts "under the impression that they can go with [their male kin] to St Louis."[58] They became stranded in smaller towns, however, because Missouri's slave code held steamboats and railroad companies liable for escaped slaves.[59] "These negroes are not received as passengers on the steamboats running on the Missouri," explained General Ewing, "the owners of the boats fear the penalties of the state laws against those who carry off slaves."[60] Train and steamboat conductors refused to allow fugitive slaves on board without military passes or orders from commanding officers.[61] As a result, families needed military passes to travel with their male kin to the training grounds and contraband camp at Benton Barracks in St. Louis.

General Brown complained in January 1864 that the women and children who had gathered at Union posts and towns constituted "a great annoyance."[62] As the commander of the District of Central Missouri, Brown barred women and children from traveling to St. Louis with male relatives.

Brown recognized that wives wished to "follow their husbands who have entered the service" but discounted their family relations and the legitimacy of slave marriages. He further stigmatized the women and children as diseased, warning military headquarters that transporting family members to St. Louis would bring to the city "about two thousand decrepid men, women, and children among whom the small pox and venereal prevails to a frightful extent."[63] Military commanders had not considered enslaved families when formulating the plan to enlist slave men and now had to respond to a migrant population of women and children attempting to follow the new soldiers.

"What shall I do with the negro women who come to this post, when their masters come after them and they refuse to go home?" the provost marshal at Wellsville asked the acting provost marshal general in February 1864.[64] Another provost marshal stationed in Mexico, Missouri, wrote to department headquarters about soldiers' wives and children who had "ran off and sought refuge here," asking, "What should be done with them?"[65] Such questions swamped the provost marshal general's office: "The inquiry made in regard to negro women and children, how they are to be cared for, is but the repetition of such inquiry by every mail, and from all parts of the department."[66]

"Some twenty five or more of the wives of men who have enlisted came into Louisiana[, Missouri,] and called upon me to protect them," reported Lieutenant Jeff Mayhall, a provost marshal stationed in Pike County. He also sought to call officials' "attention to the fact that the Soldiers (Colored) wives and families are being awfully abused, particularly those belonging to Rebels" and begged for permission to shelter soldiers' families from slave owners. He warned that his inability to provide protection had "completely put a stop to the recruiting business" and suggested that a change in policy would enable him to "recruit 300 men in this country." He concluded by telling General Pile, "You I am confident, never saw such a scene in your life. I hope I may never witness the like again."[67]

By early February 1864, the acting provost marshal general, S. S. Burdett, was receiving "almost daily" communications from local provost marshals about these appeals from soldiers' families.[68] The marshal stationed at Fuller reported, "The wife of a colored recruit came into my Office to night and says she has been severely beaten and driven from home by her master and owner. She has a child some two years old with her, and says she left two larger ones at home." She sought transportation to join her husband.[69] The provost marshal stationed at Mexico, Missouri, reported to headquarters, "I am informed that there are many cases where the negro men enlist their wives are made to do the work formerly done by the men."[70]

Information about the abuse of soldiers' enslaved families and its effect on enlistment eventually reached Secretary of War Edwin M. Stanton. Captain John Gould, a commissary officer in Lexington, Missouri, urged Stanton to intervene so that enlistment would continue. Burdett concurred, endorsing Gould's letter by noting that as soon as the enslaved population understood that the military had little legal power to interfere with these sales, the "enlistments of men having families will be entirely at an end." General Rosecrans, too, endorsed Gould's recommendation, concluding that freeing the families of enlisted men would be an act of justice.[71]

Enslaved women persisted in their pursuit of freedom, protection, and assistance from the provost marshals by entering marshals' offices, stating their situations, and petitioning the military to grant them free emancipation certificates or passes to leave the area. African American soldiers' wives, mothers, and sisters gave sworn testimony to the provost marshals, often accusing owners of being disloyal.[72] Paulina Jones received a pass for herself and two children after stating, "My husband Alfred Jones enlisted in the United States Army on the 22nd day of December 1863 at Hannibal MO. Ever since my masters family have treated me very badly & threatened to separate my children from me & that my husband should never come back to the house again & that if he did [the master] would shoot him on sight." The provost marshal certified that Alfred Jones had indeed been recruited and gave Paulina Jones a military pass and with it de facto freedom.[73]

Complaints of abuse at the hands of masters featured prominently in the testimony. Maria Brown stated that her master, Dr. Andy Brown, had struck her with a stick, causing injuries so severe that she had "to take to my bed."[74] Mary Franklin received a pass from the provost marshal in Hannibal after swearing that her husband had enlisted in the Union Army and that she had been "hired out to one Warren Finley, who has a son in the rebel army, and that the said Warren Finley did strike her." The provost marshal confirmed her husband's service and stated that Franklin "wishes to labor for herself." However, Franklin did not allege that her owner, Nancy Samuel of Marion County, was disloyal.[75]

The inclusion of physical assaults in these complaints was political work. Violence against slave women was not officially a military concern, yet Mary Franklin and other women presented assault as relevant to their cases. Such complaints collapsed the rhetorical boundaries between the private and the public realms and reclassified physical attacks on enslaved women as military matters. Removing themselves from the classification of "domestic dependents" who existed outside the body politic, Franklin and others repositioned themselves as individuals with the right to complain about physical abuse. Moreover, Franklin did not simply narrate her assault to a family member or a sympathetic white Unionist neighbor; rather, she presented her complaint to a military representative, an agent of the state. Her accusation challenged the legal prerogatives of white people to physically assault slave women and thereby revealed one of enslaved women's key political priorities—the right to physical protection.

Some provost marshals and other Union officials acknowledged the validity of enslaved women's moral claim on the men who had enlisted their husbands and sons. Enslaved women were now the kin of soldiers, they had contributed to the cause of the Union military, and they sought freedom as a matter of justice. In February 1864, the provost marshal of Louisiana, Missouri, Jeff Mayhall, implored General Pile, "If the government calls on the negro to fight her battles—in Gods name protect their wives and children while they are in the army."[76] In turn, some military officials recognized that they had an obligation to the families of soldiers. General Pile, too, advocated on behalf of soldiers' families, urging the military to send wives and children to Benton Barracks, where shelter, rations, and schooling would be provided.[77]

Despite Pile's advocacy, soldiers' families often had to find their own way to St. Louis. Almeda Patterson, for example, traveled to the city in search of paid labor after her husband, Martin, reported that she and their children were being abused. A few months after Martin Patterson enlisted, Almeda left Howard County with her young son, Will, and her half-sister. More than a year passed before they reached St. Louis; the journey included a stop in the small town of Knob Noster, where she gave birth to another child, and several months in Warrensburg. From there, Almeda made her way to St. Louis with a group of acquaintances: "We just said we was going to St. Louis and picked up and went, some women and a couple of men."[78] In St. Louis, she found work cooking for a banker.

Soldiers' families occasionally received military transport. In November 1864, a military escort accompanied a party of enlistees and several African American women, most likely family members, on their rail journey from the Missouri countryside to St. Louis. There, white lieutenant Albert

Demar of the 27th Regiment helped them as they transferred to a streetcar that would take them to Benton Barracks. As a squad of enlisted men rode on the streetcar platform, the women sat inside the car, occupying public space usually reserved for individuals classified as "white ladies." A white St. Louis resident protested this challenge to the racial segregation of his cityscape and complained because his wife "objected to ride in the same car with negroes." These St. Louis white residents insisted that the African American women ought to stand outside on the platform with the soldiers, where African American residents customarily rode in accordance with the informal practices of the city's streetcar lines. Demar responded that African American women "had as much right in the Car as white people." Demar ultimately backed down, however, and directed the women to move to the outside platform, where the enlisted men were standing.[79]

Thousands of women and children reached St. Louis and settled in at the Benton Barracks contraband camp, which General Schofield had created in 1863, removing refugees from the St. Louis Missouri Hotel. This new complex offered soldiers and families shelter, rations, and medical attention. Thousands of people, including the family members who followed and arrived with soldiers, received aid and shelter at the Barracks. Camp superintendent W. H. Corkhill noted the arrival of an "accumulation of Women and Children." Military chaplains legally married couples at the complex, providing federal acknowledgment of marital ties.[80] In addition, refugees and sick soldiers could attend a school taught by the Corkhills' daughter.[81] One student, Mary A. Bell, had relocated from Howard County to join her mother, ten siblings, and father, soldier Spottswood Rice, while he was convalescing at the hospital.[82] Two of Rice's other daughters, Mary and Cora, remained enslaved by brother and sister F. W. and Kitty Diggs in Glasgow, Missouri. In September 1864, Rice wrote to Kitty Diggs from the hospital to assert his rights as Mary's father, threatening divine retribution if Diggs refused to allow the girl to come to St. Louis: "Now I want you to understand that mary is my Child and she is a God given rite of my own and you may hold on to hear as long as you can but I want you to remember this one thing that the longor you keep my Child from me the longor you will have to burn in hell and the qwicer youll get their."[83] Spottswood Rice also used his connection to the military to assert his fatherly rights, assuring Mary and Cora that the Union Army would help him free them: "Dont be uneasy my children I expect to have you. If Diggs don't give you up this government will and I feel confident that I will get you."[84] The evidence does not reveal how Mary reached St. Louis, but we do know that she came to the city after Spottswood Rice sent these letters to Glasgow. Mary Rice Bell understood that her father, as a Union soldier, had struggled to free her from bondage. In 1937, when she was eighty-five, Mary recalled, "I love army men, my father, brother, husband and son were all army men. I love a man who will fight for his rights, and any person that wants to be something."[85]

African American Women Petition the Provost Marshals in St. Louis

After migrating to St. Louis, women continued to petition the local provost marshals. As residents of the city, these women, mobilized by the Civil War crisis and exposed to discussions of rights and freedom, pursued a wide variety of complaints. No longer enslaved, they wanted more than passes to St. Louis. The enlistment of slave men changed the grounds on which soldiers' wives could seek military assistance. Formerly enslaved women were now the kin of soldiers, and their families had contributed to the fight for the Union. Women used this moral claim as they sought inclusion in the military justice system.

Many of these female relatives found work as domestic laborers in St. Louis.[86] When disputes with employers arose, these women presented their cases to the provost marshals, framing their complaints as the economic justice owed to members of soldiers' families. One woman lodged a complaint at the St. Louis district office for "fourteen dollars & fifty cents" owed to her by W. M. Marshall. As a result, the district provost marshal wrote to Marshall and instructed him to "make immediate settlement of this claim or you will be required to appear at this office in reference to the matter."[87]

Another soldier's wife, Annie Link, who earned "her living by washing," visited the St. Louis District provost marshal when Mrs. Francis refused to settle a $5.50 debt but instead "shook the money in [Link's] face and at the same time declared she would not pay her." Standing in the marshal's office, the clerk of the provost marshal's office recorded Annie Link's statements as she contrasted her patriotism with her employer's Confederate sympathies: "Mrs. F. is a violent rebel. [Link] has heard her say that 'she wished the U.S. Soldiers were in Hell.'"[88]

By the time legislative emancipation occurred in January 1865, Missouri's formerly enslaved women had become accustomed to bringing their claims for assistance to the provost marshal. In June 1865, Lucinda Farris, a soldier's wife, visited the office of the district provost marshal in St. Louis to enlist his help in regaining custody of her fourteen-year-old daughter, Fannie, who had been sold into the Kentucky slave market during the preceding year. Farris, who had lived as a slave in Boonville, testified that her former owner had kept all of her good clothes, the "sugar and coffee her husband had bought before he left for the army," and "$26 in silver" given to her by her old mistress "on her dying bed." Despite all these thefts, Lucinda "asks no return nor remuneration—but only asks as the wife of an American soldier—James Farris—who served nearly three years . . . that her only child may be restored to her."[89] In response, the provost marshal's office attempted to persuade the owner to return Fannie to her mother.[90]

African American women also sought assistance from the provost marshals in settling disputes over Civil War enlistment bounties. Eliza Shirley was to have received $130 from the U.S. paymaster in St. Louis for the enlistment of her husband, William Shirley, "a colored Substitute." However, Eliza Shirley received only $100. In response to her complaint, the St. Louis District provost marshal's office wrote to the paymaster's office seeking corrective action.[91]

In addition, soldiers' wives brought rental disputes with white landlords before the provost marshal, revealing the creative ways in which freedwomen worked to make domestic and "civil" disputes military concerns. Once officers accepted these concerns as legitimate areas for military regulation, they often seized such opportunities to enlarge the scope of military authority. The St. Louis provost marshal claimed the power to regulate all the rental agreements between the city's African American residents and white landlords, relying on two rationales. First, officers believed they had an obligation to protect soldiers' families. Second, African Americans' legal disabilities in the civil court system justified military intervention in civilian affairs.

In May 1864 Captain Charles S. Hills, a St. Louis provost marshal, became alarmed by the number of complaints from soldiers' wives summoned before justices of the peace for failing to meet debts. Hills wrote directly to the responsible city judge to warn that according to Missouri law, the women could not be ejected from their homes—specifically, that soldiers' wives could not be "prosecuted or distressed for non-payment" of rent.[92] Justices of the peace nevertheless continued to issue "writs of eject-ment," prompting Hills to tell his superiors that if he did not interfere with these cases, families would be thrown "upon the streets." The provost mar-shal noted that these cases were "becoming common" and consequently directed the St. Louis city justices to stop all such proceedings.[93]

Missouri law protected only citizens of the state from debt prosecu-tions, and Hills was specifically concerned about the families of colored soldiers, who were not technically Missouri citizens and thus depended "on the military authorities alone to save them from the streets."[94] In August 1864, Captain Hills ordered the protection of Angeline Nelson, declaring that she was "not to be disturbed in the peaceable possession of her place of residence" and that "any further violation on the part of any one will be promptly punished."[95]

In a January 1865 case, the assistant examiner in the St. Louis District provost marshal's office collected testimony about a dispute in which an African American woman had made a first payment of six dollars to rent rooms in a tenement but the landlord refused to give her the key unless she paid an additional four dollars.[96] Two months later, Eliza Smith lodged a similar complaint against her landlord, Isaac Walker. The provost mar-shal in this dispute did not issue a military directive but advised "that her money be returned to her" less two dollars for the time she had resided on the premises.[97]

Enslaved women did not just escape slavery; they requested from mili-tary officials, as a matter of justice, freedom for themselves and for their children. Through their claims to the provost marshals, women asserted their right to establish a relationship with the state. Emancipation was more than the single January 1865 moment when the Missouri legislature eradi-cated the institution of slavery. For many of Missouri's enslaved women, the emancipation process began when they used military citizenship to seize freedom and obtain judicial hearings. Recognizing that U.S. Army officials could not ignore complaints if they wanted African American men to enlist, these women used the situation to their advantage, securing freedom and protection even while the institution of slavery persisted.

CHAPTER 4

"The First Morning of Their Freedom"

African American Women, Black Testimony, and Military Justice

IN MAY 1864, Thomas Farrell, a white man, assaulted Charlotte Ford outside of her St. Louis home. Ford, a free woman of color, had never seen Farrell before he ran up her street with the military police in pursuit. Farrell threatened to "knock me down" and struck her on the back of the head with a brick. Ford testified at Farrell's military trial: "He struck me and said 'That is the way that Jeff Davis does the business—I am a Jeff Davis man all over.'" When the military examiner asked if Farrell had been drunk, Ford wryly responded, "He was sober enough to strike me."[1]

Before the Civil War, Ford did not possess the legal right to testify about her attack in any Missouri court. The slave code forbade any African American, slave or free, from testifying against a white person. In fact, African Americans continued to be prohibited from testifying against white people in civil court until the spring of 1865, when Radical Republicans rewrote the Missouri Constitution. Ford was able to testify against Farrell in 1864 because Union officers permitted African Americans to act as witnesses in military courts.[2] Ford's act of testifying redefined her civil status.

Unable to testify against white people in the civil courts, African American women went before military courts, a venue designed to address the concerns of the military and its soldiers, to charge white residents with a variety of offenses.[3] By 1864 and 1865, African American women in St. Louis, both slave and free, routinely sought justice through the military legal system, accusing white citizens of assault, rape, kidnapping, and unfair labor practices. "This office has been crowded with applications from Negroes for redress of grievances," wrote Lucius C. Matlack, the St. Louis District provost marshal, in April 1865.[4]

Matters involving African Americans were the subject of 34 percent of all outbound correspondence pertaining to civilian complaints from the office of the St. Louis District provost marshal between May 27, 1864, and June 17, 1865. The correspondence considered for this analysis includes petitions by white Confederate sympathizers who visited the office to lodge complaints about property seized by Union troops.[5] The provost marshals exercised vigorous powers of seizure over the property of disloyal civilians. As guerrilla warfare raged across the Missouri countryside, provost marshals had no shortage of civilians who warranted investigation, and officials pursued an aggressive policy of property confiscation and civilian arrest. Under such circumstances, the fact that African American business made up such a large proportion of all civilian complaints is notable. The amount of business involving free and enslaved black residents was surprisingly large given that free and enslaved African American residents accounted for only 3.3 percent of St. Louis's 1864 population.[6]

The enthusiasm with which the black population visited the provost marshal offices emphasizes their willingness to enlist military authority, and

TABLE 1 Percentage breakdown of civilian complaints discussed in outbound correspondence from the St. Louis District provost marshal's office, May 27, 1864–June 17, 1865

Complaint Type	African American (%)		Unspecified Race (%)	
	Men	Women	Men	Women
Assault	6	1	5	2
Wages	8	2	1	1
Children	0	3	1	1
Rentals	1	1	7	11
Speech	0	1	2	1
Disturbance	1	0	5	0
Rebel Activity	0	0	0	1
Theft	4	0	2	1
Seizures/Permits	0	0	5	1
Enlistment	6	0	1	0
Overall	24	10	29	21

Each value is calculated as a percentage of the entire group of 169 letters. Complaints from men and women are counted in both categories. Seventeen percent of the letters did not mention a specific complainant. Some letters refer to "informants" or other civilians without identifying them by name.

Source: Letters Sent, Entries 1733–35, Provost Marshal Office, St. Louis District, Department of the Missouri, Record Group 393, pt. 4, National Archives and Records Administration, Washington, D.C.

ultimately, the federal power, as an entity that could dispense rights and justice in response to a variety of petitions and complaints. Free and enslaved people made broad-based "rights" claims in Civil War St. Louis, asserting their belief that federal citizenship was capacious and ought to include people such as them. They made these claims on federal power prior to the enactment of the Fourteenth Amendment, and in a state in which the Emancipation Proclamation did not apply.[7]

The complaints to the St. Louis provost marshal were gendered and racialized in specific ways. African American men were especially at risk for attack by drunken white individuals in commercial districts and other assaults in public spaces.[8] Substitute enlistment fraud and other military matters also generated a significant proportion of the correspondence concerning African American men.[9] White women were concerned largely with rental disputes, and African American women occasionally sought out help with similar matters.[10] The families of soldiers were protected from civil proceedings by Missouri law including actions to evict for nonpayment of rent.[11] There are a few instances of African American women also

TABLE 2 Percentage breakdown by demographic category of civilian complaints discussed in outbound correspondence from the St. Louis District provost marshal's office, May 27, 1864–June 17, 1865

	African American (%)		Unspecified Race (%)	
Complaint Type	Men	Women	Men	Women
Assault	24	12	16	8
Wages	34	24	2	6
Children	0	29	2	3
Rentals	2	12	24	53
Speech	0	6	6	6
Disturbance	2	0	16	0
Rebel Activity	0	0	0	6
Theft	17	0	6	6
Seizures/Permits	0	0	16	3
Enlistment	24	0	2	0

Each value is calculated as a percentage of the set of complaints originating from the specific demographic group (e.g., African American women).

Source: Letters Sent, Entries 1733–35, Provost Marshal Office, St. Louis District, Department of the Missouri, Record Group 393, pt. 4, National Archives and Records Administration, Washington, D.C.

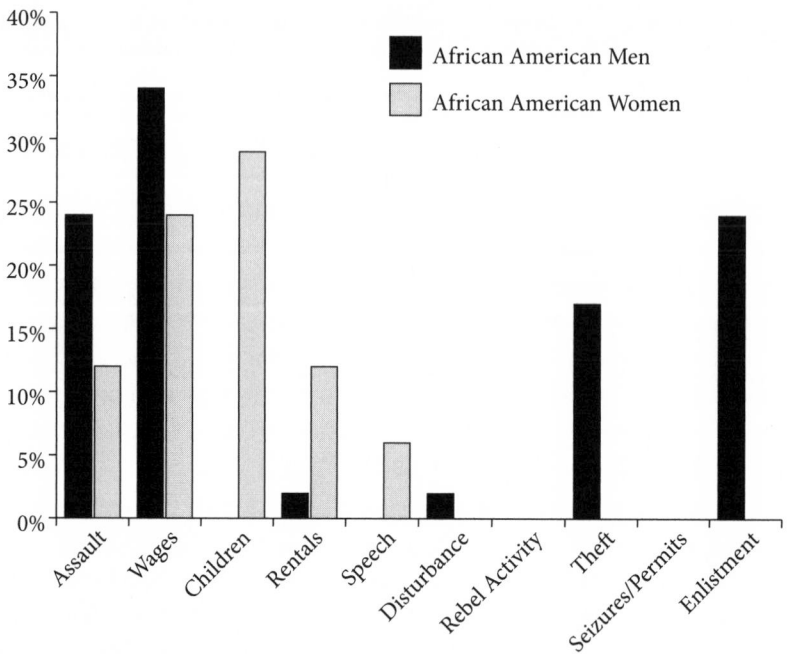

FIGURE 1. Comparison of complaint volume by type: African American women versus African American men

seeking out similar rent protections.[12] However, African American women turned much more frequently to the provost marshal for assistance in reclaiming children held in bondage, even after abolition.[13] Furthermore, African American women's wage and assault complaints often dealt with domestic labor situations, in which women were also vulnerable to abuse by employers.[14] The social and physical culture of slavery continued after the institution was legally abolished, and black women were determined to obtain full emancipation. By pressing their legal claims through the military justice system, African American women interrupted the social privileges ingrained into the local labor practices of a border city that had sanctioned slavery for decades.

The actions of African American women in St. Louis, such as Charlotte Ford, demonstrate how they used the military justice system to circumvent Missouri's black code during the Civil War. Martial law provided new opportunities for African American women living in the city to claim citizenship rights. Less than two months after he first declared martial law in Missouri, General John C. Frémont implemented the trial of civilians in

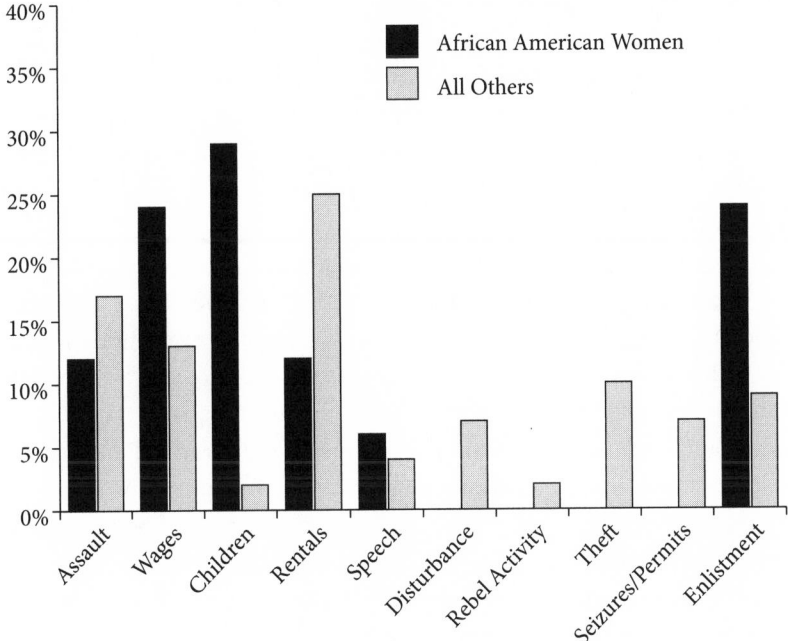

FIGURE 2. Comparison of complaint volume by type: African American women versus all other demographic groups combined.

military commissions. This practice, first used in Missouri in September
1861, spread to multiple states during the Civil War.[15]

Incessant guerrilla activity contributed to the plethora of military trials
of civilians in Missouri. Geographically, St. Louis was the headquarters of
Unionist activity in the state, while "Little Dixie," a fertile region along the
Missouri River conducive to small-scale slaveholding, spawned much rebel
activity. But Unionists and Confederate sympathizers often lived in close
contact with each other, since political factions were widely dispersed and
liberally mixed throughout the state. The army could not afford to lose control of Missouri to the Confederate-allied bushwhackers and other rebellious elements in the countryside.[16]

Missouri's internal conflict necessitated strict military control over the
civilian population of an ostensibly friendly territory. More civilians experienced military arrest in Missouri than in any other loyal state, and the
great majority of those held in military prisons were never formally tried.[17]
Trials of civilians by the armed forces, when they occurred, were an unprec-

edented invasion of military authority into civil affairs. In 1864, the U.S. Supreme Court refused to hear *Ex parte Vallandigham*, a case involving a civilian convicted by a military commission. Not until two years later, in *Ex parte Milligan*, did the Supreme Court rule that military tribunals could not try civilians unless the alleged offense had occurred "in areas of military activity."[18] Prior to *Milligan*, the Union's wide application of military law in Missouri allowed African American women to bring civil grievances before military officials such as the provost marshals.

The St. Louis office of the provost marshal resolved most grievances through correspondence, threats of military power, or even short confinements in military jails.[19] On at least two occasions, however, the provost marshal conducted formal military trials of white men, with their African American female accusers testifying in support of the United States.[20] The majority of the records documenting visits by African American women to the St. Louis District provost marshal's office are dated between January 1864 and April 1865. The office closed its doors to African American applicants in the spring of 1865 when the Missouri legislature rewrote state statutes to admit black testimony in civil courts.[21]

To make their claims, African American women occupied the physical space of military offices. These women stood alone before the military courts, nearly always choosing to initiate complaints and petition military officers unmediated by husbands, brothers, or fathers. Republican contract ideology defined the husband and father as the head of household and thus responsible for household dependents. Black women entered the military justice system as complainants and witnesses, asserting an ideology of self-ownership.[22]

Before the St. Louis provost marshals, African American women claimed several rights, including the right to custody of their children, the right to be paid for their labor, and the right to seek state protection from bodily assault.[23] The claims made by enslaved, contraband, and free African American women to military officials throughout Missouri reveal the political work performed by black women as they attempted to reconfigure their civic existence during the Civil War. Provost marshal courts offered black residents, deprived of the right to witness in the civil system, the chance to be heard by a state official.[24]

Enslaved African American men may have avoided bringing complaints to the provost marshal's office because men who reported traitorous masters were pressured to enlist in one of Missouri's African American regiments.

In August 1864, a slave man reported his master's disloyal actions. According to a St. Louis newspaper, the man "stated that his master was a rebel, and requested that the Captain give him free papers." In response, the provost marshal "filled up a certificate of enlistment" and "told him to go out to Benton Barracks, and he would be free."[25] General Schofield designated the provost marshals as enlistment agents, essentially turning them into recruitment officers for the U.S. Colored Troops in Missouri.[26] For African American men, though, enlistment into the Union military would separate them from their families. Enlisted African Americans were unable to physically protect or economically support family members. African American men had family responsibilities; free and enslaved families relied upon the labor and income of family members. Many enslaved families lived independently, compensating their slave owners for the arrangement with a set payment each month. These families had to earn money for rent and food for their dependents. Family survival was itself an act of resistance against slave power. African American men were torn between the duty to sustain their families and joining the Union Army to participate in the military destruction of slavery. Because the provost marshal held enlistment power, enslaved men had reason to be cautious in approaching the provost marshal with complaints.

Demographics may also play a part in explaining why black men did not complain on behalf of their wives and children. Steamboat workers and other black male laborers in the city likely had left their families elsewhere, as had many of the men serving with the Union Army in St. Louis.[27] Further, a significant number of black men who dealt with the provost marshal's office were military substitutes whom tricksters had attempted to swindle. A large proportion of the black male residents living in Missouri were involved with the Union Army, either as soldiers or as employed contraband workers. Meanwhile, many of the black women working in St. Louis were the family members of soldiers, and were not residing with their soldier husbands, brothers, or fathers in military camps or on the front lines.

Men and women both reported physical assaults to the provost marshal. African American women reported rape and physical violence at the hands of employers. In contrast, African American men most often appeared as complainants in unpaid labor disputes, the forcible impressments of African American men as substitute soldiers, and physical confrontations in which white men—not necessarily employers—attacked African American men.[28]

Martial Law

Although African Americans used it to further their own freedom and rights of citizenship, the provost marshal system was not instituted to improve black civil rights. The Union military had imposed martial law to hunt down traitors, and Missouri commanders had to contend with a local insurgency in addition to incursions by the Confederate Army from Arkansas. The provost marshals made rooting out Confederate sympathizers their main concern, and to that end turned to the testimony of both free and enslaved African Americans. The military information offered by African Americans played a critical role in the pursuit, capture, and prosecution of Confederate sympathizers. African American witnesses were often the sole providers of information that military officials could use to hunt down and prosecute disloyal activity. One wartime telegraph, for example, urged military officials to interview "a negro woman who knows the facts" about a family that had hidden escaped Confederate prisoners. But, the military telegraph warned, "This is all negro information."[29]

For enslaved women, reporting masters' suspicious activities to Union officials offered a means of escape. Hulda, a forty-year-old woman from the Missouri countryside, lived with her six-month-old son, Abraham; a three-year-old girl, Cloe; and four other related children in the household of Boyle Elliot, a known rebel with four relatives serving in the Confederate Army. Hulda's young children probably limited her ability to travel far as she searched for a provost marshal willing to hear her case. In February 1864, a Union sympathizer wrote in support of Hulda and her children to the provost marshal general, "These poor people know that they have been held in violation of law for more than two years. They have made nightly journeys to neighboring towns and military stations in search of imaginary Pro Marshals." The writer dramatically concluded, "The state of their minds is such that they cannot be reduced to slavery again in the first morning of their freedom without the use of the severest means."[30]

In St. Louis, however, the seat of the headquarters of the U.S. Army's Department of the Missouri, African American women could much more easily find military officials to whom they could report suspected disloyalty. In September 1864, military officials solicited Julia Hawkins, a free African American woman, to serve as a witness to the "disloyal conversation & practices" of Terry Kingsland, a "well known and rabid Secessionist."[31] The presence of U.S. Army troops as well as provost marshals' offices protected African American informants from Confederate retribution.

African Americans had a strong incentive to report suspicious behavior. The Second Confiscation Act of 1862 allowed the military to confiscate enslaved people owned by disloyal owners. Lincoln's Emancipation Proclamation did not free any enslaved people in Missouri as it did not apply to the loyal slave states. But Missouri provost marshals issued certificates of freedom to slaves who fell under the province of the Second Confiscation Act.[32]

Enslaved African Americans used the Union military's need for information about Confederate sympathizers as a strategy to earn a hearing before military officials. The goal of the enslaved informant was to gain freedom and strike a blow against slave owners. In 1862, Virginia and Mary Catherine, enslaved women living in Marion County, reported to Union forces that their master, "Old Man Caldwell," had supplied Confederate irregulars with gunpowder. After Union forces confiscated the powder, Caldwell told Mary Catherine that "he was going to put an end to me" and "blow my *damned* brains out." The two women fled to Union forces in Palmyra, where they testified that Caldwell had murdered a Union man.[33]

In effect, elite St. Louis families that supported the Confederacy discovered that their households had been infiltrated by potential Union spies. Enslaved women were an integral part of the domestic space of Confederate households, with the opportunity to hear and view disloyal activity hidden from outsiders. "Miss Lucy, our 'intelligent contraband' watches everything so closely that we do nothing but lie," wrote Zaidee Bagwell, a white teenage resident of St. Louis to a Confederate officer in 1863.[34] Bagwell accurately feared that those who "closely watched" her courier would capture her letter. In fact, the letter was captured that same month and turned over to the provost marshal general in St. Louis.[35] Bagwell was subsequently arraigned and tried before a military commission for encouraging rebellion and offering aid to Confederate forces.[36] Bagwell had reason to be wary of her domestic servant. Military officials arrested and prosecuted the friends, mothers, and wives of Confederate soldiers, who, like Zaidee Bagwell, corresponded with acquaintances and male relatives by post.[37] Bagwell may have been investigated or arrested on the basis of her servant's testimony.

In fact, with the aid of martial law and sympathetic commanders, African American residents of St. Louis aggressively pursued freedom by reporting the disloyal acts of their current and former owners to the provost marshal. Julia Chamberlain, a slave of Jesse Underwood, swore in June 1864 that her master "is an avowed rebel." Chamberlain asserted that she had overheard him "express himself in favor of the rebellion" and that he "gave material aid and comfort to rebels in arms."[38] Another woman, Eveline Mericks, testified that her master had left home to fight for the South and that her mistress had "received letters from him off and on during the times he has been absent." The St. Louis provost marshal reported that in return for her testimony, "Eveline thinks she ought to have emancipation papers and be free."[39] Similarly, Sarah Campbell, a contraband who worked as a laundress at a St. Louis military prison, reported to the prison commander that her former master had involved himself in the Minute Men, a club that organized in St. Louis with the goal of holding Missouri for the South. The prison commander noted in his correspondence with the provost marshal general that Campbell "would now like to obtain her free papers if possible."[40]

Members of St. Louis's black community often had known each other prior to arriving in the city and could testify regarding each other's former owners. In July 1864, African American Patrick Rogers swore that Mary Early was the former slave of an Arkansas rebel who was "an aider and abettor of rebels in arms against the Federal Government." Early had been captured by U.S. forces in Arkansas in the summer of 1863, and on the basis of Rogers's testimony, Captain Charles S. Hills, the St. Louis District provost marshal, granted Early "free papers."[41]

Notably, enslaved women were not pressured to enlist in the military when they visited the provost marshal. Instead, many took the opportunity to seek improvements in the legal status of themselves or their kin. Jane Ciss leveraged her visit to Hills into a bid to reclaim her enslaved children. In May 1864, Ciss asked for official recognition of her contraband status. James W. Ferguson, a private in the 68th U.S. Colored Troops, swore that he had known Ciss for "about twelve years back in Warren and Montgomery Counties"; that her "late owner," Benjamin Ciss, was a rebel and guerrilla soldier who was "most of the time in the bush"; and that Benjamin Ciss's son had enlisted in the Confederate Army. Another soldier, Robert Custer, swore that he had known Jane when he was enslaved on a Montgomery County farm about half a mile from her home. Before Custer "left the neighborhood" in February 1864, he heard Benjamin Ciss "frequently uphold the rebel cause in conversation with his neighbors."[42] On the basis of these two affidavits, Hills declared that Jane Ciss was entitled to contraband status and "the protection of all officers of the United States."[43]

Jane Ciss then traveled about sixty miles west to the provost marshal at Warrenton, where she used her new contraband status to try to free her children, who were still held by her former master. The provost marshal at Warrenton asked the St. Louis office to forward the affidavits of the two African American soldiers to "establish the fact that her children are in the hands of a Disloyal person."[44]

In a city long accustomed to slavery and its social practices, enslaved women now possessed the power to initiate the arrest and incarceration of slave owners, challenging the patriarchal prerogatives claimed by slave masters. In April 1864, "two negro girls" swore out affidavits charging their former master, Thomas Gardiner of St. Louis, with disloyalty and accusing him of hosting "Rebel soldiers." As a result, the provost marshal general ordered men from the U.S. police office to arrest Gardiner and subject him to military examination. Gardiner was held for a time in Myrtle Street Prison, a building, ironically, once used as a "slave pen" for a slave-trading business.[45] These two women worked to destroy the household hierarchies that were a necessary component of the slave system. By reporting their masters to the provost marshal, the enslaved women moved the politics of the household into the public space of a military court.

Thomas Gardiner suffered the social humiliation of losing control of his "girls." The ideology of slavery was based on a gendered system, in which white men manufactured both political legitimacy and cultural capital through their display of mastery over their household dependents. Within antebellum pro-slavery ideology, the construction of the appropriate Republican citizen was dependent on the successful display of mastery. Those men who did not own enslaved people claimed the identity of "master" through the control of their "domestic dependents"—that is, white women and children.[46] Gardiner's "girls" attacked not only the slave system but also Gardiner's right to claim the identity of "citizen." His formerly enslaved women refigured themselves as the true patriots, claiming for themselves the identity of citizens while working to classify Gardiner as a traitor not worthy of inclusion in the national body politic.[47]

The military's hunt for disloyalty turned the city's social structures upside-down. Fugitive slave women transformed themselves into patriots by informing on disloyal residents, while elite members of society were subject to military justice and imprisonment on the basis of black testimony. Bernard Lynch, who had run a large slave-trading business out of downtown St. Louis, had escaped to the Confederacy after Union troops occupied the city early in the war. The Union military confiscated his slave pen, turned it into a military prison, and held former slave owners and supporters of the slave system there.[48] This transformation exemplified how city landmarks that had sustained the infrastructure of slavery morphed into symbols of liberation. Elite disgust at the disruption of racial hierarchies in St. Louis was reflected in the 1862 words of Anne Ewing Lane, the daughter of an eight-term mayor and a southern sympathizer: "The dutch & the darkeys are the only free people here now."[49]

The petitions and complaints of freedwomen articulated political priorities that were informed by their gendered experiences under slavery. Now they had means to remake the world and assert their vision of freedom. For formerly enslaved women, this vision rejected the routine practices of slavery, including the loss of their children to the slave trade, beatings at the hands of their masters and mistresses, and the lack of compensation for their labor. Familiarized with the military justice system, African American women used the office of the provost marshals to press a multitude of claims previously impossible under the Missouri slave code.

Child Custody Cases

From the earliest years of the Civil War, African American women petitioned the provost marshal for custody of their children. African American women who claimed custody of their children challenged the basis of the nineteenth-century North American slave system, which sustained itself with the legal principle that the status of the child would follow the mother. The institution of slavery violently appropriated the reproductive potential of African American women, legally classifying their children as subject to forced labor, captivity, and sale. Freedwomen sought to recover their children from captivity and white control.[50]

In wartime Missouri, the unprecedented ability to use a governmental agency to gain custody of enslaved or indentured children marked a revolutionary change in the options available to African American women. As early as September 1861, a free black mother asked the provost marshal's office to adjudicate a dispute with a St. Louis resident in an effort to free her son, Theodore, from slavery. The woman claimed that Dr. J. B. Burnett had agreed to give Theodore to her if she paid him eight hundred dollars within six months. The doctor apparently reneged on his agreement and had Theodore continue to nurse Burnett's sickly son.[51]

By January 1862, the provost marshal had begun to intervene more actively to return African American children to their mothers' care. Contraband Georgiana Carnes proved that she had been tricked out of the custody of her children, Isabella and Arthur, and the marshal ordered that the children "be delivered into her possession forthwith."[52] Though Carnes was successful, she, like other African American women, had to navigate a complex system of military law in order to gain custody of her children.

In January 1865, a woman named Margaret reported to the St. Louis district provost office that she could not locate her daughter, Betsy. In the spring of 1863, Betsy, a twelve-year-old indentured worker, was in the possession of Mrs. Haisley. Nearly two years later, however, Margaret had frequently visited Mrs. Haisley's home but could not locate her child or obtain any information as to where the girl had gone. The St. Louis district provost marshal demanded that Mrs. Haisley explain "what has become of the child and where it is at this time."[53]

One case, initially brought before the St. Louis provost marshal by America Smith, was eventually tried before a military commission. Freedwomen who approached Union forces ran the risk of involuntary separation from their children through indentures. Superintendents at contraband camps occasionally facilitated the placement of child refugees in homes as indentured servants, separating them from adult relatives.[54] In 1863, when Smith was living at the Helena, Arkansas, contraband camp with her seven-year-old daughter, Anna, Charles Frank visited the camp in search of a young domestic servant. He persuaded America Smith to allow him to take Anna to his St. Louis home, promising that she would live "with his wife to keep her company. . . . He said his wife would keep and learn her a great deal." Although Smith was reluctant, the camp superintendent advised that Smith "had better let the man have her."[55]

America Smith followed her child to St. Louis a few weeks later and spent nearly two months searching for her daughter. Desperate, she initiated proceedings against Frank at the provost marshal's office. He was arrested and formally interrogated in the provost marshall's office. Unsatisfied with Frank's answers and suspicious that Frank had sold the child into the Kentucky slave market, military officials incarcerated the man in one of the city's military prisons. Frank claimed that he had given Anna Smith to a man whom he met in a saloon and whose name he had forgotten. The case eventually went to a military commission trial, where America Smith testified against Frank. The commission ultimately found Frank innocent, revealing the limits of the military justice system to serve the interests of African American complainants, but he did spend several months in jail during the proceedings.[56]

With the end of legal slavery in Missouri in January 1865, St. Louis mothers who had been separated from slave children engaged the provost marshal's office to assert their new custody rights. With abolition, Governor Thomas Fletcher immediately proclaimed that all of Missouri's enslaved people were now free.[57] Some masters, however, refused to comply. On April 18, 1865, Matilda Williams filed a complaint alleging that Winrod Snyder had refused to release her daughter. The district provost marshal, Lucius C. Matlack, summoned Snyder to explain why he was holding Emma M. Williams in his custody "against the consent of her mother."[58] Similarly, in April 1865, Ellen Carter sought to regain custody of her seven-year-old daughter, Elizabeth, who remained illegally enslaved near Columbia in Boone County. The district provost marshal forwarded Carter's case to his superiors in the provost marshal general's office because the case fell outside of his geographic jurisdiction.[59]

Several African American women used the St. Louis provost marshal's office to reunite their families after the eradication of slavery in Missouri. Children were often hired out to different households or geographically separated from their parents to discourage escape attempts. In April 1865, a number of women applied to the St. Louis district provost marshal for assistance in regaining custody of their enslaved children who had been stranded in the Missouri countryside.[60]

Assault Cases

Recall Charlotte Ford and her assault at the hands of the brick-wielding "Jeff Davis man." The assault occurred on May 29, 1864, when Farrell struck Ford on the head with the brick, shouting, "That is the way that Jeff Davis does the business—I am a Jeff Davis man all over."[61] U.S. policemen had been pursing Farrell when he came upon Ford in the alley outside of her St. Louis home. The military police most likely arrested Farrell, incarcerated him in a local military prison, and notified the local St. Louis provost marshal of these developments. Captain Hills promptly charged Farrell with "committing an assault on the person of a colored woman," writing to headquarters that Farrell posed a threat to the city as one of the "most desperate leaders" of a group "calculated to bring serious trouble upon the city of St. Louis by their hostility to all persons of color."[62]

As this incident illustrates, military officials patrolled, arrested, and imprisoned white citizens who assaulted black residents in St. Louis. The military arrested these white assailants despite the fact that the civil courts, along with the city's police system, continued to operate throughout the Civil War. Lincoln's suspension of habeas corpus had enabled military authorities to arrest civilian assailants like Thomas Farrell without the need for formal charges or a trial.[63]

By the summer of 1864, the African American residents of St. Louis were aware of their ability to report physical attacks to a sympathetic provost marshal's office. In the majority of these assault cases, the military authorities in St. Louis did not formally try civilians before military commissions. In October of that year, Mary Ann Higgins "got on a spree" on the St. Louis levee, and, "filling her apron with rocks, amused herself by throwing stones at the head of every negro who passed." After receiving complaints, the provost guard "proceeded to the battle field and captured her in the act."[64] Military guards arrested Higgins and brought her to the provost marshal's office, where she was charged with "committing an assault on an unoffending negro on the levy." John B. Means, the clerk and assistant examiner, sent Higgins to the "Female Prison on St. Charles Street."[65]

Provost marshals issued charges after arresting prisoners, but such charges were only initial classifications of wrongdoing, not formal charges such as those brought by military commissions. Local provost marshals then forwarded the evidence to superiors in the provost marshal general's office in St. Louis, where officials generally had three options: trying the assailant before a military commission; turning over the collected affidavits and the prisoner to the civil court system; or releasing the prisoner on parole. Most of those who faced charges were either turned over to the civil courts or released from the military prisons.[66]

The assault on Charlotte Ford was both a performance of an ideology and an attack on her gender and her race. Ford's ability to live free in the city of St. Louis offended Farrell's sensibilities as a "Jeff Davis man." Farrell may have targeted Ford as a symbol of the wartime destruction of slavery. The migration of formerly enslaved people to St. Louis had already altered the demographics of the city by the time of the assault in May 1864. Yet Farrell's aggression was not directed toward a genderless freedperson—Farrell specifically attacked an African American woman. The mere presence of African American women in the city should not have bothered a "Jeff Davis man," since black domestic workers were commonplace in antebellum St. Louis. However, the disruption of racial hierarchies and the potential that Ford might obtain the privileges that accrued to white "ladies" prompted his display of violence. His physical violation demonstrated his contempt for her gender, her race, and her potential freed status.

A military trial resolved Farrell's case in September 1864, after it was forwarded up the chain of martial justice. Farrell had weakened his position by cheering for Jefferson Davis during the incident, thus opening himself up to the charge of disloyalty to go along with assault and battery.[67] The commission found Farrell guilty and sentenced him to hard labor for six months. But Major General William S. Rosecrans, the commander of the Department of the Missouri, "disapproved of the proceedings" and ordered Farrell released from custody on September 15, 1864.[68]

Ford's act of testifying against Farrell was an assertion of her right to live in St. Louis without the fear of white violence. Other women joined in the effort to establish not just their right to be free from assault but also their rights to both physical and verbal respect. In September 1864, an African American woman went before Hills to report a verbal assault by John Conner, a white civilian. Hills responded to her complaint by arresting Conner and charging him with "using grossly disloyal Language" and "insulting an Innocent & inoffensive colored woman." Hills had originally written *lady*, but either he or his clerk crossed out the word and replaced it with *woman*.[69] In essence, this complainant attempted to claim the respect that accrued to white women and the identity of a lady in the context of living in a slaveholding state.

Captain Hills took affidavits and forwarded the collected evidence as well as the prisoner to his superiors. In his letter to headquarters, Hills noted that the victim was an African American woman "who on account of having no white witnesses is by the laws of the state, debarred from redress in civil courts." Hills's impulse was to classify the African American woman as a "lady," but either he or his superior officers apparently were not prepared to grant an African American woman that identity and its attendant gender and class privileges associated with middle- and upper-class white womanhood.[70]

Military authorities charged Conner with verbal assault and disloyalty. His use of "grossly disloyal Language" — distinct from the charge of "insulting" language—probably justified this unusual military case.[71] The charge of disloyalty warranted military interference in civilian race relations.

The outcome of the case is unknown, but the incident delineates the circumstances in which the provost marshal charged white civilians for race-based attacks or verbal insults. Like Farrell, Connor was accused of disloyal behavior. In both cases, the provost marshal relied on the charge of disloyalty to justify the military's expansion of juridical authority into civilian race-based affairs.

Military officials occasionally went beyond investigating white civilians who assaulted free or contraband African Americans. In one instance, the provost marshal interfered with a slave owner's physical punishment of an enslaved woman. Mrs. Edwards was investigated for her "cruel beating of a negro woman," Hannah, in February 1864. A U.S. policeman reported to his captain that Mrs. Edwards "has the reputation of being a violent rebel."[72] Once again, the outcome of the case is unknown, but Mrs. Edwards's Confederate sympathies may have made Hannah subject to military appropriation under the Second Confiscation Act.

By 1864, the St. Louis provost marshal's office was vigilant about the prosecution of white-on-black assaults. It willingly collected sworn affidavits from African American residents about white violence and arrested white civilians for making racial insults. The St. Louis provost marshal's office and the African Americans who testified against white citizens posed a challenge to the privileges of whiteness found in the city's civil court system.

Three African American women swore affidavits attesting to John Ferguson's assault (possibly sexual) on Rebecca Seldona in January 1865.[73] Ferguson owned tenements in Clabber Alley, a section of St. Louis occupied by low-income white residents as well as African Americans.[74] The provost marshal asserted that Ferguson had "committed a great crime" and "is deserving of some punishment," but because all the witnesses to the assault were "colored persons," the civil courts could not punish Ferguson.[75] Ferguson was charged with "assault with intent to commit a great bodily injury on the person of a colored person" and incarcerated in the Gratiot Street Prison.[76] Within the week, the provost marshal general turned Ferguson and his case materials over to the civil courts because Ferguson's offense was "one for the Civil Authorities to determine."[77]

In at least one instance, the St. Louis district provost marshal dealt with the attempted rape of an African American woman. In March 1865, landlord William Quinn attempted to rape his tenant in addition to assaulting an African American man. The marshal forwarded the testimony, along with the prisoner, to the headquarters of the provost marshal general. Like Ferguson, William Quinn was turned over to the civil authorities for trial.[78]

African American women who worked as domestic laborers often lived in their white employers' homes, leaving them particularly vulnerable to physical violence. In one such 1864 case, Samuel Sommers and Margaret Carter were arguing in his kitchen when, Carter later testified, he "jumped up and took a rolling pin off the table" and struck her "twice in the stomach." Carter "took the rolling pin from him and laid it on the table" and accused him of stealing five dollars from her. In response, Sommers "took a knife off the table and said he would cut her damned throat for her."[79]

African American women understood freedom to mean that employers could not beat employees. Slave owners had routinely subjected enslaved women to domestic violence. Indeed, physical violence sustained the institution of slavery. It was within this context that black women like Margaret Carter worked to assert their own visions of freedom and citizenship. In a similar case later the same year, Jane Jones reported her employer's physical violence to the provost marshal, although her initial goal was to acquire back wages. Jones, a twenty-year-old free black woman, had lived and worked in the St. Louis household of Mr. and Mrs. John Gordon for about fifteen months when she left after "John came into the room where I was and shook and kicked me for going into his room after some article." She briefly left the Gordon household but later returned to "obtain the balance due me." Jones testified that Mr. Gordon "was continually threatening to whip or strike me" and that she left the household because she "was afraid of Mr. Gordon abusing me." Emily Partridge Eaton, a white woman serving as president of the Freedmen's Relief Society of St. Louis, asked military authorities to assist Jones. In response, the St. Louis district provost marshal arrested and examined Mrs. Gordon but dismissed the case after finding "no cause of action against her."[80]

The civil courts continued to perform the political work of constructing racial difference. Missouri's legal culture sanctioned physical abuse by white people of black bodies. Legal statutes imposed a variety of physical penalties on both enslaved and free black Missourians.[81] This state-sanctioned corporal punishment was based not simply on slave status but on racial identity.

Local sheriffs or city marshals routinely punished free African Americans convicted of criminal offenses with lashing. Petit larceny, defined by Missouri's laws as stealing up to ten dollars in goods or cash, was a common charge in the St. Louis courts in this time period and one for which Missouri law treated white and black women differently. White residents could receive imprisonment for up to one year or a fine of up to one hundred dollars. African American women, free or enslaved, who were not pregnant were subject to twenty-one lashes. (Pregnant women were spared the lash and instead received up to twenty-one days in prison.)[82] In June 1864, the St. Louis Recorder's Court sentenced Emma Anderson, an enslaved woman, on charges of petit larceny: she received "four stripes at the hands of the City Marshal."[83] The same court sentenced a free black woman to five stripes as late as February 1865: Eliza Clay, a free African American woman, received that punishment after pleading guilty to petit larceny.[84] African American men who were convicted of attempted rape were castrated.[85] These physical punishments, encoded in the criminal code prior to the Civil War, were used to attack the masculine and feminine identities of African Americans at the same time that they were finding new recognition and status in the military legal system.

Labor Disputes

When the military justice system in St. Louis intervened in labor situations, it involved itself in an issue unrelated to the conventional domain of martial law. In June 1864, when the marshal ordered a slave mistress to allow Eliza Moore to visit her sick mother "once each day," the matter had nothing to do with the issue of disloyalty.[86] Nevertheless, by seeking and obtaining the provost marshal's intervention, African American women used the military justice system to undermine the institution of slavery. Martial law gave military officials wide authority to interfere in the lives of St. Louis residents, and in this case, an enslaved woman relied on military power to force a labor compromise with her owner.

Freedwomen's distinctive experience as laborers in the city informed the complaints they made to provost marshals. Like other cities in slave-holding states, the enslaved population in St. Louis skewed toward women, who tended to work as laundresses, cooks, and domestic servants.[87] The demand for African American women workers resulted from the numerous household jobs available in the city. The labor performed by freedwomen was quite similar to their work prior to emancipation. As enslaved women gained their freedom, they used the provost marshal's office to force formal wage arrangements with their employers. This power to insist on the regular payment of wages for labor was one way freedwomen asserted their new status.

Provost marshal Charles S. Hills wrote to one such employer in July 1864, "Madam, This colored woman has filed a complaint at this office that you are indebted to her for 5 months labor." Hills ordered the employer to pay the claimant six dollars and threatened to "collect this claim by Military authority unless settled immediately."[88] In another instance, a marshal informed John Bennett that his former servant, Sarah Gales, had complained about an "unsettled account of wages" and asked him to "call at this Office on Monday."[89]

Employers in St. Louis agreed to pay wages to African American women who were still enslaved because the city offered numerous opportunities for escape. Refusing to pay wages brought the real possibility of losing entirely the services of the enslaved workers. Jennie Blanton was enslaved by Charles Tyler in Lafayette County until May 6, 1864, when Tyler gave her to Mary Cursley. Blanton labored for Cursley until the fall of 1864, when the two women moved to St. Louis. At that point, according to Blanton, "Mrs. Cursley promised me wages if I would remain with her."[90]

Military authorities were aware of the legal disabilities that prevented African Americans from seeking justice from the civil courts in disputes with white employers. Helen Jackson "lodged a complaint" after a Mrs. Demas refused to pay her wages, claiming that Jackson had stolen one of her silver spoons. The marshal told Demas that "if there is any proof [Jackson] has stolen the spoon," the matter could be pursued in the civil courts, whereas Jackson "cannot resort to civil law to collect the money due her." He ordered Demas to pay.[91]

African American freedwomen also used the provost marshal's office to assert their right to property accumulated while they were enslaved. According to Harriet Hampden, Charles Hunt had freed her in January 1865 but "refused to give me any of my clothing except what I had on my person at the time." The provost marshal ordered Hunt to give Hampden her clothing and to pay her ten dollars compensation "for her time and trouble in getting her clothing from him."[92]

The St. Louis provost marshals made no assumption of coverture in these wage complaints. In almost all of the cases, women made complaints against employers for unpaid wages in their own names, not in the names of their fathers or their husbands. In only one case did a woman make a joint wage complaint with her husband, and in this instance, Anna and Levi Clark were pursuing separate grievances. Levi Clark made a complaint against Asa Gates over wages for taking care of his horses. Anna Clark swore that Gates had employed her to cook for him for three months at sixteen dollars per month, but after a week had insisted that she wash and iron, in return for which she demanded an increase of four dollars per month.[93] In total, these complaints demonstrate that African American women used the provost marshal's office to force wage compromises during the transition to free labor.

The End of Martial Law

The end of martial law meant that African American women could no longer turn to the provost marshals for justice. In the spring of 1865, the general commanding the Department of the Missouri directed the orderly transfer of power from the military courts back to civil law.[94] Martial law officially ended in Missouri with a joint declaration of Commanding General John Pope and Governor Fletcher on March 7, 1865.[95] But the military courts did not immediately abdicate the civil responsibilities they had adopted during the Civil War.

In the November 1864 elections, Radical Republicans gained power in Missouri, capturing the governor's office and setting the stage for the creation of a new state constitution.[96] One of the first tasks of the January 1865 Constitutional Convention was the abolition of slavery, and official celebrations took place in St. Louis on January 14.[97] The new constitution also gave African Americans the right to testify in Missouri's civil court, a decision that even the Radicals hotly debated.

The convention's consideration of the proposal to allow such testimony demonstrated that the value of African Americans' wartime testimony before provost marshals was key to the delegates' support for the change. Delegate Captain Gustavus St. Gemme, an assistant provost marshal, argued that "he had had opportunity of testing the capacity of negroes to testify" and that if this testimony was "good in a military sense, there could be no objection to it civilly." St. Gemme believed that African American witnesses were "well qualified to give evidence" and that delegates who opposed the amendment were a "slur on the military." Other supporters of the amendment pointed specifically to the military value of African American testimony: noted one, "Many negroes had been compelled to carry food to bushwhackers in the bush," and certain "traitors, bushwhackers and rebels" were "convicted on the testimony of negroes, but . . . could never be reached otherwise."[98]

The political discussion about the admission of African American testimony against white persons entered the city's mass media. Prior to the convention, St. Louis's *Daily Missouri Democrat*, a strongly pro-Union and pro-Republican paper, published a front-page letter under the pseudonym Justinia that urged the repeal of the section of the Missouri legal code that prohibited African Americans from testifying against white persons.[99]

Just two days later, on the convention's second day, the *Democrat* noted John Ferguson's attack on Rebecca Seldona. In the civil courts, Seldona "could have no redress," but "the military officers are no respectors of colors, and in many cases have received the sworn statements of negroes against whites."[100]

After vigorous debate, the delegates passed a "Declaration of Rights" that removed the racial bars to witness testimony.[101] Missouri voters ratified the new constitution on June 6.[102] The Union Army could no longer cite legal restrictions against testimony to justify adjudicating cases brought by African American complainants.

In the spring of 1865, the St. Louis provost marshal's office began "gradually" adjusting "towards the proper functions of a military bureau only."[103] In April 1865, Matlack, the St. Louis District provost marshal, asked Missouri's secretary of state about the new law "making people of color equal before the law in Civil Courts." He needed reassurance and advice on the "present standing before the law of Americans of African descent in Missouri." Cases involving such persons accounted for "much of the local business of the office" and caused "frequent collision with the civil rights of the Citizens." In particular, Matlack wanted to know whether "the negro" could "be a party to suits in the Civil Courts against white persons" for assault, debt, and the "restraint of personal liberty" and whether African Americans could testify against white persons in the civil courts.[104]

Reassured that African Americans were equal before the law, Matlack published an official notice in two St. Louis newspapers describing the new law and the altered role of the provost marshal's office. The office would no longer deal with claims "from Negros for redress of grievances or collection of claims." All people of color could now testify in the civil courts against white people and were "subject to the same fines, penalties and punishment for offenses or crimes as white persons." Consequently, "no complaints nor claims of the negro will be entertained or prosecuted at this Office Nor at any other office in this District when the Civil Courts are in operation."[105]

"For Rent," declared an April 14, 1865, article in the *Daily Missouri Republican*. The provost marshal's offices and their accompanying "necessary war evils" had moved out of their prominently located headquarters at the corner of Fifth and St. Charles in downtown St. Louis. The building was closed up, with "large handbills placed on the window panes advertising the rooms for rent."[106]

African Americans had lost their access to the military courts, but they had gained entry to the official courts of the state apparatus. African American women's political work had paid off. They had stood before provost marshals, claimed a civil identity, and asserted their right to establish a relationship with the state. Before a military-legal official, a man who represented federal power, enslaved and free women argued for their due wages, charged white men with assault, and asked for state assistance in reclaiming custody of their children. The assertion of such rights was one way in which freedwomen made citizenship claims on the state. Harriet Hampden, Helen Jackson, Charlotte Ford, and countless other women achieved a measure of justice denied to them by the civil courts. These formerly stateless women had claimed a nation.[107]

CHAPTER 5

The Legacy of Slave Marriage

Freedwomen's Marital Claims and the Process of Emancipation

NANCY RICHARDS TESTIFIED THAT she married her soldier husband at Benton Barracks in November 1863 because he told her that "he greatly feared he would not come out of the war alive, and in that case he wished her to be legally possessed of all that was, or might be his." Until 1863, Richards had lived as a slave in the city of St. Louis and in neighboring St. Charles County. She and James Richards had been engaged for two years before he decided to enlist. The promise of a bounty may have encouraged him to ensure that the marriage was conducted by a military chaplain and recorded by the U.S. Army. James and Nancy Richards lived together as "man & wife" at Benton Barracks and were "so regarded by [his] comrades." As he had feared, James did not survive the war, but their military marriage guaranteed that his widow was legally entitled to his bounty and pension.[1]

The assertion of marital rights was one way in which freedwomen such as Nancy Richards experienced the process of emancipation. "Marriage," both under slavery and in the postwar period, had more to do with who had the power to name it and to break up those marriages than with the familial attachments of the two individuals involved. African American women attempted to seize the power to name their own marriages, a power that was intimately bound up with the process of emancipation.

Freedwomen's marital claims comprised part of their project to construct a civic identity. Citizenship forms its meaning through everyday experiences in which people test the boundaries of their rights and obligations, and marriage was one of those experiences.[2] The identity of citizen is not constructed through dealings with an abstract state entity. The gendered nature of citizenship is constructed in part by the rights and responsibilities assigned to "married women" by husbands, communities, and the legal system.[3]

Freedwomen constructed their identities as citizens, and realized their civil status, through interactions with these entities. Their marital claims were made in dialogue with the Union Army, the Federal Pension Bureau, divorce law, and the African American church and community. Asserting their definitions of marriage within these arenas, freedwomen worked to emancipate themselves from slaveholders, patriarchal authority, church authority, and state authority.[4]

Prior to emancipation, slave owners played a coercive role in the formation and separation of families. For formerly enslaved women, the ability to choose their family and then maintain those family ties was critical to their definition of freedom. Formerly enslaved women had experienced the horror of the slave trade and the violent separation of enslaved families on both the local and the interstate levels, with the latter often transferring human property to faraway cotton-rich states "down the river" such as Louisiana, Texas, and Mississippi.[5] Unlike nineteenth-century white feminists, who focused on the legal disabilities of marriage, African American women fought to have marital legitimacy conferred on their relationships. But both groups fought for the right of individual women to make their own choices in forming or reforming definitions of family.[6]

Military Marriages, Romantic Decisions, and the Meanings of Freedom

Commanders and chaplains associated with African American regiments as well as Freedmen's Bureau officials advocated formal remarriage for men and women who had been married while enslaved. Not infrequently, these white men were ordained Protestant ministers with views of sexuality and marriage that they paternalistically applied to the formerly enslaved population.[7] William A. Pile, the commander of black troops in Missouri, was typical in that his opposition to slavery went along with racially prejudiced assumptions about the sexual behavior of the enslaved population. A Methodist minister and a former commander of Radical Republican white troops from St. Louis, General Pile recognized the military's obligation to support the families of African American enlistees and consequently ordered Union officers to bring the soldiers' wives and children to the contraband camp at Benton Barracks.[8]

In November 1863, Pile testified before the American Freedmen's

Inquiry Commission that it was "uniformly true" that freedpeople wished to legally marry. While many formerly enslaved people indeed sought to take advantage of the option to marry, Pile and other military officers attempted to impose their own morality and visions of marriage on the freed population. "The first thing to be done," Pile stated, "and one of the most important things to be done . . . is to impress upon them the importance of the family relation." Pile wanted the military to encourage "domestic obligations" between husbands and wives.[9] Union officers commonly took the attitude that the former bondspeople lacked a "proper" understanding of marriage and needed "help" to form families.[10]

However, Pile and other military officials also accepted the existence of black families.[11] But military marriages were not simple acts of Union benevolence toward freedpeople. The Union military promoted marriage to support a specific vision of gendered norms and sexual monogamy that reinforced the concept of a male head of household who was responsible for providing for his family. Despite this middle-class vision of female dependency, Union military officers often expected both African American women and children to labor outside of the household, both in agriculture and as laundresses and cooks for the army. In fact, Union officers and later Freedmen's Bureau officials used marital contracts to enforce wage labor agreements.[12]

As the recruitment of enslaved men attracted the families of soldiers to Union military camps throughout the border states, many Union commanders refused to aid these refugees. In recruitment centers for African American men, such as Camp Nelson in central Kentucky, commanders drove away wives and children, many of whom had recently escaped from slavery or wartime violence, refusing to allow them sanctuary. During the summer and fall of 1864 hundreds of African American women and children were barred from Camp Nelson.[13]

The military recognition of slave marriage represented a modest improvement over the wholesale rejection of women and children from military camps. In April 1863, John Eaton Jr., the superintendent of military camps in Tennessee and northern Mississippi, required that contraband husbands and wives who wished to live together must legalize their slave marriages in formal ceremonies conducted by military chaplains. In March 1864, Adjutant General Lorenzo Thomas issued Special Order no. 15, which extended this policy throughout the Union military.[14] Military marriages conferred official recognition that the formerly enslaved population possessed families, and this acknowledgment opened the possibility that the Union military might have a wider obligation to soldiers' families.

Despite the Union military's promotion of slave marriages, commanders continued their efforts to remove African American women from camps and even cities. Further, long-term couples who had married while enslaved faced Union officials who would not recognize their marriages. Officers combined prejudices about sexual immorality with their concerns about vagrancy to justify women's forcible removal from Union-occupied cities such as Natchez, Mississippi.[15] Commander William Pile was exceptional in that he encouraged the migration of women and children to St. Louis.

The freedwomen's interest in marriage was typically distinct from and often at odds with the Union Army's goals for the institution, but the freedpeople were pleased to have the option of legal marriage. That said, they did not want the military to govern their familial or sexual choices. The enslaved population held a variety of familial goals that did not necessarily conform to the vision of marriage promoted by Union officers and chaplains.[16]

"Weddings, just now, are very popular, and abundant among the Colored People," reported A. B. Randall, a military chaplain stationed in Little Rock, Arkansas, to the adjutant general on February 28, 1865. The community had learned of Special Order no. 15 and reacted with enthusiasm to the public recognition of African American marriages. Randall noted that in the preceding month, he had married twenty-five couples, most of whom had been "living together for years."[17] But the military did not approve of all African American marriages. Randall discouraged soldiers from marrying women the men had met at camp, preferring to conduct ceremonies for slave couples of long standing. This military policy may have been a response to the sexual stereotypes imposed on young, unattached African American women.

In Helena, Arkansas, Colonel John G. Hudson was so alarmed at marriages between soldiers and refugee women that he issued a special order revoking all marriages conducted by the post chaplain, J. I. Herrick, in February 1865. Hudson was particularly concerned that "the enlisted men of this command, are much in the habit of marrying Common place women of the town."[18]

Colonel Hudson carefully tracked soldiers living with their wives while serving in his regiment. He directed all his company commanders to forward all applications for marriage certificates made at the Helena post for his "approval or disapproval"; soldiers in all marriages "that are disapproved of . . . will not be allowed to Stay out of Quarters nights." Hudson also prohibited any soldier from "send[ing] for his wife" without military permission.[19]

Relationships and marriage ceremonies involving soldiers and contraband women living at Helena were quite popular despite the orders of Union commanders. Freed from the restrictions imposed by slave owners, African American women at contraband camps exercised new freedoms by choosing their own husbands. Hannah Johnson met and married her husband, Chatman Pryor, while his regiment was stationed at Helena, and they "lived as man and wife, she outside of camp, until he died." A fellow private remembered Hannah as "a ginger-cake, chunky woman" whom Pryor had married about two years after arriving in Helena.[20]

Military recognition of slave marriages to some extent legitimated the presence of soldiers' families at or near military posts. Jane Carter left Pike County, Missouri, joined her enlisted husband in Baton Rouge, Louisiana, and "lived with the soldier for nearly a year, in a little cabin in close proximity to the company camp, and while the soldier was still in service." According to Carter, the regimental officers would not allow her to live with her husband unless she participated in a marriage ceremony.[21]

Enslaved people had resisted their owners' efforts to govern familial and sexual relationships. During the Civil War, however, enslaved women escaped their slave homes with men who were not the husbands assigned by owners. In Franklin County, Missouri, the owner of Simon and Lorenda Williamson whipped them both several times in an attempt to break up their relationship. As a soldier, Simon Williamson cast off his other slave wife, a woman named Silva, and claimed Lorenda as his spouse, sending Lorenda and his daughter letters and money.[22]

Jane Barker recalled that her Missouri mistress "did not want her to marry"; consequently, "no white persons" were present at her marriage to Cain Barker, which was performed by an African American Methodist minister in Knox County. Jane Barker subsequently escaped with her husband after he enlisted in the Union Army. They traveled together with Union troops until she was put off their boat in Cape Girardeau with the other women and children. She "parted with him on the bow of the boat," and her husband's last words to her were a request to not hire out her two children and a promise to send money as soon as he received his wages. While enslaved, Cain Barker had also married a woman named Charlotte.[23] Emancipation allowed many freedpeople the chance to make romantic choices unencumbered by the decisions of slave owners.

Federal Pension Law and the Marital Claims of African American Civil War Widows

Enslaved African American women who did not receive the privilege of legal marriage found themselves at a disadvantage if their husbands perished in the war. The legal wives of black soldiers became eligible for pensions. In April 1864, Congress eased the burden of proof for freedwomen seeking pensions after the massacre of African American soldiers at Fort Pillow, Tennessee, about forty miles north of Memphis on the Mississippi River. The Battle of Fort Pillow became notorious because Confederate general Nathan Bedford Forrest permitted white Union men to surrender but oversaw the slaughter of about two hundred of the three hundred African American soldiers remaining at the fort. Although Forrest, later a founding member of the Ku Klux Klan, denied that he murdered the soldiers, people witnessed the massacre and reported the war crimes.[24]

The publicity surrounding the shocking deaths at Fort Pillow may have encouraged lawmakers to grant pensions to the bereaved relatives of the dead men. As amended in July 1864, the Pension Statute granted pensions to African American widows of soldiers if two reliable witnesses swore that the couple "habitually recognized each other as man and wife, and lived together as such for a definite period not less than two years."[25] Military pensions provided a monthly income that could make a substantial difference in war widows' economic situation, and women began to submit claims even before the Confederacy surrendered. The right to a widow's pension was an extension of privileges associated with legal marriage and thus was central to the civic identity emancipated widows attempted to construct.[26]

African American war widows had no direct economic claim on the state; rather, their economic entitlement flowed through the marital bond. The Pension Bureau had to legitimize slave marriages before widows could receive the economic benefits of their marital rights. The 1864 Pension Statute provided that the government could confer ex post facto legality on slave marriages, meaning that Pension Bureau investigators defined which of its newest citizens' marital customs would be considered legitimate after the Civil War. Special investigators from the Pension Bureau separated slave relationships into legal marriages and criminal cohabitation. As a consequence, the distribution of widows' pensions depended on how the federal government and its agents defined legitimate slave marriages.[27]

African American women whose slave marriages had been ratified by military chaplains were likely to receive military pensions. For example, Sarah Adams married her husband, James, in a ceremony performed by Chaplain W. H. Corkhill at Benton Barracks and subsequently received her widow's pension.[28] Similarly, Sallie and Champ Smith had married in 1850 and lived as a couple until his enlistment in November 1863. In March 1864, they had a military marriage ceremony, also performed by Corkhill, thereby removing all concerns that their slave marriage was irregular—or that any other relationships Champ may have had while enslaved might have counted as marriage—and smoothing the way for Sallie's claim to Champ's pension after his death in September 1864. Two months later, Sallie Smith appeared before a clerk of the St. Louis County Court to apply for a widow's pension. Now residing on Almond Street, Smith retained a legal firm to handle her pension application and gathered witnesses to testify on her behalf, demonstrating that she possessed the legal acumen needed to prove her claim.[29]

Cynthia Buford's pension application offers another example of the power of a military ceremony to legitimate claims. Nathaniel and Mary Buford had married roughly a decade before the war in Callaway County, Missouri, where they were enslaved, and had two children, Bettie and Ellen, in 1853 and 1857, respectively. Mary Buford died in 1862 or 1863, and Nathaniel subsequently met Cynthia Colwell and married her in an 1864 ceremony conducted by a military chaplain. Nathaniel died of malaria in September 1865, and Cynthia applied for a Civil War pension shortly thereafter, easily winning approval in 1867. Under an 1879 law, children up to age sixteen were entitled to Civil War pension funds, and this money could be paid in a lump sum even after the children had reached adulthood. When Bettie and Ellen applied for minors' pensions under that provision, they were rejected on the grounds that their mother was not Nathaniel Buford's legal wife—in effect, that they were illegitimate.[30] Cynthia Buford's short but documented legal marriage trumped Mary Buford's claim even though Mary and Nathaniel had been married for much longer and had children together.

In many cases, however, the chaos and dislocation of war prevented African Americans from formalizing their relationships. In some instances, one or both partners could not escape slavery; at other times, problems such as shelter, food, illness, and caring for children took priority over marriage ceremonies. The U.S. Pension Bureau did not require claimants to have undergone a legal ceremony but also awarded pensions to women who could prove the existence of their slave marriages. In October 1868, Eliza Perkins, a resident of St. Louis, applied for a widow's pension. She had married Thomas Perkins in Lincoln County in a slave ceremony conducted by an African American minister. Two former neighbors, Richard Bland and Helen Reach, who had been enslaved in Lincoln County, swore before the clerk of the St. Louis County Court that they had witnessed the marriage and that Eliza and Thomas were considered by "all their acquaintances" to be a married couple. Eliza Perkins was admitted onto the pension rolls in January 1869 despite having no legal proof of her marriage.[31]

Similarly, Charlotte and Henry Washington had married in an 1856 ceremony performed by an African American minister in St. Louis. Two months after Henry's August 1866 death of cholera while at Jefferson Barracks near St. Louis, Charlotte applied for a pension. Several African American witnesses collected by Charlotte backed up her claim, including two soldiers from her husband's regiment, testifying before a notary public at the St. Louis County Court.[32]

The Federal Pension Bureau, Sexual Respectability, and the Definition of Legal Marriage

The primary determination of success for an African American widow attempting to receive a Civil War pension was her ability to prove the legality of her marriage. As in the Buford case, a wife who could prove her claim could wipe out the history of enslaved family life. Ann Smith, for example, was certified and received a widow's pension in December 1868 but was dropped from the rolls in 1874 after a pension investigator concluded that she had made a fraudulent claim. She and Robert Smith had begun their relationship while enslaved in Montgomery County and had two daughters, Ann and Sophia. Millie Crockett, who attended the births of both children, testified that the children were the daughters of Robert Smith. However, the Pension Bureau investigator reported that neither the Smiths' owners nor members of the local enslaved community considered the couple married but that Robert Smith had "just took up with her."[33] The government rejected Ann Smith's attempt to assert her definition of marriage, delegitimizing her children and invalidating her self-identification as a wife. Her experience suggests that in the years following the Civil War, pension investigators, acting for the federal government, increasingly regulated the moral lives of war widows.[34]

In addition, African American communities recognized that not all romantic attachments resulted in marriage and had specific definitions of various sorts of nonmarital relationships such as "taking up" or "sweethearting." Brenda Stevenson has suggested that the practice of polygamy may have been more common than scholars have recognized. What freedpeople considered legitimate intimate relationships did not necessarily accord with the legal definition of marriage.[35]

Ann Smith's removal from the pension rolls demonstrates the role a particular definition of sexual respectability played in the governmental allocation of pensions. Robert Smith's former owner, Joseph Poindexter, contended that she was not named Ann Smith but Ann Best, after the name of her owner, John Best, and characterized her as "a low character." Poindexter thus used constructions of illicit sexual behavior to delegitimate Ann Smith's claim on the federal government.[36] In the absence of a marriage ceremony performed by a Union chaplain, white owners' testimony carried great weight in determinations of pension eligibility. But slave owners had often resisted their chattel's attempts to marry and had inflicted punishment on men and women who did so. Consequently, enslaved people did not consider white permission for, or attendance at, a slave marriage to be a reliable or objective determinant of family bonds.

In addition, Robert Smith's mother contested Ann Smith's right to a widow's pension. With the backing of Robert's brother, Umstead, and his wife, Robert's mother claimed that Robert had never married Ann.[37] Competing social and financial interests existed within enslaved communities and even within families, and parents at times objected to their children's marriages, further reducing the likelihood of a neighborhood consensus. Under slavery, marriage was defined by those who could impose and destroy romantic and familial attachments. As part of the process of emancipation, African American women attempted to seize that power for themselves. In the case of Ann Smith, the Federal Pension Bureau investigated and imposed its own definition onto her relationship with Robert Smith. Mary and Sophia, Robert Smith's children, were declared to be illegitimate and according to federal pension laws were not the children of Robert Smith. Fluid understandings of marriage in the slave community placed freedwomen at a disadvantage in their struggle to get their marriage recognized by the federal government. Concepts such as "took up" could define anything from a casual relationship to an informal marriage.[38]

When more than one widow applied for a soldier's pension, the Pension Bureau had to resolve apparent bigamy.[39] Lorenda Williamson and her daughter, Missouri Ann, initially collected a ten-dollar-a-month pension after Simon Williamson's death—a substantial supplement for a woman who only a few years earlier had lived as a slave on a Franklin County farm.[40] But after a year, the federal government suspended Lorenda's stipend when Silva Williamson filed her own claim on the grounds that she had married Simon Williamson in a slave ceremony.[41]

Confronted with a second slave wife, the Pension Bureau assigned a special investigator to research the purported marriages of Lorenda, Silva, and Simon. From 1869 to 1881 the bureau conducted three different investigations to resolve the marital status of the two widows. In the third and final investigation, the agent ruled that Silva was the "only true and legal wife" of Simon. From the perspective of the state, this ruling transformed Lorenda's status from that of a legal wife into an immoral woman who had engaged in criminal cohabitation.[42]

Pension Bureau agents nullified slave marriages based on state-imposed definitions of sexual respectability.[43] As a consequence, certain war widows were deprived of the economic benefits of marriage, including pensions. The allocation of widows' pensions reveals an important aspect of how legal marital status and its converse, constructions of criminal sexual behavior, shaped the civil rights of emancipated women in post–Civil War America.[44]

Shifting definitions of legal marriage played a crucial role in the long-delayed resolution of the Williamson case. After the third and final investigation, the bureau struck Lorenda from the pension rolls. The special investigator concluded in his 1881 report that Lorenda was a "woman of bad reputation, who no doubt had frequent and criminal intercourse with the soldier." He recognized that Lorenda had "several children" by Simon, but dismissed them as "illegitimate" and declared that Lorenda was viewed as no more than a "common prostitute" among the enslaved population.[45] Lorenda not only lost her pension, the state also stripped her of her marital identity.

In contrast, Silva's reputation for sexual respectability was a key factor in the government's decision to acknowledge her as the legitimate widow. While enslaved, Lorenda had married a man and separated from him before her relationship began with Simon. She testified that her first husband left her for another woman.[46] Lorenda could not legally divorce her first husband, but this did not prevent the pension investigator from construing her relationship with Simon as an act of bigamy or adultery. Silva did not have any other husbands to explain away, whereas Lorenda had to convince the pension investigator that her first marriage had truly dissolved. The pension investigators failed to take into account that Lorenda, like other enslaved persons, could not legally marry or petition the court for a divorce. The circumstances of slave life blurred the distinctions between married couples and illicit relationships. Special investigators, however, ignored the diversity of familial relationships under slavery. They imposed firm distinctions between sexually virtuous slave women and those widows they identified as morally suspect.[47]

To make these distinctions, agents researched the sexual histories of the contesting widows. The Pension Bureau erased the history of slavery, attributing to slave women an agency they never actually possessed. Investigators conducted extensive interviews with family members, the former slave owners, and others in the African American community in which a couple had lived during slavery.[48] It was through collection of such testimony that Silva won the pension. In 1850, Simon formally married Silva in a ceremony that was conducted in her master's home by a Methodist class leader. Several people who had grown up with Silva strengthened her claim by testifying not only that she was sexually monogamous during her marriage to Simon but also that Simon was the only man with whom she had ever had an intimate relationship.[49] Notably, these distinctions were the conclusions of the Pension Bureau officials and not always consistent with African American community views and values.

Lorenda, however, argued that Simon never accepted Silva as his true wife. According to Lorenda, Simon married Silva in 1850 because he had impregnated her, and Silva's father subsequently forced a wedding on Simon. She emphasized that Simon viewed Silva as a casual relationship, claiming that, "we all teased him a good deal about his running around among the girls."[50] Lorenda also claimed that despite marriage to Silva, Simon "was running backwards and forward between her and me." Throughout the first half of the 1850s, Simon apparently maintained sexual relationships with both Silva and Lorenda.

Notably, Simon's sexual behavior did not alter his own potential economic claims on the state. But like other widows, Lorenda had to prove the legitimacy of her marriage to collect her pension. Lorenda testified that she was informally married to Simon in June 1848, although the best evidence indicates Simon did not devote himself to Lorenda until the late 1850s. According to Lorenda, she bore Simon a child every year, and by 1858 she had given birth to thirteen of Simon's children.[51]

Lorenda and her witnesses also claimed that Simon permanently separated from Silva and devoted himself to Lorenda several years before the Civil War. A former slave testified that Simon and Lorenda attended a religious camp meeting together and were acknowledged as a married couple. In contrast to Silva, however, Lorenda and Simon did not participate in a formal marriage ceremony. Rather, Simon and Lorenda began married life by living together as a family.[52] In the end, Silva's sexual respectability and her formal marriage ceremony convinced the special investigator that Lorenda was an interloper into the legitimate marriage of Simon and Silva.[53]

Silva's challenge might not have been successful but for an 1873 change in the pension laws that narrowed the grounds for successful claims. The government previously accepted slave marriages as legitimate if two witnesses testified that the soldier and his wife had recognized each other as married for a minimum of two years before the soldier's enlistment. In other words, Lorenda did not need a ceremony or community acknowledgment of her marriage; she only needed two former neighbors who testified that she and Simon recognized each other as husband and wife.[54]

The 1873 law, however, shifted the power to define a marriage away from the two central figures in the relationship. The Pension Bureau now required evidence that a man and woman had undergone a formal marriage ceremony or had been habitually "recognized by their neighbors" as joined in marriage. The affidavits of two witnesses no longer sufficed. After 1873 the widow had to depend on the "habitual" recognition of her mother-in-law, her former master, her neighbors, and her own kin to convince the pension investigator that she was a "legal" wife.[55] Any interested party could question a couple's marital legitimacy.

The Williamson case exemplifies how this change in evidentiary procedure allowed the state to drop widows from the pension rolls even after they had been recognized as legal wives. Every person's opinion from Lorenda's old neighborhood was imbued with legal significance. Predictably, residents of Franklin County disagreed as to whether Lorenda was the wife of Simon at the time of his death. Silva's former master and her friends and relatives all insisted that Silva was the only "real" wife of Simon up to his enlistment in the Union Army.[56]

Pension agents expected a community consensus of marital status to emerge from their investigations, but this expectation did not take into account the realities of slavery. The imposed diaspora of the internal slave trade separated couples and confused marital boundaries. In addition, community consensus was not a foregone conclusion. Neighbors and relatives could—and did—disagree about the legitimacy of slave unions.

Masters frequently attempted to impose their decisions on the personal lives of enslaved people. As noted earlier, Lorenda's master testified that he whipped Lorenda and Simon several times to keep them apart.[57] Lorenda's marriage to Simon was subject to contestation before as well as after the Civil War. Throughout all of the investigations, Lorenda continued to insist that she was Simon's wife. Furthermore, the evidence in the pension file demonstrates that Simon himself recognized Lorenda as his wife. To substantiate her claim, Lorenda gave the pension investigator letters that Simon had sent her during the Civil War.[58] While stationed in St. Louis, Simon wrote to Lorenda,

> My Dear Wife
> I am well at this time and I hope to find you and the children the same way. My Love to my Mother. Brother Paul is well. Wanting to see you all very bad. . . . I want to hear from my other two children. . . . From Your Husband Simon Williamson[59]

In his letters Simon promised to send Lorenda his pay, thus demonstrating that his death deprived Lorenda of his economic support. He also concerned himself with the education of their youngest daughter, Missouri Ann, advising Lorenda to "try and give Missouri a little Schooling."[60] The letters demonstrate that at the time of his death, he viewed Lorenda as his wife, and he acknowledged himself to be the father of Missouri Ann.

Lorenda also testified that after Simon ran away to join the army, her master "gave her a severe whipping, because Simon had gone." Missouri slave owners often punished the wives of men who escaped to enlist in the Union Army.[61] From this evidence, we can conclude that Lorenda's master targeted her as a significant woman in Simon's life. Simon may have heard about his former master abusing Lorenda, because he traveled back to the farm to help Lorenda escape from slavery.[62]

Simon's wartime letters indicated that he planned to rejoin Lorenda after the war. In one letter, he worried that he would be unable to locate his family members: "Stay at that place as long as you can so that I will know where to find you when I come." Simon, however, died of sickness in December 1864. He would not survive the war and would never return to the woman he thought of as his wife.[63]

The creation of the widows' pensions implied that the state owed the wives of deceased soldiers a basic level of economic support. Lorenda believed that she was entitled to claim this support from the state. However, as a formerly enslaved African American woman—with a suspect sexual history in the eyes of the Pension Bureau—she found herself at a disadvantage in her ability to establish herself as a "legal wife." African American women who most closely adhered to the normative sexual behavior expected by the white pension investigators held an advantage in the determination of pension cases. Lorenda had a much harder time claiming the mantle of respectability because she had engaged in a relationship against the wishes of her slave owner. Silva, in contrast, had a much easier time engaging in the politics of respectability because her relationship was sanctioned by slave owners and the elders in her community.

The federal government bestowed the civil right of marriage unevenly on emancipated women. Both Lorenda and Silva experienced a transformation in their legal status from slave to citizen. Both women claimed their right to a military pension, and they both pushed the state to recognize that, as the wives of a soldier, they were owed an economic obligation for their husband's military service. But although each of these women had borne Simon's children and cohabited with him, the state stripped Lorenda of her pension and reassigned it to Silva.

The Gibson Marriage: Same-Sex Marriage, Passing, and the Performance of Gender

African American women employed fluid definitions of marriage both before and after emancipation, as Jane Gibson's experience suggests. Gibson's story is unusual because she married a woman passing as a man, with the wedding taking place in an African American Methodist church not long after the end of the war. Yet Gibson's life is also typical in that she ended up arguing for her preferred definition of marriage before a state representative. What at first might seem extraordinary in fact reveals the negotiation of an expanding range of sexual and marital choices after the Civil War.

Before the Civil War, Gibson was enslaved by "old Tom Cordy" in the countryside six miles from Warrenton, Missouri. Gibson described Spencer Camp, who was enslaved by a neighbor, as "the first man I ever had"; although she "was not married to Camp" by ceremony, she "lived with him as his wife about a year and a half." The couple had one child who died young. After Cordy bought another man, Henry Gibson, Jane "quit Spencer Camp and took up with Henry," and they had a daughter, Martha. According to Jane Gibson, she and Henry also did not formally marry but lived together as husband and wife for a year and a half before he "ran away to go in the army" in 1863. Jane Gibson moved to Warrenton as the "War was breaking up."[64]

Enslaved women had little control over their sexual lives and familial relations. During the time in which she was enslaved, Jane bore two children fathered by her slave owner, Lucy and a son named Add.[65] Held in bondage, enslaved women were subject to sexual abuse by the men who held absolute power over their lives. Slave masters and their male relatives faced few social consequences, and no legal repercussions, if they sexually assaulted those women who were defined by the law as property.[66]

When Jane Gibson applied for her pension, a special examiner who investigated her past found that Gibson had married another person soon after the Civil War. Jane Lewis, an African American woman, passing as a man, came to Warrenton with her two young daughters, Julia and Sadie. Jane Lewis was known in town as James, or "Jim" Lewis, and was married to Jane Gibson in the fall of 1866 by the Reverend Henry Jones in a local African American Methodist church known as Wesley Chapel. James/Jane Lewis wore a white suit for the marriage ceremony and afterward the couple took a "bridal tour to Montgomery City" and "settled down to housekeeping" in Warrenton.[67] Benjamin Fields attended the marriage ceremony and remembered that the couple married in the log church around "three years after 'freedom.'" Fields asserted that James/Jane Lewis and Jane Gibson lived together for approximately five months before separating.[68]

As exemplified in Jane Gibson's life history, emancipation brought greater agency to African American women in their choices of marital partners. Women took advantage of their newfound freedom to create their own definitions of family. Her pension application revealed a life filled with complicated conceptions of sexuality, respectability, and marriage. Lucy

Edwards knew Jane Gibson from the time she was "set free" and moved to Warrenton. She recalled that the marriage of James/Jane Lewis to Jane Gibson was "a peculiar marriage" and that the wedding had taken place in front of a full church audience. Edwards, an attendee at the wedding, remembered that James/Jane Lewis "looked like some kind of a man," elaborating that, "they all said he wasn't but he was dressed like a man." Lucy Edwards recalled how they had talked to her "about their troubles" with their children shortly before their separation. According to Edwards, after they separated James/Jane Lewis relocated to St. Louis, and Jane Gibson did not remarry or take up with any other person.[69]

It is not clear how Jane Gibson or James/Jane Lewis defined their relationship. Years later, James/Jane Lewis's child Sadie defined her mother as a woman, while reporting that Jane Gibson said her mother "always wore breeches and that she was a woman and a man."[70] Samson Edwards, who later married Julia, another daughter of James/Jane Lewis, recalled that his mother-in-law wore "men's clothes" in Warrenton and was known as Jim Lewis until "she was examined by some men up there." Edwards also claimed that his mother-in-law was later prosecuted in St. Louis for wearing men's clothing.[71] In 1901, Jane Gibson asserted about her former husband, "To tell the plain truth he was half man and half woman."[72] George Carrico, a resident of Warrenton, asserted that James/Jane Lewis "was said to sometimes wear a dress and call himself 'Jane' and sometimes pants and called himself 'James' Lewis."[73]

The marriage of two African American women in a black Methodist church underscores women's expanded agency and range of marital and sexual choices immediately following the Civil War. As a freedperson, James/Jane Lewis had the opportunity to travel and create new gender identities. As a freedwoman, Jane Gibson had much greater power to choose her marital and sexual relationships. But freedwomen's sexual and marital choices often conflicted with the definition of marriage promoted and enforced by the state through the Pension Bureau.

Jane Gibson found that both her experiences under slavery and her choices after freedom would be construed as immoral by the Pension Bureau. Around 1893, Gibson moved to St. Louis to find work, where she was reunited with her soldier husband, Henry Gibson. They lived together for a number of years before they legalized their marriage by undergoing a religious ceremony in 1897. After her husband's death, Jane Gibson applied for her pension, asserting that she had not married any other man.

The Pension Bureau researched Jane Gibson's marital history, to determine if she was eligible for a pension under the existing statutes. To qualify for a pension, Jane needed to have married Henry Gibson prior to 1890. Her assertion that she was married to Gibson before his enlistment was critical to the legality of her pension claim. Under the pension statutes, any marriage to a man other than her soldier husband would have invalidated her claim. The special examiner was confused by her relationship with James/Jane Lewis, but due to the fact that Lewis had been labeled as a woman in her death certificate, he determined that her marriage ceremony in the Warrenton Methodist church was not legal in the eyes of the law and therefore could not interfere in her pension claim. Notably, the pension investigator found that her pre–Civil War relationship with Henry Gibson was not a "marriage" but was simply a "took-up" relationship. Thus, Jane Gibson was labeled as disrespectable by government bureaucrats and denied a soldier's pension.[74]

Divorce as Emancipation:
Sinai Johnson versus Demas Johnson

A Contentious Marriage

For Sinai Johnson, the years during and after the war included a series of emancipations from patriarchal authority—in her marriage, her church, and her community. After a series of violent incidents, she left her husband, Demas, and initiated a divorce case against him.[75] Sinai Johnson filed her divorce suit on the ground of cruel and inhuman treatment in the St. Louis Circuit Court against her husband, Demas Johnson, in March 1868. In her divorce petition Sinai asserted that her husband had assaulted her with a broomstick, choked her, and threatened to kill her.[76] Testifying in her divorce trial, Sinai Johnson described a violent household. She accused Demas of beating her and locking her out of her home. In her testimony, Sinai observed that if she wanted to "see a friend," her husband would "fall out about it" and told her that she "should not go to see anyone without his permission."[77] Sinai Johnson's marital separation and consequent divorce from her husband represented a series of emancipations from the patriarchal authority that she found in her marriage, her church, and her community.

Sinai Johnson first left her husband in 1862, after an extended violent incident. One night, after getting Demas his dinner, she told him that she wanted to return some sewing work that she had finished. Demas Johnson forbade her to leave the house and then "broke a broomstick" over her head and shoulder and "shoved" her out the door. Neighbors Rufus H. and Matilda Pettiford attempted to investigate and approached the Johnson household, but, as Sinai testified, Demas "kept me locked up and beat me to his own satisfaction."[78]

After returning from work the next day, Demas beat Sinai severely with a stick in the street in front of several neighbors. When her son-in-law, Charleton H. Tandy, learned that Sinai had been "beat nearly to death," he entered the Johnson home, giving Sinai the opportunity to run to the house of a neighbor, Cloe Jackson. According to Jackson, Demas chased her "with a piece of crate in his hand." This beating left Sinai permanently injured: "I am a cripple now in my shoulder." She moved in with her daughter and son-in-law but returned to her husband after Demas promised "to do better."[79]

Sinai Johnson "left him for good" on May 11, 1864, after another violent incident: Demas Johnson "took up a big hatchet & run me out of the house." In response, Sinai fled to her daughter and son-in-law's room and remained there all night. In the morning, Demas raised a chair and "said I could not stay there. If I did he would kill me." Her daughter, Missouri Tandy, confronted Demas Johnson, saying "father this is my mother & you shant hurt her."[80]

Both Sinai and Demas Johnson were well-established members of the upper stratum of St. Louis's African American community. She was a free woman of color who had lived in the city for sixteen years when she married Demas in 1849. He won his freedom in 1850, and over the years the couple worked and accumulated property. Sinai Johnson viewed herself as an active participant in this accumulation of capital, selling pies and whiskey at Jefferson Barracks. By 1868, the couple owned two houses, one of which rented for about thirty dollars a month, while the other was worth about fifteen hundred dollars.[81]

In 1868, Demas Johnson reunited with his first wife, Elizabeth Jackson, whom he had married as a young man in Virginia. After a minister performed their wedding, Demas and Elizabeth lived together for approximately ten years and had three children. After Elizabeth and the children were sold to a new owner in Texas, Demas had no knowledge of them for twenty-five years, when he learned that they were alive and living in Kentucky. He testified that in light of that knowledge, he had a duty to support

Elizabeth. By the time of the Johnsons' divorce trial, Elizabeth and Demas were living together in St. Louis.[82]

The case of *Johnson v. Johnson* raised a marital question that other formerly enslaved people also faced. Emancipation reestablished relationships between spouses who had been separated under slavery, and some men and women had to choose between former and current husbands or wives. Members of the African American community had no clear consensus over the definition of marriage, especially when those marriages had not been legalized with formal postemancipation ceremonies.[83] As the Johnson case illustrates, contestations about marital status could mushroom into neighborhood conflicts.

Marital Rights, Obligations, and the African American Church

Several of the African American residents of St. Louis who testified in the 1868 *Johnson v. Johnson* divorce trial belonged to one of the city's African American churches, the Eighth Street Baptist Church, as did Demas and Sinai Johnson. Eighth Street's minister, the Reverend John R. Anderson, married Demas and Sinai Johnson in 1849, and Demas was an assistant deacon.[84] Men who testified for Demas Johnson included Edmund Collins, a church deacon, and Rufus Pettiford, a trustee of the church.[85]

Rev. Anderson was a leader of St. Louis's antebellum black community, and members of his church played a prominent role in the struggle for civil rights. In 1837, Anderson was working as a typesetter for noted abolitionist Elijah P. Lovejoy when Lovejoy's office was attacked by rioters and his printing press thrown into the Mississippi River.[86]

Sinai Johnson's daughter, Missouri, married Charleton H. Tandy in 1859, and he supported his mother-in-law throughout her marital struggles and in her divorce case. "I have always given her shelter," he testified.[87] Tandy also organized an 1870 boycott against St. Louis's racially segregated streetcars.[88] As part of a younger generation at the Eighth Street Church, Tandy advocated black autonomy in congregational governance, and in his position as Sunday school superintendent, he replaced white instructors with African Americans.[89] His civil rights work suggests a connection between the politics of marriage and struggles for civil rights.

The black Baptist church community shaped the perception of marital rights and obligations held by Demas and Sinai Johnson as well as their fellow community members. Congregants at their church became involved in the Johnsons' marital struggles.[90] The Reverend Edward L. Woodson, another leader of St. Louis's African American community, took a pastoral role and visited their house "frequently to talk with each of them as a minister." Woodson encouraged Sinai Johnson to return to Demas after their separation, but Sinai told him that she was "afraid he would kill her."[91] Woodson testified for Sinai Johnson during her 1868 divorce trial, while another minister, Henry Thomas, testified for Demas.[92] Although African American churches established definitions of legitimate marriages, prescriptive standards of marital behavior, and gendered ideals within marriage, competing definitions existed within the same church community.

After the 1862 assault, the Eighth Street Baptist Church conducted a disciplinary trial against Demas Johnson for his physical abuse of Sinai Johnson. The trial was directed by Rev. Anderson and witnessed by two to three hundred church members.[93] Among those in attendance was Tandy, who asserted that Demas Johnson admitted that he had physically injured Sinai Johnson and "asked her forgiveness."[94] Demas's witnesses, including Collins, another attendee, disputed this contention. According to Collins, Demas admitted that he had "a piece of a crate in his hands but [said] that he did not strike her with it."[95]

The divorce transcript reveals gender conflict within the St. Louis Baptist community. Several church members encouraged Sinai Johnson to return to her husband despite his threats. When Sinai Johnson attempted to store "her things" at Rufus and Matilda Pettiford's house, Rufus objected and "told my wife it was wrong to let them remain," forcing Sinai to remove her property. Pettiford believed Demas was "a good provider for his family" and repeatedly "expostulated" with Sinai, asking her to return to her husband. Deacon Collins, too, "tried to induce" Sinai Johnson to return home.[96]

None of Demas's witnesses contended that his marriage to Sinai was illegitimate or void as a consequence of his slave status in 1849. Several of his supporters pointedly noted that he wanted Sinai to return after the 1864 separation. Demas Johnson's witnesses accused Sinai Johnson of violating the prescriptions for proper wifely behavior by calling her husband a "black nohow," "a black devil & a black dog" and by saying that he "was no man at all." Eliza Davison claimed that she had heard Sinai Johnson say "she would as soon be in bed with a snake as be in bed with Demis [sic]."[97] Demas Johnson represented a specific gendered authority and power that promoted one definition of the proper behavior of wives. Sinai Johnson and her allies contested this definition of marriage.

Gender Conflict and Sinai Johnson's Claim of Legal Marriage

Sinai Johnson testified at her divorce trial, "I thought we might live together till he tried to disgrace me by saying we were never legally married."[98] With such a statement, Demas Johnson was attempting to redefine his relationship with Sinai Johnson to classify her as an individual who was not entitled to any of the cultural status or economic benefits that accrued to legal wives. This argument threatened Sinai's economic rights and her social standing because as a legal wife, Sinai Johnson could make claims on marital property and social respectability.

Demas Johnson reiterated in the public courtroom that he viewed his first marriage as the legitimate union and his second as false. His lawyers asked the St. Louis Circuit Court to declare the marriage void as a result of his slave status at the time of the ceremony. The court refused to accept this rationale, and the jury granted Sinai Johnson her divorce and fifteen hundred dollars' worth of the couple's fifty-five hundred dollars in marital property.[99]

Demas Johnson's lawyers appealed the ruling to the Missouri Supreme Court, again asserting that his marriage to Sinai Johnson should be declared invalid based on his enslaved status at that time, and that Sinai thus had no claim on the marital property. Demas Johnson wished to leave his real estate to his first wife, Elizabeth Jackson, and their children. His lawyer argued that "the misfortune of slavery should not be made a punishment on the old wife, whom he is compelled to support, by all the tender feelings that a man can have for the mother of his children and his first love."[100] But the high court noted that after he was emancipated, Demas "continued to live and cohabit with [Sinai] and constantly acknowledged her as his wife"; it thus declared the marriage valid.[101]

In so doing, the court granted ex post facto legality to Sinai and Demas Johnson's marriage, holding that formerly enslaved people had the right to marry "from the moment of freedom." Demas Johnson had continued to live with Sinai for approximately thirteen years after he was freed in 1850: this cohabitation, along with the community's recognition of the union, affirmed the legitimacy of the marriage.[102]

The court's decision confirmed Sinai Johnson's status as a married woman. On a practical level, the state invested Sinai with economic rights—her claim to marital property. Likewise, for African American war widows, collecting a pension demonstrated political currency or at least the acknowledgment of an economic citizenship.[103]

*   *   *

African American women attempted to redefine marriage according to their own needs and preferences during and immediately following the Civil War. As the power to delineate families moved from slave owners to the state, African American women found opportunities to assert their own definitions of marriage within the confines of state-imposed conceptions of respectability and arbitrary government interests. State institutions possessed the power to define legal marriage: they could allocate civil protections to some people while placing others outside of family circles.

African American women advocated a variety of marital choices, challenging at times both state and community standards of marriage. State institutions repeatedly refused to recognize the marital complications caused by the legacy of slavery and the slave trade, while gender struggles within the African American church and community presented another area of contestation. The struggle for marriage choices signified a series of emancipatory challenges as freedwomen worked to enact their visions of freedom.

Epilogue

ST. LOUIS RESIDENT Lucy Ann Davis narrowly escaped a return to slavery with the assistance of an unauthorized intervention by military forces in April 1863. Shortly after apprehending and incarcerating her husband, two slave catchers found Davis living in a St. Louis household and attempted to force her to return to her owner. Union soldiers stationed at a military post observed the group as it passed by, "severely beat" the two men, and freed Davis.[1]

After the initial assault on her freedom, Lucy Ann Davis opted to remove herself from the reach of her would-be abductors. Her master persisted in his attempts to recapture Davis, and he sent more slave catchers to the St. Louis house where she had taken up residence. According to another resident of the household, "Yesterday some men came with still another paper to arrest her. . . . But the property was gone. The property wants to be safe."[2]

Nothing more is known of Lucy Ann Davis's movements until six years later, when she and her husband, Anderson Davis, filed an antisegregation suit against the Missouri Railroad Company, a St. Louis streetcar operator. On April 15, 1869, Lucy Ann Davis had boarded a streetcar on Olive Street to ride to her residence in the western part of St. Louis. As she opened the door to enter the car, the conductor "forced, crowded, pushed, ejected and threw" her from the vehicle, violently refusing her access to public transport.[3]

Lucy Ann Davis was a member of a population mobilized by the wartime destruction of slavery.[4] In the years following the war, Davis was one of several African American women to use the civil courts to contest racial segregation on the St. Louis streetcars. As early as May 1866, Martha Turner

pressed a suit for two thousand dollars in damages against the People's Railway Company after she was thrown "with great force and violence" from
a moving streetcar.[5] Over three months in 1867, four more women sued
streetcar operators. In what may have been an organized civil rights protest,
Susan Taylor and Frances Watson attempted to sit inside a streetcar on the
same day in May 1867. Attorneys for the Missouri Railroad Company argued
that Taylor and Watson had entered the car "without any intent of riding,
well knowing at the time that the defendant had set apart the front platform
for negroes to ride on."[6] In each case, the streetcar company agreed to pay
costs plus one cent.

Frances Watson's husband, Abraham Watson, had boarded the car
with his wife, yet he remained on the outside platform while Frances sat
inside, causing all but three white people to leave the car. This procession of
St. Louis residents, enacting an ideology of white supremacy, walked along
the car until it stopped at the company's stables, at which time the superintendent came aboard and ordered the Watsons to leave.[7] Frances Watson
had performed an act that was unavailable to Abraham: she had claimed
the status of a lady by entering the streetcar's interior. Common carriers
such as railroads segregated space according to gender and class status in
the antebellum and immediate postwar years.[8] According to racial custom in St. Louis, white "ladies" possessed the privilege of sitting within the
streetcars. By claiming this particular space in the cityscape and asserting
her right to occupy that space, Frances Watson claimed the respectability
attached to the identity of a lady and insisted on recognition of that identity.
Her actions constituted an assertion of her gender and her right to sit as an
equal with other St. Louis women.

The battle over the streetcars intensified. On June 4, 1867—the same
day that the *Daily Missouri Democrat* announced that St. Louis's streetcar
companies had "rescinded the orders" barring African Americans from sitting inside the cars—Jane Reese, a "well dressed" seamstress, hailed a streetcar at the corner of Fourth and Olive Streets. The conductor stopped the
car for her, and as she took hold of the railing to board the back platform,
the conductor "rang the bell and dragged her along, at the same time trying
to push her off." Reese was dragged for about thirty feet and was severely
injured. Two weeks later, she sued.[9] A few weeks after Reese's attack, another
African American woman, Caroline Williams, who was pregnant and had
a child in her arms, was pushed off a streetcar. She, too, sued.[10] African
American women challenged the racial hierarchies of the antebellum era

when they asserted their gender and constructed their identities as "ladies" in the post–Civil War years.

African American women claimed a gender as part of the process of emancipation. Formerly enslaved women fought to be recognized as wives of soldiers, as sisters, as mothers, and most of all as people, not property. The community carried on the struggle for freedom that had begun during the war. As Davis and other women worked to deconstruct the slaveholding nation, they promoted their own vision of American citizenship.

African American women performed these political actions in a context in which Missouri's black men, unlike their counterparts in South Carolina and elsewhere, were not enfranchised until the 1870 ratification of the Fifteenth Amendment. In addition, Missouri's African American population had little ability to bring labor or other complaints to Freedmen's Bureau courts or military officials during Reconstruction.[11]

Missouri's wartime provisional government ended with the January 1865 inauguration of Republican governor Thomas C. Fletcher and other officials elected in November 1864. Missouri's Radical Republicans led the fight for abolition in January 1865 and for ratification of the Thirteenth Amendment to the U.S. Constitution the following month. Then they turned their attention to drafting a new state constitution, which was ratified in June and which eliminated the old black codes and granted African Americans full civil rights except suffrage rights and the right to hold public office. The constitution also provided that public funds would be used to establish segregated black schools. Federal authorities took particular note of the fact that Missouri's constitution allowed black testimony in the civil courts.[12]

The U.S. Bureau of Refugees, Freedmen, and Abandoned Lands, popularly known as the Freedmen's Bureau, initially established a regional headquarters in St. Louis. However, in October 1865, the bureau's commissioner, Major General Oliver Otis Howard, concluded that the bureau did not need to maintain a presence in Missouri because of the legal changes already enacted. Scattered Freedmen's Bureau activity continued in the state, but it lacked military support.[13]

But freedpeople still had to contend with racial violence, wage theft, and illegal enslavement of children.[14] In the summer of 1867, Fanny Wilson's former master, Peter Colman, threatened her life when she attempted to take custody of her children. Wilson first sought help from the Freedmen's Bureau in Memphis but was told that they could not assist her. She then turned to Governor Fletcher, writing to him in August 1867 that Colman had told her that the children "are his property and he will kill—me or anybody else that tries to take them away from him." The governor referred her letter to Freedmen's Bureau agents in St. Louis, who noted "There are no U.S. Troops in Missouri"; since they were unable to take the case, Memphis was the "nearest post." Her complaint was then forwarded to Washington, D.C., where Howard searched for available agents. All of the bureau's Tennessee officers were occupied with their duties, so Howard passed the complaint to Kentucky, where the assistant commissioner sent an agent, accompanied by two U.S. soldiers, to investigate the situation.[15]

Despite the withdrawal of military authorities from Missouri and lack of resources to assist St. Louis's African Americans, they continued to pursue civil rights. On October 2, 1865, men and women gathered at the Eighth Street Baptist Church to found the Missouri branch of the National Equal Rights League. A committee of seven prominent African American men was elected to organize future mass meetings throughout the state. The league prioritized the removal of racial restrictions on suffrage for men and the establishment of an "efficient" public school system for African American children.[16] Although it is quite possible African American women voted during this meeting, it is notable that the Missouri Equal Rights League presented a gendered argument in support of the enfranchisement of black men. Members petitioned the Missouri Assembly, pointing to African Americans' military service as evidence of their loyalty to the nation. But when Radical Republicans in the legislature submitted an amendment to give black men the vote to the Missouri electorate in 1868, voters rejected it.[17]

Black public life nevertheless expanded in St. Louis and other areas. Attendees at the meeting that led to the formation of the Equal Rights League had also discussed "the great want of a colored newspaper" in the city.[18] Within a few years, the *Freedmen's Opinion* and the *New Era* and the magazine *American Sunday School Worker* had all begun publication out of St. Louis.[19] Black clubs and societies proliferated: one African Methodist Episcopal minister noted in 1866, "There are more societies, benevolent and otherwise, than I ever saw in any city before."[20] African American women participated in this blossoming of black associational life, participating in a diverse group of religious and benevolent groups. Lucy Delaney, for example, not only served in religious and Masonic organizations but also participated in the Col. Shaw Women's Relief Corps, an auxiliary to the Grand Army of the Republic, a Union veterans' group that aligned itself with Republican organizations and candidates.[21] Societies celebrating drama and literature appeared in the 1870s. Eliza Barnes served as the secretary for the Unique Literary Club, which met once a month.[22] In the religious sphere, African American women demanded to be recognized for their participation in services. At the 1872 General Conference of the African Methodist Episcopal Church, "the feminine Methodists of St. Louis" petitioned for "official sanction" of their religious speech by public ordination.[23]

*   *   *

In the crisis of the Civil War, freedwomen developed a gendered conception of citizenship that was firmly rooted in their wartime struggle to destroy slavery. The actions of African American women reveal their political priorities, which included protection from physical violence, family reunification, custody of children, and the freedom to choose marital, romantic, and sexual partners. After the violence of the slave system, concerns about bodily liberty and protection from physical abuse were of the utmost importance to freedwomen.

Emancipation itself was a gendered process. After slave enlistment began in Missouri, men were freed in return for their military service, but their female relatives had to find a separate path out of slavery. Despite these barriers, freedwomen worked to construct a civil status through multiple and complementary claims. African American women claimed space in Union camps and military courts. They made social claims on a gendered identity when they asserted their status as soldiers' wives and mothers. They inserted themselves into the national imaginary by claiming the cultural identity of patriot.

For enslaved women, the personal was political. They worked to transform "domestic" disputes with slave owners into military matters. This creative effort to transform the politics of the household into military concerns allowed women entrance into Union camps and military courts. Freedwomen constructed a civil existence, asserting their vision of citizenship to win inclusion in the body politic. The struggles of these women clarify the central role of the legacy of slavery and the gendered process of slave emancipation in the construction of American citizenship rights.

Notes

ABBREVIATIONS

BME   Berlin, Ira, Joseph P. Reidy, and Leslie S. Rowland, eds. *The Black Military Experience*. Ser. 2 of *Freedom: A Documentary History of Emancipation, 1861–1867*. New York: Cambridge University Press, 1982.

CMCF   Court Martial Case Files, Record Group 153, National Archives and Records Administration, Washington, D.C.

CR   *Christian Recorder*

CWA   Contested Widow's Application no.

CWPF   Civil War Pension Files, Record Group 15, National Archives and Records Administration, Washington, D.C.

DM   Department of the Missouri, Record Group 393, National Archives and Records Administration, Washington, D.C.

DMD   *Daily Missouri Democrat*

DMR   *Daily Missouri Republican*

DS   Ira Berlin, Barbara J. Fields, Thavolia Glymph, Joseph P. Reidy, and Leslie S. Rowland, eds. *The Destruction of Slavery*. Ser. 1, vol. 1 of *Freedom: A Documentary History of Emancipation, 1861–1867*. New York: Cambridge University Press, 1985.

IA   Invalid's Application no.

IC   Invalid's Certificate no.

LR 94   Letters Received, Record Group 94, ser. 12, National Archives and Records Administration, Washington, D.C.

LR 2593   Letters Received, ser. 2593, Department of the Missouri, Record Group 393, Pt. 1, National Archives and Records Administration, Washington, D.C.

LR 2786   Letters Received, ser. 2786, Provost Marshal General, Department of the Missouri, Record Group 393, Pt. 1, National Archives and Records Administration, Washington, D.C.

LS   Letters Sent, Provost Marshal Office, St. Louis District, Department of the Missouri, Record Group 393, pt. 4, National Archives and Records Administration, Washington, D.C.

NARA   National Archives and Records Administration, Washington, D.C.

OR	U.S. War Department. *The War of the Rebellion: A Compilation of Official Records of the Union and Confederate Armies.* 128 vols. Washington, D.C., 1880–1901.
PMG	Provost Martial General, Department of the Missouri
Provost Marshals' File	Union Provost Marshals' File of Papers Relating to Individual Civilians, Record Group 109, National Archives and Records Administration, Washington, D.C.
RG	Record Group
Robinson Court Martial	"Proceedings of a General Court Martial Convened at St. Louis Missouri, August 5, 1863, for the Trial of Col. W. P. Robinson, 23rd Reg. Missouri Volunteer Infantry," NN-222, Box 1527, Record Group 153, Court Martial Index, 11-00 Ser., 1859–68, National Archives and Records Administration, Washington, D.C.
Statutes at Large	U.S. Congress. *Statutes at Large, Treaties, and Proclamations of the United States of America, from December 5, 1859, to March 3, 1863.* Vol. 12. Boston: Little, Brown, 1863.
ULR	Unentered Letters Received, ser. 2594, Department of the Missouri, Record Group 393, pt. 1, National Archives and Records Administration, Washington, D.C.
USCI	U.S. Colored Infantry
USCT	U.S. Colored Troops
WA	Widow's Application no.
WC	Widow's Certificate no.
WGFL	Ira Berlin, Steven F. Miller, Joseph P. Reidy, and Leslie S. Rowland, eds. *The Wartime Genesis of Free Labor: The Upper South.* Ser. 1, vol. 3 of *Freedom: A Documentary History of Emancipation, 1861–1867.* New York: Cambridge University Press, 1993.

INTRODUCTION

1. Statement of Charlotte McNeil to George E. Leighton, Provost Marshal, St. Louis, June 5, 1862, F-1371, Provost Marshals' File, M345-187.

2. Ibid.

3. Ibid.

4. W. M. H. Judd, U.S. Police Officer, to George E. Leighton, Provost Marshal, St. Louis, June 6, 1862, F-1371, Provost Marshals' File, M345-187.

5. The right to petition was one of the few formal political tools available to women in the early republic and antebellum periods (Kerber, "I Have Don . . . Much," 100–103).

6. After the Civil War, Freedmen's Bureau agents generated language about "rights" in response to complaints from freedpeople, such as a "positive" right to custody of children (Kate Masur, *Example for All the Land*, 76). O'Donovan found in her study of southwest Georgia that freedwomen brought complaint cases involving personal issues and family life to bureau officials "fifteen times more frequently than did black men" (*Becoming Free*, 197). For gendered analyses on the activities of women in the Freedmen's Bureau, see Farmer-Kaiser, *Freedwomen and the Freedmen's Bureau*; Rosen, *Terror in the Heart*, 38–39, 52–53, 58–59, 224–25; Bercaw, *Gendered Freedoms*, 145–56; Frankel,

Freedom's Women, 111–12, 135–43; Schwalm, *Hard Fight for We*, 234–35, 253–54, 260–66. Cimbala discusses the bureau's actions in promoting equality under the law in *Under the Guardianship of the Nation*, 194–216. For background on the history of the Freedman's Bureau's courts, see Bentley, *History of the Freedmen's Bureau*, 152–68. Nieman examines the judicial authority of the Freedmen's Bureau as well as labor and wage complaints to bureau courts in *To Set the Law in Motion*, 144–47, 181–89.

7. Bercaw, *Gendered Freedoms*, 75–78.

8. Parrish, *Turbulent Partnership*, 20; Oakes, *Freedom National*, 155–59; Foner, *Reconstruction*, 37. For descriptions of martial law, see Mark E. Neely, "Missouri and Martial Law," in *Fate of Liberty*, 32–50; Witt, *Lincoln's Code*, 187–99; Randall, *Constitutional Problems under Lincoln*, 147–57.

9. Gerteis, *Civil War St. Louis*, 142; Gerteis, *Civil War in Missouri*, 12–13; Phillips, *Missouri's Confederate*, 260–61.

10. Cimprich, *Slavery's End in Tennessee*; Hyman and Wiecek, *Equal Justice under Law*, 232–47, 257–66; Rose, *Rehearsal for Reconstruction*.

11. St. Louis shared several characteristics with the slave city of Baltimore, which was also located in a border state. Martha S. Jones discusses the "in-between character" of Baltimore in "Leave of Court," 57.

12. Adler, *Yankee Merchants*; Galusha Anderson, *Story of a Border City*; Gerteis, *Civil War St. Louis*; Parrish, *Turbulent Partnership*; Arenson, *Great Heart of the Republic*; McKerley, "Citizens and Strangers."

13. Mark E. Neely, *Fate of Liberty*, 32–50; Gerteis, "Friend of the Enemy," 166–68; Gerteis, "Outrage on Humanity."

14. Cultural citizenship is a set of social and cultural practices that establish claims to a place in the body politic. See Flores and Benmayor, "Constructing Cultural Citizenship"; Rosaldo, "Cultural Citizenship, Inequality, and Multiculturalism."

15. For the gendered ways in which freedwomen attempted to reclaim a measure of control over their lives, see Bercaw, *Gendered Freedoms*; Frankel, *Freedom's Women*; Schwalm, *Hard Fight for We*.

16. Glymph, "This Species of Property."

17. *Confiscation Act of 1862* (Second Confiscation Act), approved July 17, 1862, *Statutes at Large*, 589–92.

18. Loyalty is, of course, subjective. Some scholars point out that many Missourians who were found to be disloyal under martial law would not have described themselves as such. See Phillips, "Question of Power."

19. Feimster, "General Benjamin Butler"; Feimster, "Rape and Justice."

20. Downs, *Sick from Freedom*; Downs, "Other Side of Freedom"; Schwalm, "Surviving Wartime Emancipation."

21. Schultz, *Women at the Front*.

22. These claims and petitions can be found in two record groups at NARA. The first includes three letter books generated by the St. Louis district provost marshal between May 1864 and June 1865. This record group is divided into three archival subgroups: "Letters Sent," Entry 1733 (May–October 1864), "Letters Sent," Entry 1734 (October 1864–April 1865) and "Letters Sent," Entry 1735 (April–June 1865), Provost Marshal Office, St. Louis District, DM, pt. 4. The second record group is the Union Provost Marshals' File of Papers Relating to Individual Civilians, which is available as National Archives Microfilm Publication M345. These documents were sent to the War Department from Union Army provost marshals and placed in Record Group 109, the War Department

Collection of Confederate Records. Much of the material deals with the patrol and punishment of Confederate sympathizers. The Missouri State Archives has created a searchable database of the Missouri materials: http://www.sos.mo.gov/Records/Archives/ArchivesDb/provost/ (accessed January 2, 2015).

23. Historical actors are capable of forming alternative conceptions of the "rights and privileges" to which they see themselves as entitled. Scholars have noted the presence of a lay rights consciousness in American discourse. See Hartog, "Constitution of Aspiration"; Clark, "Sacred Rights of the Weak," 464n2.

24. In the past twenty-five years, one of the most popular presentations of Civil War history was Ken Burns's television documentary series, *The Civil War*, but it omits the perspectives of enslaved people.

25. Kelley, *Race Rebels*, 9–10.

26. Scholarly debates have raged over the question of who or what freed the enslaved population. A contentious panel at the 1992 Annual Meeting of the American Historical Association highlighted these scholarly disputes over the respective roles of Abraham Lincoln and the wartime actions of enslaved people. See Berlin, "Who Freed the Slaves?"

27. Louis P. Masur, *Lincoln's Hundred Days*; Foner, *Fiery Trial*.

28. The Fourteenth Amendment bestowed birthright citizenship on the formerly enslaved population. While some scholars may conceptualize citizenship solely as a question of sovereign recognition of individuals, others have more broadly theorized citizenship as a social process. Canning and Rose have argued that citizenship forms its meaning through social practices in which people test the boundaries of their rights and obligations ("Gender, Citizenship, and Subjectivity"; see also Somers, "Citizenship").

29. Asen suggests that discourse theory may answer the question of how people enact citizenship ("Discourse Theory of Citizenship"; see also Mezey, "Law as Culture"; Bennett, *Banning Queer Blood*, 6–7). West explores how the performance of citizenship includes "cultural contestations" over the body itself (*Transforming Citizenships*, 6–7, 16–19).

30. On "performance genealogies" and the interaction of history and memory, see Roach, *Cities of the Dead*.

31. On performance as embodied action, see Diana Taylor, *Archive and the Repertoire*. For insights on embodied experience and colonial interactions in the early Atlantic world, see Kopelson, *Faithful Bodies*.

32. Boris, "Citizenship Embodied." This book relies on gendered critiques of citizenship and republican political theory. For scholarship on the gendered nature of citizenship in the United States, see Basch, *In the Eyes of the Law*; Cott, *Public Vows*; Kerber, *No Constitutional Right*. Nancy Bercaw, *Gendered Freedoms*, applies the gendered analysis of citizenship to the study of slave emancipation. For a discussion of the gendered aspects of republican political theory, see Pateman, *Sexual Contract*; Smith-Rosenberg, "Discovering the Subject." On the pro-slavery rhetoric derived from republican ideology in the antebellum South, see McCurry, "Two Faces of Republicanism."

33. VanderVelde, *Mrs. Dred Scott*, 309–19; Arenson, *Great Heart of the Republic*, 82–106; Ehrlich, *They Have No Rights*, 141–45; Fehrenbacher, *Dred Scott Case*, 339–65.

34. Kerber, "Meanings of Citizenship."

35. See Kerber, "Separate Spheres"; Fraser, "What's Critical about Critical Theory?" Boydston, *Home and Work*, demonstrates how women's household labor becomes invisible when it is falsely separated from the larger economic system. Elsa Barkley Brown, "Negotiating and Transforming," argues that African American women and even chil-

dren participated in community decisions. Furthermore, the African American church operated as a political site by providing an organizing location for parades, rallies, and conventions.

36. This book builds on work that locates enslaved people as critical actors in the destruction of slavery, beginning with Du Bois's classic study, *Black Reconstruction in America*, and continued by the critical work performed by the documentary editors at the Freedmen and Southern Society Project—in particular, *DS*; *WGFL*; *BME*. For scholarship on the role played by gender in the process of wartime emancipation, see Schwalm, *Hard Fight for We*; Frankel, *Freedom's Women*. On the construction of gender and the politics of southern households, see Bercaw, *Gendered Freedoms*; Edwards, *Gendered Strife and Confusion*. For a study of labor and African American women situated in a southern city from Reconstruction to the first decades of the twentieth century, see Hunter, *To 'Joy My Freedom*.

37. Edwards, *People and Their Peace*; Edwards, "Status without Rights"; Gross, *Double Character*. In contrast to scholarship that examines the role of enslaved people within the judicial system, Penningroth, *Claims of Kinfolk*, finds that the enslaved population developed concepts of property ownership primarily through social relations, outside of formal legal frameworks.

38. Gross, "Beyond Black and White," 643. Yvonne M. Pitts provided insights about this historical method and referred me to Gross's article. Pitts, *Family, Law, and Inheritance*, applies this methodology to reveal the role of enslaved people in the contestation of wills in Kentucky.

39. Edwards, "Status without Rights," 366.

40. Gross, "Beyond Black and White," 643.

41. I am indebted to Leslie A. Schwalm for directing me to the National Archives and Records Administration in Washington, D.C., and its wealth of sources. Her scholarship in *Hard Fight for We* presents a model of how to employ military sources and Civil War Pension Files in the study of U.S. slave emancipation. Other scholars who have influenced my methodology in their use of records at the National Archives include Bercaw, *Gendered Freedoms*; Frankel, *Freedom's Women*. I have also relied heavily on the edited volumes of primary sources collected from the National Archives and published in *DS*; *WGFL*; *BME*.

42. Astor, *Rebels on the Border*, 125, 144; Oakes, *Freedom National*.

43. Novak, "Legal Transformation of Citizenship," describes the differences between antebellum state citizenships, which entitled one to associational privileges of "status and membership," versus the national citizenship ratified by the Fourteenth Amendment and featuring the federal protection of rights. See also Kate Masur, *Example for All the Land*, 5–7; Vorenberg, "Citizenship and the Thirteenth Amendment."

44. The constitutional changes of Reconstruction introduced the federal protection of personal liberties that had previously been the province of individual states (Finkelman and Gottlieb, "Introduction," 10–11). On the need for historians to examine the constitutional history of Reconstruction through the critical analysis of both the "new legal history" and a "new constitutional history," see Vorenberg, "Reconstruction as a Constitutional Crisis." Finkelman, "Rehearsal for Reconstruction," analyzes black migration to northern free states, the struggle for racial equality, and the antebellum roots of the Fourteenth Amendment.

45. Kantrowitz, *More Than Freedom*; Nieman, "Language of Liberation." For a treatment of the ways in which the black population was committed to the principle of equal-

ity in Washington, D.C., during Reconstruction, see Kate Masur, *Example for All the Land.*

CHAPTER 1. "I TOLD MY MISTRESS THAT
THE UNION SOLDIERS WERE COMING"

1. Thompson, *Story of Mattie Jackson*, 11.

2: Borderland scholarship has demonstrated how categories of people who do not legally possess citizenship rights can utilize cultural assertions of citizenship claims to assert a place in the national state. See Flores and Benmayor, *Latino Cultural Citizenship*; Saldívar, *Border Matters*; Valerio-Jiménez, *River of Hope.*

3. Canning and Rose, "Gender, Citizenship, and Subjectivity." Although the United States, as a sovereign entity, had made clear through the Supreme Court's *Dred Scott v. Sandford* decision (1857) that African Americans in Missouri were not citizens, St. Louis's black population contested this restrictive notion of citizenship until the passage of the Fourteenth Amendment.

4. Performative actions such as raising flags can function as "civic engagements" that "stabilize normative political identities" (Bennett, *Banning Queer Blood*, 6–7). Diana Taylor directs us to consider how "the performance of a claim contributes to its legality"—for example, Neil Armstrong's embodied performance of bringing the U.S. flag to the moon (*Archive and the Repertoire*, 21). The transformation of U.S. citizenship during the Civil War was informed by a struggle over the ownership of bodies. In such struggles over citizenship, Stryker emphasizes that "what is at stake is not just what conventionally counts as political activity . . . but the very configurations of body, sense of self, practices of desire, modes of comportment, and forms of social relationship that qualify one in the first place as a fit subject for citizenship" (*Transgender History*, 51). See also West, *Transforming Citizenships*, 6–7, 16–19.

5. Kerber, "Presidential Address," 16–17.

6. For the politicization of the household during the Civil War and Reconstruction eras, see Glymph, *Out of the House of Bondage*; Edwards, *Gendered Strife and Confusion.*

7. Martha S. Jones uses the formulation of a "public culture" to avoid the problematic idea of a "public" sphere that can exist separately from the "private" realm (*All Bound Up Together*, 211n13). For a feminist analysis of the liberal understandings of the "public sphere," see Fraser, "Rethinking the Public Sphere"; Fraser, "What's Critical about Critical Theory?"

8. On the legal status of enslaved people within antebellum American households, see Fede, *People without Rights*; Morris, *Southern Slavery and the Law*; Pitts, *Family, Law and Inheritance*, 34–37; Bardaglio, *Reconstructing the Household.*

9. On the importance of cultural rhetoric in constructing the class and racial aspects of the legitimate American subject, see Smith-Rosenberg, "Dis-Covering the Subject." For a contemplation on the meaning of female citizenship and the relationship of women to the nation-state, see Kerber, *No Constitutional Right*. Black nationalism in the United States informed struggles for full citizenship and equality during the revolutionary and antebellum years; see Alexander, *African or American?*

10. On slave trading in St. Louis and Lynch in particular, see Galusha Anderson, *Story of a Border City*; Gerteis, *Civil War St. Louis*, 170.

11. Galusha Anderson, *Story of a Border City*; Gerteis, *Civil War St. Louis*, 170.

12. Burke, *On Slavery's Border*; Hurt, *Agriculture and Slavery*; Trexler, *Slavery in Mis-*

souri; McLaurin, *Celia, a Slave*. For comparisons with another slave border state (Maryland) with a major port city (Baltimore), see Fields, *Slavery and Freedom*. Emancipation and grassroots political activities of African Americans in rural areas throughout the Confederate South are detailed in Hahn, *Nation under Our Feet*. Schwalm, *Hard Fight for We*, explores women's critical role in asserting a gendered vision of freedom. For more on the transformation from slavery to freedom in South Carolina, see Saville, *Work of Reconstruction*; Rose, *Rehearsal for Reconstruction*. For Military emancipation in rural Georgia, see O'Donovan, *Becoming Free*. For an international comparison of emancipation, see Scott, *Degrees of Freedom*.

13. Primm, *Lion of the Valley*, 132–33, 143–44.

14. The city of St. Louis's population was 160,773 in 1860 (Joseph C. G. Kennedy, *Population of the United States in 1860*, 297). On the rapid urbanization of antebellum St. Louis and the city's prominence in the steamboat trade, see Adler, *Yankee Merchants*, 71, 93, 110; Primm, *Lion of the Valley*, 138–39, 201. For St. Louis's significance as a nineteenth-century American city, see Arenson, *Great Heart of the Republic*.

15. Wade, *Slavery in the Cities*. In 1860, African Americans comprised 3.3 percent of the population of St. Louis County (which includes the city of St. Louis). The county had 6,211 people of color (4,346 enslaved and 1,865 free) (Joseph C. G. Kennedy, *Population of the United States in 1860*, 294). For comparisons with other slave cities in the late antebellum period, see Myers, *Forging Freedom*; Cynthia M. Kennedy, *Braided Relations, Entwined Lives*; Schafer, *Becoming Free, Remaining Free*. The relatively marginal role of urban slavery in St. Louis before the war resembled the situation in Atlanta and other southern cities, especially when contrasted with the way slavery dominated society in the rural South (Hunter, *To 'Joy My Freedom*, 8–9). For how the growth of the white working class affected the political environment in Baltimore, New Orleans, and St. Louis leading up to the Civil War, see Towers, *Urban South*.

16. Buchanan, *Black Life on the Mississippi*, 15–16, 19–51, 53, 62.

17. Christensen, "Black St. Louis," 83–84; Day and Kedro, "Free Blacks in St. Louis"; Greene, Kremer, and Holland, "Slaves without Masters"; Clamorgan, *Colored Aristocracy of St. Louis*; Keckley, *Behind the Scenes*, 60–62.

18. Greene, Kremer, and Holland, *Missouri's Black Heritage*, 85–86; "Account of Visits by the American Freedmen's Inquiry Commission to the Contraband Camp at Benton Barracks, Missouri, and to Two Schools in St. Louis," December 3, 1863, 0-328, LR 2593, in *WGFL*, 584–85; Galusha Anderson, *Story of a Border City*, 333–37. On African Americans during the war who "created a school board . . . in establishing a school system for blacks," see Christensen, "Race Relations in St. Louis," 125; see also Christensen, "Black St. Louis," 34, 35.

19. Wade, *Slavery in the Cities*, 30–32.

20. Ibid., 24–25. Men were more in demand as farm laborers in rural areas. In St. Louis, the percentage of the enslaved population that was female was 54.5, 52.3, and 63.9 in 1840, 1850, and 1860, respectively (Wade, *Slavery in the Cities*, 330). In contrast, by 1860, the enslaved population in St. Louis County (outside of the city), consisted of 1,210 males and 1,211 females (Joseph C. G. Kennedy, *Population of the United States in 1860*, 297).

21. VanderVelde, *Mrs. Dred Scott*, 78–79; Gerteis, *Civil War St. Louis*, 7–15; Seematter, "Trials and Confessions."

22. Gerteis, *Civil War St. Louis*, 7–17; Tanner, *Martyrdom of Lovejoy*, 77; Trabscott, "Elijah Parish Lovejoy."

23. William Wells Brown, *Narrative of William W. Brown*, 26, 28.

24. VanderVelde, *Mrs. Dred Scott*, 231; VanderVelde and Subramanian, "Mrs. Dred Scott," 1040–41, 1076, 1083; Kaufman, *Dred Scott's Advocate*, 139–43.

25. Farmer-Kaiser, *Freedwomen and the Freedmen's Bureau*, 96–140; Zipf, *Labor of Innocents*, 69–70, 84–105. Recent scholarship has found that suits were more commonly filed by enslaved female litigants in Latin America, where they could sue not only over freedom but also over sexual violence and exploitation (Komisaruk, *Labor and Love in Guatemala*, 85, 92–98).

26. Documents associated with 301 freedom suits filed in the St. Louis courts are available in Freedom Suits Case Files, 1814–60, *St. Louis Circuit Court Historical Records Project*.

27. *Laws of the Territory of Louisiana; Laws of the State of Missouri*.

28. Helen, a slave, to Hamilton R. Gamble, [ca. 1826], quoted in Moore, "Ray of Hope Extinguished," 6–7. See also *Missouri v. Walker, et al.*, March 1826, Case no. unavailable, *St. Louis Circuit Court Historical Records Project*.

29. Quoted in Moore, "Ray of Hope Extinguished," 5; *Dorinda, a Woman of Color v. Simonds, John Junior*, March 1826, Case no. 42, *St. Louis Circuit Court Historical Records Project*; Kennington, "River of Injustice," 79.

30. Pitts, *Family, Law, and Inheritance*, 34–38; *Marguerite, a Free Woman of Color v. Chouteau, Pierre Sr.*, July 1825, Case no. 26, *St. Louis Circuit Court Historical Records Project*. For background on the Chouteau family, see VanderVelde, *Mrs. Dred Scott*, 188–91.

31. "From the Genius of Universal Emancipation: Important Decision," *Freedom's Journal*, December 14, 1827.

32. On the definition of antebellum black public culture, see Martha S. Jones, *All Bound Up Together*, 5, 211n13.

33. For an examination of the role of sexual violence in struggles for citizenship rights during Reconstruction, see Rosen, *Terror in the Heart*.

34. *Wash, Polly v. Mahegan, Joseph M.*, November 1839, Case no. 167, *St. Louis Circuit Court Historical Records Project*; Delaney, *From the Darkness*, 16, 23–24; Kennington, "River of Injustice," 65–66, 70. Polly Wash's other daughter, Nancy, escaped slavery after her owner took her to Niagara Falls. She then married a Canadian farmer, enabling her to live in freedom and to birth her children "without the sin of slavery to strive against" (Delaney, *From the Darkness*, 17, 18).

35. *Britton, Lucy Ann by Her Next Friend Polly Wash v. Mitchell, David D.*, November 1844, Case no. 18, *St. Louis Circuit Court Historical Records Project*. The court clerk used the name Britton instead of Lucy Ann Berry's actual name.

36. Delaney, *From the Darkness*, 26, 33–34; VanderVelde, *Mrs. Dred Scott*, 196–99.

37. Delaney, *From the Darkness*, 36–38. On the communication networks of enslaved St. Louis residents, see Kennington, "River of Injustice," 66–71.

38. Delaney, *From the Darkness*, 62–63; Guy, "Synoptical Biography." For more information on nineteenth-century African American women's affiliational lives in Missouri, see McKerley, "Heroines of Jericho."

39. Delaney, *From the Darkness*, 62–63, v, 15.

40. See Martha S. Jones, *All Bound Up Together*, 12, 23–57, 66–67; Dunbar, *Fragile Freedom*, 48–69; Harris, *In the Shadow of Slavery*, 72–95; Schwalm, *Emancipation's Diaspora*, 36, 158–74.

41. Galusha Anderson, *Story of a Border City*, 13; Stevens, *History of Central Baptist Church*, 10, 29–31, 39; VanderVelde, *Mrs. Dred Scott*, 300, 302.

42. Stevens, *History of Central Baptist Church*, 11. On the uses of Turner's Hall during the Civil War, see Primm, *Lion in the Valley*, 246; Gerteis, *Civil War St. Louis*, 80, 81, 103, 323.

43. Cottrol, *Long, Lingering Shadow*, 80–109; McCurry, "Two Faces of Republicanism." For examinations of nineteenth-century southern legal culture, see Edwards, *People and Their Peace*; Bardaglio, *Reconstructing the Household*. For the background on the law of master and servant and the legal governance of the household, see Tomlins, *Freedom Bound*, 372–75, 519, 526–37; Kerber, *No Constitutional Right*, 11–15. For the reaction in St. Louis to the *Dred Scott* decision, see Arenson, *Great Heart of the Republic*, 94–102. Attorney and future U.S. senator Henry S. Geyer refined his racially exclusive arguments in the St. Louis licensing case of Charles Lyons, a free black arrested for living in the state without a license (VanderVeld, *Mrs. Dred Scott*, 244–46, 305, 309; see also Kaufman, *Dred Scott's Advocate*, 145–46, 198–200; Arenson, *Great Heart of the Republic*, 89).

44. For analysis of the similar historic and widespread assertions of federal citizenship by antebellum African Americans in Boston, see Kantrowitz, *More Than Freedom*.

45. *Frank Leslie's Illustrated Weekly*, June 26, 1857; "Dred Scott Free at Last, Himself and His Family Emancipated," *St. Louis Daily Evening News*, May 26, 1857; Kaufman, *Dred Scott's Advocate*, 142, 223–28; VanderVelde, *Mrs. Dred Scott*, 321–22, 324, 441n45; Arenson, *Great Heart of the Republic*, 96–97, 115, 207.

46. General Assembly of the State of Missouri, "Negroes and Mulattoes: An Act Concerning Free Negroes and Mulattoes," section 8, approved March 14, 1835, 14, Office of the Secretary of State, Missouri State Archives, Jefferson City; revised in General Assembly of the State of Missouri, "Free Negroes: An Act More Effectually to Prevent Free Persons of Color from Entering into the State, and for Other Purposes," section 12, approved February 23, 1843, Missouri State Archives; Arenson, *Great Heart of the Republic*, 115; Greene, Kremer, Holland, *Missouri's Black Heritage*, 64; Bellamy, "Free Blacks in Antebellum Missouri," 219; "Free Men and Women of Color in St. Louis City Directories, 1821–1860," *St. Louis Public Library: Premier Library Sources*, http://previous.slpl.org/libsrc/freemen.htm (accessed January 3, 2015); "List of Free Negroes, Licensed by the County Court of St. Louis County," Dexter P. Tiffany Collection, Missouri History Museum, St. Louis; Kaufman, *Dred Scott's Advocate*, 228.

47. General Assembly of the State of Missouri, "Negroes and Mulattoes: An Act Concerning Free Negroes and Mulattoes," sections 21, 22, approved March 14, 1835, cited in Jenkins, "Freedom Licenses." For the pertinent legislation, see *Revised Statutes* (1835), 413–17; *Laws of the State of Missouri, Twelfth General Assembly*, 66–68; *Laws of the State of Missouri, Fourteenth General Assembly*, 104, all cited in Bellamy, "Free Blacks in Antebellum Missouri"; VanderVelde, *Mrs. Dred Scott*, 244–46.

48. "An Act More Effectively to Prevent Free Persons of Color from Entering into This State, and for Other Purposes," February 23, 1843, cited in Buchanan, *Black Life on the Mississippi*, 9, 13, 24.

49. Ibid., 24–25.

50. Litwack, *North of Slavery*, 30–63. Martha S. Jones finds that "African American claims-making was at the center of antebellum legal culture" in 1850s Baltimore ("Leave of Court," 68). The assertion of rights in the legal arena, such as the right to travel freely, preceded the Civil War and Reconstruction.

51. *Seaton Stoner v. State of Missouri*, September 23, 1835, *St. Louis Circuit Court Historical Records Project*. Stoner was sentenced under General Assembly of the State of

Missouri, "Negroes and Mulattoes: An Act Concerning Free Negroes and Mulattoes," sections 21, 22, approved March 14, 1835, cited in Jenkins, "Freedom Licenses."

52. *Seaton Stoner v. State of Missouri*, 4 Mo. 614 (1837).

53. "Free People in Missouri," *Colored American*, September 26, 1840.

54. For a discussion of the free black community in Boston and the development of a inclusive federal citizenship, see Kantrowitz, *More Than Freedom*, 5–9, 28–40. Kate Masur explores how black activists in Washington, D.C., asserted a capacious civil equality during Reconstruction (*Example for All the Land*, 5–79). See also Vorenberg, *Final Freedom*.

55. Gerteis, *Civil War St. Louis*, 23; Kaufman, *Dred Scott's Advocate*, 145–46, 200; VanderVelde, *Mrs. Dred Scott*, 244–45.

56. "Judge Krum's Opinion," *St. Louis Weekly Union*, December 16, 1846; VanderVelde, *Mrs. Dred Scott*, 244; Primm, *Lion of the Valley*, 186, 188.

57. *Ordinances of the City of St. Louis, 1835*, cited in Goldin, *Urban Slavery*, 135.

58. Hadden, *Slave Patrols*, 53–55; Curry, *Free Black in Urban America*, 84–87.

59. Hadden, *Slave Patrols*, 41–42, 51–61, 76–84.

60. *State v. Frank Johnson*, April 1843, Case no. 174, Circuit Court Case Files, "Case of Frank Johnson," *St. Louis Circuit Court Historical Records Project*; "Some Ten Free Mulattoes . . . ," *St. Louis New Era*, December 31, 1842, reprinted in "Glances at Southern Papers," *Emancipator*, April 20, 1843; Briscom, "Francis Johnson."

61. "State v. By Habeas Corpus Act," for John Rudd, filed July 20, 1854, Court of Criminal Corrections, Missouri Historical Society, St. Louis.

62. *Lackland, James B., City Attorney v. Dougherty, James, City Recorder* (1851), Missouri Supreme Court Case Files, Missouri State Archives.

63. *St. Louis Weekly Union*, November 13, 1846, quoted in Kaufman, *Dred Scott's Advocate*, 145.

64. Scharf, *History of Saint Louis*, 585–86.

65. "An Act Respecting Slaves, Free Negroes, and Mulattoes," February 16, 1847, cited in VanderVelde, *Mrs. Dred Scott*, 406n13; Gerteis, *Civil War St. Louis*, 22–23; Kaufman, *Dred Scott's Advocate*, 144–46; VanderVelde, *Mrs. Dred Scott*, 245.

66. Adler, *Yankee Merchants*, 71, 93, 110; Primm, *Lion of the Valley*, 138–39, 201.

67. Efford, *German Immigrants*; Kristen Anderson, "German Americans"; Levine, *Spirit of 1848*; Zucker, *Forty-Eighters*, 65–66, 105–9; Rowan, *Germans for a Free Missouri*; WGFL, 552–53.

68. Towers, *Urban South*, 143–44, 206.

69. Burke, *On Slavery's Border*, 5, 94–107, 118–26; Jeremy Neely, *Border between Them*, 31–34; Hurt, *Agriculture and Slavery*, 273–300; Trexler, *Slavery in Missouri*, 53–56, 170–72, 206–7.

70. Joseph C. G. Kennedy, *Population of the United States in 1860*, 283, 297; Trexler, *Slavery in Missouri*, 44, cited in Kaufman, *Dred Scott's Advocate*, 172.

71. Galusha Anderson, *Story of a Border City*, 9; Frémont, *Story of the Guard*, 27; J. B. Frémont to George Julian, May 1, 1862, in *Letters of Jessie Benton Frémont*, 320.

72. Thomas, *From Tennessee Slave to St. Louis Entrepreneur*, excerpted in *"Ain't but a Place,"* ed. Earley, 49.

73. Jud Bemis to Stephen A. Bemis, St. Louis, April 13, 1862, Bemis Family Papers, 1861–65, Bemis Collection, Missouri History Museum, St. Louis.

74. Arenson, *Great Heart of the Republic*, 112; Phillips, *Missouri's Confederate*, 238; Gerteis, *Civil War St. Louis*, 73, 79, 87–88.

75. Arenson, *Great Heart of the Republic*, 112–13, 114; Parrish, *Frank Blair*, 90–91; Gerteis, *Civil War St. Louis*, 84, 97; Phillips, *Missouri's Confederate*, 243–44, 247; Primm, *Lion of the Valley*, 232–33.

76. Parrish, *Frank Blair*, 90; Gerteis, *Civil War St. Louis*, 79–96.

77. Phillips, *Damned Yankee*, 106–7; Gerteis, *Civil War St. Louis*, 89.

78. Gerteis, *Civil War St. Louis*, 85, 87, 92.

79. Phillips, *Missouri's Confederate*, 244; Phillips, *Damned Yankee*, 153; Gerteis, *Civil War in Missouri*, 12–13; Gerteis, *Civil War St. Louis*, 90; Parrish, *Frank Blair*, 95. Taylor defeated Unconditional Unionist candidate John How. The previous mayor, O. D. Filley, was a Republican.

80. Arenson, *Great Heart of the Republic*, 111; Phillips, *Missouri's Confederate*, 230–32, 244.

81. Primm, *Lion of the Valley*, 233; Gerteis, *Civil War St. Louis*, 79, 89–90, 92, 111–12.

82. Winter, *Civil War in St. Louis*, 39; Snead, *Fight for Missouri*, 155; Wagner, *Good Order and Safety*, 23; Hager, *Dred and Harriet Scott*, 53.

83. Arenson, *Great Heart of the Republic*, 115; Hager, *Dred and Harriet Scott*, 54.

84. April 20, 1861, St. Louis County Court Records, *St. Louis Circuit Court Historical Records Project*.

85. April 23, 1861, in ibid.; Hager, *Dred and Harriet Scott*, 54; Arenson, *Great Heart of the Republic*, 115.

86. Peregrine Tippett, "Protest against Licensing Negroes," May 27, 1861, Tiffany Collection; Arenson, *Great Heart of the Republic*, 115.

87. August 19, 1861, St. Louis County Court Records, *St. Louis Circuit Court Historical Records Project*.

88. February 27, August 4, 1862, both in ibid.

89. May 1, 1863, in ibid.

90. "Free Negro Bonds, 1862–1864," Tiffany Collection.

91. Arenson, *Great Heart of the Republic*, 111–14; Gerteis, *Civil War St. Louis*, 79–96.

92. Arenson, *Great Heart of the Republic*, 116–17; Gerteis, *Civil War St. Louis*, 100–115; Galusha Anderson, *Story of a Border City*, 102, 159, 160; Rombauer, *Union Cause*, 174; Winter, "Like Sheep in a Slaughter Pen."

93. Galusha Anderson, *Story of a Border City*, 98–102, 106–19.

94. Ibid., 98–102, 106–19, 181; Gerteis, *Civil War St. Louis*, 338. On the mob violence and excitable crowds that gathered in the streets of St. Louis during this time, see Webb, *Battles and Biographies of Missourians*, 50; Rombauer, *Union Cause*, 238–40.

95. Parsons, *Memoir of Emily Elizabeth Parsons*, 74. For bibliographic information on Parsons, see Brockett, *Woman's Work*, 272–78.

96. Anne Ewing Lane to Sarah Sidney Glasgow, January 12, 1862, William Carr Lane Collection, Missouri History Museum, St. Louis.

97. On the increased resistance, both symbolic and material, of the enslaved population during the Civil War, see Schwalm, *Hard Fight For We*, 75–76, 88–97, 104–7, 126–27; Hunter, *To 'Joy My Freedom*, 4–6, 13–20.

98. Thompson, *Story of Mattie Jackson*, 10.

99. Ibid., 6, 8.

100. Ibid., 11.

101. Ibid.

102. Ibid., 13.

103. Ibid., 12.

104. Captain G. Granger, Judge Advocate, St. Louis, to Major Eaton, St. Louis Arsenal, September 10, 1861, Thomas Grider File, F-1333, Provost Marshals' File, M345-11.

105. Thompson, *Story of Mattie Jackson*, 12.

106. Mattie Jane Jackson may have found shelter at a building on Elm Street run by a group affiliated with the Ladies' Union Aid Society. Rooms in the back of the St. Louis house were set aside for African American war refugees. See Corbett, "Refugees of War," 87; Parrish, *History of Missouri*, 3:71–72.

107. Thompson, *Story of Mattie Jackson*, 12–13.

108. Ibid., 12–14.

109. Bernard G. Farrar, Provost Marshal General, to Police Commissioners of St. Louis, March 3, 1862, in *OR*, ser. 1, vol. 8, 584; Rombauer, *Union Cause*, 174–75.

110. Gerteis, *Civil War St. Louis*, 267.

111. Mark E. Neely, "Missouri and Martial Law," in *Fate of Liberty*, 32–50; Witt, *Lincoln's Code*, 187–99; Randall, *Constitutional Problems under Lincoln*, 147–57.

112. Mutti Burke has observed that Missourians increasingly relied on the Office of the Provost Marshal as court systems failed under the strain of the bushwacker fighting in the countryside (*On Slavery's Border*, 275). For the guerrilla warfare in Missouri, see Astor, *Rebels on the Border*, 113–19, Sutherland, *Savage Conflict*, 14–16, 18–25, 58–65, 125; Fellman, *Inside War*; Jeremy Neely, *Border between Them*, 96–131.

113. *OR*, ser. 1, vol. 3, 466–67; "The Beginning of the End," *Harper's Weekly*, September 14, 1861, 578; "General Fremont's Proclamation—Emancipation," *Frank Leslie's Illustrated Newspaper*, September 21, 1861. Lincoln overruled Frémont's emancipation policies but accepted the general's institution of martial law. General Henry W. Halleck, Frémont's successor as commander of the Department of the West, specifically requested permission to establish martial law and received formal authorization to suspend the writ of habeas corpus on December 2, 1861. Military commanders in Missouri often took actions that resembled martial law before it was officially established. On May 15, 1861, General William S. Harney invoked a "higher law" when he refused to answer a writ of habeas corpus issued by U.S. district judge Samuel Treat concerning a military prisoner, Captain Emmet McDonald, who had been taken during the Camp Jackson Affair (Mark E. Neely, *Fate of Liberty*, 32, 36–38; Gerteis, *Civil War St. Louis*, 113, 128–31).

114. Arenson, *Great Heart of the Republic*, 121; Gerteis, *Civil War St. Louis*, 355n53; Primm, *Lion of the Valley*, 243.

115. Gerteis, *Civil War St. Louis*, 149–61; Arenson, *Great Heart of the Republic*, 120–22.

116. On the enactment of the Second Confiscation Act, see Louis P. Masur, *Lincoln's Hundred Days*, 58–64, 66–67. For background on the Office of the Provost Marshal and enforcement of martial law in St. Louis, see Arenson, *Great Heart of the Republic*, 131–35; Primm, *Lion of the Valley*, 242–244.

117. Gerteis, *Civil War St. Louis*, 128; Mark E. Neely, *Fate of Liberty*, 35, 36, 38, 41, 44, 49, 168–69.

118. Mark E. Neely, *Fate of Liberty*, 168–69.

119. Gerteis, *Civil War St. Louis*, 132, 169; "St. Louis Declared under Martial Law," *CR*, August 24, 1861; "Police Commissioners' Report," April 29, 1862; Winter, *Civil War in St. Louis*, 39; Major General John Charles Frémont, U.S. Volunteers, St. Louis, to His Excellency, Hamilton Gamble, Governor of the State of Missouri, August 18, 1861, in *Supplement*, pt. 3, vol. 1, ser. 93, 42–43.

120. A janitor at the courthouse removed the flag the following day. Arenson, *Great*

Heart of St. Louis, 112–13, 114; Primm, *Lion of the Valley*, 242; Gerteis, *Civil War in Missouri*, 8–11; Gerteis, *Civil War St. Louis*, 77, 79, 85, 87, 90.

121. W. J. Davis, St. Louis, letter to the editor, April 12, 1865, in "For the Christian Recorder: St. Louis Correspondence," *CR*, June 3, 1865.

122. Gerteis, *Civil War St. Louis*, 170.

123. Thompson, *Story of Mattie Jackson*, 14–15.

124. Confiscation Act of 1862 (Second Confiscation Act), approved July 17, 1862, in *Statutes at Large*, 589–92. The enforcement of the First and Second Confiscation Acts in Missouri is discussed in further detail in chapter 2.

125. Major Jonathon N. Herder, 1st Missouri Infantry, Provost Marshal, Camp Gamble, St. Louis, to Brigadier General Davidson, Commanding St. Louis Division, August 28, 1862, Rebekah McCutchen File, F-1198, Provost Marshals' File, M345-182.

126. Thomas T. Gantt, endorsement on John F. Tyler to Captain Griffing, September 20, 1862, in *DS*, 438.

127. Testimony of John H. McCutchen, St. Louis, October 14, 1862, J. H. McCutchen File, F-1198, Provost Marshals' File, M345-182.

128. Major General Samuel R. Curtis, St. Louis, to Brigadier General Davidson, October 9, 1862, J. H. McCutchen File, F-1198, Provost Marshals' File, M345-182.

129. R. J. Howard, St. Louis Custom House Official, to Major General Samuel R. Curtis, Commander of the Department of the Missouri, October 10, 1862, in *DS*, 437–38.

130. Eliot, *Story of Archer Alexander*, 60–61, 63, 64–66, 68.

131. Ibid., 60–61, 63, 67–68.

132. Ibid., 70–71.

133. Ibid., 72–73; Confiscation Act of 1862.

134. Louisa Alexander to Archer Alexander, November 16, 1863, in Eliot, *Story of Archer Alexander*, 78–79.

135. Ibid., 79–82.

136. W. B. Napton Diary, October 13, 1864, in Napton, *Union on Trial*, 217–18.

137. *Western Sanitary Commission*, 110, 134.

138. Galusha Anderson, *Story of a Border City*, 251.

139. For the significance of geographic mobility to the definition of freedom, see Cohen, *At Freedom's Edge*; Camp, *Closer to Freedom*, 12–34.

140. Testimony of William Dicks, September 28, 1863, in *State of Missouri v. Aaron Brown and Jane Dicks*, Court John Young, Justice of the Peace (Recorders Court), Microfilm MA-544, Archives of the St. Louis Circuit Court Project, Missouri State Archives, St. Louis.

141. Ibid.

142. Testimony of William Dicks, September 28, 1863, Testimony of Walter E. Dill, Clerk of the Jessie Bell, September 30, 1863, both in ibid.

143. Testimony of Hugh Murphy, September 28, 1863, in ibid.

144. Testimony of Lawrence Harrigan, St. Louis Police Officer, September 28, 1863, in ibid.

145. Testimony of William Dicks, September 28, 1863, in ibid.

146. Christensen, "Black St. Louis," 52; Testimony of John F. Hume, Esq., Editor of the *Missouri Democrat*, American Freedmen's Inquiry Commission, 1863, p. 144, Roll 201, M-619, LR 94; Galusha Anderson, *Story of a Border City*, 262. George Lipsitz claims that in 1880 the city held the distinction of being the "third largest urban black population in the nation, behind Baltimore and Philadelphia" (*Sidewalks of St. Louis*, 17). In 1860,

St. Louis's 3,297 African Americans accounted for 2.04 percent of the population. By 1870, the city had 22,088 black residents, or 7.10 percent of the total (Primm, *Lion of the Valley*, 332; Greene, Kremer, and Holland, *Missouri's Black Heritage*, 69; Corbett, "Missouri's Black History," 21).

147. Bethiah P. McKowen to "My Dear Son," St. Louis, July 1, 1862, in McKowen, "Civil War Letters," 247.

148. Schwalm, "Overrun with Free Negroes."

149. Alice (Negro Contraband) File, August 27, 1863, F-1461, Provost Marshals' File, M345-4.

150. Schwalm, *Emancipation's Diaspora*, 77–80; WGFL, 572.

151. Samuel Sawyer, Superintendent of Contrabands at Helena, Ark., to Brigadier General Prentiss, Commander of the District of Eastern Arkansas, St. Louis, March 16, 1863, S-239 1863, LR 2593, in *WGFL*, 566.

152. Samuel Sawyer, Superintendent of Contrabands at St. Louis, to Major General Curtis, Commander of the Department of the Missouri, April 18, 1863, S-284 1863, LR 2593, in *WGFL*, 568–70; Schwalm, *Emancipation's Diaspora*, 76–80.

153. Christensen, "Black St. Louis," 38, 83–85, 86, 97, 112–13.

154. Testimony of Ladies' Contraband Relief Society, [December 2, 1863], filed with O-238 1863, LR 94, in *WGFL*, 583.

155. Blassingame, "Recruitment of Negro Troops"; Fellman, "Emancipation in Missouri"; *BME*, 183, 187–90.

156. Testimony of Nancy Edwards, December 9, 1903, April 23, 1904, Testimony of Mary Ross, April 1, 1904, both in James Edwards File, Co. F, Reg. 6, USCI, IA 842.583, IC 593.662, WA 792.546, WC 579.665, CWA 756.051, CWPF.

157. Christensen, "Black St. Louis," 44; Gerteis, *Civil War St. Louis*, 277, 283, 287, 288–89, 290.

158. Testimony of Claiborne Holiday, August 14, 1894, in Thomas Hughes File, Co. G, Reg. 67, USCI, WC 249.568, CWPF.

159. Testimony of Nancy Watts, March 27, 1894, in Thomas Hughes File, Co. G, Reg. 67, USCI, WC 249.568, CWPF.

160. Emily Elizabeth Parsons to "My Dear Mother," Benton Barracks Hospital, March 12, 1864, in Parsons, *Memoir of Emily Elizabeth Parsons*, 132; Testimony of the Ladies' Contraband Relief Society before the American Freedmen's Inquiry Commission, [December 2, 1863], filed with O-328, LR 94, in *WGFL*, 166; "Colored Recruits at Benton Barracks," *DMD*, January 20, 1864. See also *Western Sanitary Commission*, 110; Parsons, *Memoir of Emily Elizabeth Parsons*, 5, 6, 72; Galusha Anderson, *Story of a Border City*, 262.

161. Testimony of Elizabeth Brooks, September 22, 1871, in Joshua Brooks File, Co. E, Reg. 56, USCI, WA 156.637, WC 155.265, CWPF.

162. Emily Elizabeth Parsons to "My Dear Mother," March 18, 1864, Parsons to "Dear Kittie," March 16, 1864, both in Parsons, *Memoir of Emily Elizabeth Parsons*, 135, 133.

163. Testimony of Rev. Edward Woodson before the American Freedmen's Inquiry Commission, December 1, 1863, filed with O-328 1863, LR 94, in *WGFL*, 580–81. For more on African American churches and benevolent societies, see Bellamy, "Free Blacks in Antebellum Missouri," 224; "Churches"; Christensen, "Race Relations in St. Louis," 124–25; W. R. Revels, "St. Louis, Mo., Correspondence," *CR*, July 21, 1866.

164. "Obituary of Ara Moore," May 7, 1864, *CR*. For more on African American women

benevolent workers in St. Louis, see "Ladies of the Preachers' Aid Society," *CR*, September 20, 1862.

165. "Colored Ladies' Soldiers' Aid Society," *DMD*, December 17, 1864; Emily Elizabeth Parsons to "Dear Mother," Benton Barracks Hospital, April 4, 9, 1864, in Parsons, *Memoir of Emily Elizabeth Parsons*, 138–40.

166. "Final Report of the Western Sanitary Commission," 125, quoted in Day and Kedro, "Free Blacks in St. Louis," 129. On the role of gender and the Civil War contraband aid movement, see Faulkner, *Women's Radical Reconstruction*.

167. *Western Sanitary Commission*, 133–34; Testimony of the Ladies' Contraband Relief Society before the American Freedmen's Inquiry Commission, [December 2, 1863], filed with O-328, LR 94, in *WGFL*, 161–66; Testimony of Rev. Edward Woodson before the American Freedmen's Inquiry Commission, December 1, 1863, filed with O-328 1863, LR 94, in *WGFL*, 580–81; Parrish, "Western Sanitary Commission"; Forman, *Western Sanitary Commission*, 131. On schools established in Civil War St. Louis by the American Missionary Association, see Richardson, "American Missionary Association."

168. Emily Elizabeth Parsons, Memphis, to "Darling Mother," n.d., in Parsons, *Memoir of Emily Elizabeth Parsons*, 62.

169. Galusha Anderson, *Story of a Border City*, 266.

170. "Outrages by Contrabands at Carondelet," *DMR*, January 6, 1863; J. G. Forman, Secretary of the Western Sanitary Commission, to M. E. Strieby, St. Louis, February 22, 1865, quoted in Christensen, "Black St. Louis," 285n106; *OR*, ser. 3, vol. 4, pt. 1, 371; 558.

171. *OR*, 3, 4, 1, 371. The contrabands hired out from Benton Barracks are discussed in *WGFL*, 558.

172. "Inquest Regarding Death," *DMR*, January 6, 1863.

173. J. G. Forman, Secretary of the Western Sanitary Commission, to M. E. Strieby, St. Louis, February 22, 1865, quoted in Christensen, "Black St. Louis," 285n106.

174. "Outrages by Contrabands at Carondelet," *DMR*, January 6, 1863.

175. Testimony of Minerva Moore, May 14, 1901, in Alfred Moore File, Co. A, Reg. 68, USCT, WA 726.393, CWA 738.121, CWPF.

176. Emily Elizabeth Parsons to "Dear Mother," Mississippi River, February 13, 1863, in Parsons, *Memoir of Emily Elizabeth Parsons*, 55.

177. A.R.G., "A Voice from the South-West: Advancement of the Cause of Liberty: Review of Colored Regiment at Benton Barrack, St. Louis, Mo. Items, &c.," *CR*, January 30, 1864.

178. W. J. Davis, St. Louis, letter to the editor, April 12, 1865, in "For the Christian Recorder: St. Louis Correspondence," *CR*, June 3, 1865.

179. Camp, *Closer to Freedom*, 12–28.

180. Thompson, *Story of Mattie Jackson*, 22, 30.

CHAPTER 2. "A NEGRO WOMAN IS RUNNING AT LARGE IN YOUR CITY"

1. Luther T. Colbir, Chillicothe, Mo., to F. A. Dick, Provost Marshal General, St. Louis, February 8, 1863, F-1141, Provost Marshals' File, M345-55.

2. For this new public's political participation, see Elsa Barkley Brown, "Negotiating and Transforming the Public Sphere."

3. "Interview with Betty Abernathy," 6. On Union troops stationed in Civil War Missouri, see Parrish, *Turbulent Partnership*; Fellman, *Inside War*; Phillips, *Damned Yankee*.

4. For the cultural meanings of the word *contraband* for northerners during the Civil War, see Kate Masur, "Rare Phenomenon of Philological Vegetation." The concept of the "negro contraband" entered the nation's lexicon after the passage of the Confiscation Acts. On wartime emancipation in Missouri, see Burke, *On Slavery's Border*, 279–99; Schwalm, *Emancipation's Diaspora*, 51–57.

5. Confiscation Act of 1861 (First Confiscation Act), approved August 6, 1861, in *Statutes at Large*, 319. For the congressional debate on the First Confiscation Act, see Siddali, *From Property to Person*, 70–94. On General Benjamin Butler's treatment of the contrabands in Tidewater Virginia and the passage of the First Confiscation Act, see *DS*, 15–16.

6. Confiscation Act of 1862 (Second Confiscation Act), approved July 17, 1862, in *Statutes at Large*, 589–92. For the congressional debate on the Second Confiscation Act, see Siddali, *From Property to Person*, 120–44. The military treatment of escaped slaves was complicated by congressional legislation passed by Radical Republicans in March 1862 that prohibited military personnel from contributing to or assisting in their return to slave owners. See *Statutes at Large*, 354, cited in *DS*, 22, 402.

7. *DS*, 259.

8. For an analysis of enslaved women as wartime refugees, see Schwalm, *Emancipation's Diaspora*, 64–66. Enslaved people often attempted to escape to Union lines in family groups (Schwalm, *Hard Fight for We*, 88–97). Nancy Bercaw has found a "gendered construction of liberty" in the early period of wartime emancipation. Young men were the most likely to leave farms and plantations and run to Union lines. On the gendered patterns of escape to Union lines, see Camp, *Closer to Freedom*, 123–27; Bercaw, *Gendered Freedoms*, 21–23, 24–26; Frankel, *Freedom's Women*, 19–25, 31–35.

9. Schultz, *Women at the Front*.

10. Thomas T. Gantt to Brigadier General William S. Harney, U.S. Army, Commanding the Military Department of the West, St. Louis, May 14, 1861, in *OR*, ser. 1, vol. 3, 372–73. For further information on Gantt, see Gerteis, *Civil War St. Louis*, 177–78, 189–90, 261–62, 270–71.

11. Thomas T. Gantt to Brigadier General William S. Harney, U.S. Army, Commanding the Military Department of the West, St. Louis, May 14, 1861, in *OR*, ser. 1, vol. 3, 373.

12. General Gideon J. Pillow, Commanding General, Headquarters, Army Liberation, New Madrid, Mo., to Major General Leonidas Polk, C.S. Army, August 1, 18, 1861, in *OR*, ser. 1, vol. 3, 626, 660. For an additional report from General Pillow regarding enslaved laborers at work on fortifications, see Brigadier General Gideon J. Pillow, C.S. Army to Major General Leonidas Polk, C.S. Army, August 20, 1861, in *OR*, ser. 1, vol. 3, 665.

13. Brigadier General M. Jeff Thompson, New Madrid, Mo., to Brigadier General Gideon J. Pillow, CSA, November 16, 1861, in *OR*, ser. 1, vol. 3, 714.

14. Ibid., 466–67; *DS*, 397–98; Gerteis, *Civil War St. Louis*, 149–61; Volpe, "Frémonts and Emancipation."

15. Sutherland, *Savage Conflict*, 17–25; Astor, *Rebels on the Border*, 113–19; Fellman, *Inside War*; Jeremy Neely, *Border between Them*, 96–131.

16. Major General H. W. Halleck to unknown, in Correspondence, *OR*, ser. 1, vol. 8, pt. 1, 463.

17. "General Orders, No. 32," December 22, 1861, in ibid., 464.

18. Major General Samuel R. Curtis, St. Louis, to General Loan, Jefferson City, Mo., September 29, 1862, in *OR*, ser. 1, vol. 13, 688.

19. Major General Samuel R. Curtis, Headquarters, Department of the Missouri, St. Louis, to Brigadier General John M. Schofield, October 1, 1862, in ibid., 695; Major

General H. W. Halleck to General Samuel R. Curtis, St. Louis, March 23, 1862, in *OR*, ser. 1, vol. 8, 636–37.

20. Major General H. W. Halleck, St. Louis, to Major General John Pope, New Madrid, Mo., March 21, 1862, in *OR*, ser. 1, vol. 8, 629.

21. Camp, *Closer to Freedom*, 125; Frankel, *Freedom's Women*, 17.

22. Schwalm, *Emancipation's Diaspora*, 60.

23. "Cathy Williams' Story," 222; see also Tucker, *Cathy Williams*, 33–35.

24. Major Henry S. Eggleston, 1st Wisconsin Cavalry, Wittsburg, Ark., report, August 9, 1862, in *OR*, ser. 1, vol. 13, 203.

25. Glymph, "This Species of Property," 58; Schwalm, *Hard Fight for We*, 90.

26. Captain J. W. Towner, Co. F, 9th Iowa Volunteers, Calvey, Franklin County, Mo., to Lieutenant Colonel H. J. Herron, Pacific, Franklin County, Mo., December 20, 1861, and Enclosed Petition to Slave Property of Langston F. Goode to Major General H. W. Halleck, Commanding the Department of the Missouri, St. Louis, December 16, 1861, H-140, Pacific, Mo., December 23, 1861, F-1329, Provost Marshals' File, M345-107.

27. H. W. Halleck, General Orders, no. 3, for the Department of the Missouri, November 20, 1861, in *OR*, ser. 1, vol. 8, 370; Major General H. W. Halleck to Colonel William P. Carlin, Commander, Ironton, Mo., January 9, 1862, ULR, in *DS*, 424. See also Gerteis, *Civil War St. Louis*, 172.

28. This description and explanation of Halleck's Exclusion Orders (General Orders, No. 3) was written by Colonel Blair and published in the *Missouri Democrat*, November–December 1861. This description of the exclusion orders was quoted by Major George E. Waring Jr., Commanding Frémont Hussars, Camp Halleck, Rolla, Mo., to Acting Major General Alexander Asboth, Commanding the 4th Division, December 19, 1861 (*OR*, ser. 1, vol. 8, 451–52).

29. Major George E. Waring Jr. to Acting Major General Alexander Asboth, December 19, 1861, enclosed in Asboth to Colonel W. Scott Ketchum, December 23, 1861, A-68 1861, LR 2593, 421–22.

30. Major General H. W. Halleck to Colonel William P. Carlin, January 9, 1862, in *DS*, 424.

31. Berlin, "Who Freed the Slaves," 111–13.

32. H. R. Gamble to Major General H. W. Halleck, December 10, 1861, M-79 1861, LR 2593, in *DS*, 419.

33. Genl. Orders, no. 6, November 29, 1861, vol. 446/1135 DMo, General and Special Orders and Post Orders, ser. 1100, Post of Rolla, Mo., RG 393, pt. 4, NARA, in *DS*, 419.

34. Lieutenant Colonel John S. Phelps, Rolla, Mo., to Colonel G. W. Dodge, December 2, 1861, ULR, in *DS*, 418.

35. Major George E. Waring Jr. to Acting Major General Alexander Asboth, December 19, 1861, enclosed in Asboth to Colonel W. Scott Ketchum, December 23, 1861, A-68 1861, LR 2593, in *DS*, 421–22; Asboth, Circular no. 2, Headquarters, 4th Division, December 18, 1861, enclosed in Asboth to Ketchum, December 18, 1861, A-69 1861, LR 2593, in *DS*, 420–21.

36. Major General H. W. Halleck, St. Louis, to General Alexander Asboth, Rolla, Mo., December 26, 1861, in *OR*, ser. 1, vol. 8, 465; Halleck to Asboth, December 26, 1861, vol. 10 DMo, 109–10, Letters Sent by Major General Henry W. Halleck, ser. 2576, DM, pt. 1, in *DS*, 423; Halleck to Colonel William P. Carlin, January 9, 1862, ULR, in *DS*, 424.

37. J. G. Porter, Medical Director, Southwest Division, Springfield, Mo., to Brigadier General J. G. Totten, Commanding Southwest Division, September 6, 1862, F-1185, Provost Marshals' File, M345-44.

38. *OR*, ser. 1, vol. 8, 370; Major George Waring Jr., Camp Halleck, Rolla, Mo, to Acting Major General Alexander Asboth, December 19, 1861, enclosed in Asboth to Colonel W. Scott Ketchum, December 23, 1861, A-68 1861, LR 2593, in *DS*, 421.

39. Fisher, *Gun and the Gospel*, 42, 166; Parrish, *Turbulent Partnership*, 33, 34, 52–54.

40. Brigadier General Ben McCulloch, Springfield, Mo., to General S. Cooper, C.S. Army, November 19, 1861, *OR*, ser. 1, vol. 3, 742–43.

41. Mendenhall, *Missouri Ordeal*, 67.

42. *WGFL*, 564; see also *OR*, ser. 1, vol. 3, 742–43; Fisher, *Gun and the Gospel*, 42, 167–68. Confederate reports claimed that the formerly enslaved people belonged to both "Union men as well as secessionists" (Brigadier General Ben McCulloch, Springfield, Mo., to General S. Cooper, Adjutant and Inspector General, C.S. Army, November 19, 1861, in *OR*, ser. 1, vol. 3, 742–43). "The federals left eight days since with their [thousand] men . . . taking negroes belonging to Union men" (McCulloch to J. P. Benjamin, Secretary of War, November 19, 1861, in *OR*, ser. 1, vol. 8, 686). General H. W. Halleck wrote of his frustration with the "Kansas Jayhawkers" to Secretary of War E. M. Stanton on March 25, 1862, in *OR*, ser. 1, vol. 8, 641–42.

43. Burke, *On Slavery's Border*, 283; Benedict, *Jayhawkers*; Jeremy Neely, *Border between Them*; Earle, *Bleeding Kansas*.

44. Margaret J. Hays to Mother, Westport, Mo., November 12, 1861, in Doerschuk, "Extracts from War-Time Letters," 100.

45. Fellman, *Inside War*, 66.

46. "Proceedings in the Case of the Taking of the Slaves of Jas. M. Hunter," October 7, 1861, F-1345, Provost Marshals' File, M345-137.

47. Major General H. W. Halleck, St. Louis, Department of the Mississippi Headquarters, to E. M. Stanton, Secretary of War, Washington, D.C., March 25, 1862, in *OR*, ser. 1, vol. 8, 641–42.

48. Williams, "Narrative of Andrew Williams."

49. John T. Burris, Report on the August 23, 1862, Skirmish at Hickory Grove, Mo., August 27, 1862, in *OR*, ser. 1, vol. 13, 253–55.

50. John T. Burris, "Expedition from Fort Leavenworth, Kansas, through Jackson, Cass, Johnson, and La Fayette Counties, Missouri," September 8–23, 1862, in *OR*, ser. 1, vol. 13, 267–68.

51. Lieutenant Colonel John T. Burris, Commanding, to Major T. J. Weed, Camp Curtis, Jackson County, Mo., November 4, 1862, in *OR*, ser. 1, vol. 13, 779.

52. Unionist H. S. Lipscomb to Major General J. C. Frémont, August 9, 1861, L-9 1861, Letters Received, ser. 5502, Headquarters in the Field, Western Department, RG 393, pt. 1, in *DS*, 414–15.

53. Bernard G. Farrar, Provost Marshal General, to Police Commissioners of St. Louis, March 3, 1862, in *OR*, ser. 1, vol. 8, 584.

54. Ibid.

55. Gerteis, *Civil War St. Louis*, 272. For the debate and passage of the Second Confiscation Act, see Siddali, *From Property to Person*, 227–50. For the enforcement of the Second Confiscation Act in Missouri, see Gerteis, *Civil War St. Louis*, 270–93. The Militia Act, passed on July 17, 1862, freed the families of any men employed by the Union Army as long as masters were disloyal (Militia Act of 1862, in *Statutes at Large*, 597–600, cited in *BME*, 5, and in *WGFL*, 272).

56. Gerteis, *Civil War St. Louis*, 271.

57. R. J. Howard to Major General Samuel R. Curtis, October 10, 1862, St. Louis Custom House Official to the Commander of the Department of the Missouri, October 10, 1862, and endorsement by Colonel Thomas T. Gantt, September 20, 1862, both in *DS*, 437–38, cited in Gerteis, *Civil War St. Louis*, 270. See also Colonel John F. Tylor to Captain Theodore L. Griffing, September 20, 1862, and endorsement by Gantt, September 20, 1862, RG 393, pt. 2, NARA, cited in *DS*, 438.

58. Gerteis, *Civil War St. Louis*, 273.

59. *DS*, 403; *WGFL*, 402; Gerteis, *Civil War St. Louis*, 27, 471; General Orders, no. 35, Headquarters, Department of the Missouri, December 24, 1862, Orders and Circulars, RG 94, ser. 44, NARA, in *DS*, 441–44; Gerteis, "Friend of the Enemy," 166–68; Gerteis, "Outrage on Humanity."

60. General Orders, no. 35, in *DS*, 442, 444; Article of War, March 13, 1862, in *Statutes at Large*, 354. The article of war in question states, "All officers or persons in the military or naval service of the United States are prohibited from employing any of the forces under their respective commands, for the purpose of returning fugitives from service or labor, who may have escaped from any persons to whom such service or labor is claimed to be due." General Halleck used this congressional act, passed by Radical Republicans, to justify the severance of the military from all affairs of slavery (*DS*, 22, 402). General Curtis referred to this additional article of war when he issued his General Orders No. 35 on December 24, 1862 (*DS*, 443–44).

61. According to *Revised Statutes* (1856), chapter 168, section 6, 1577, 1579, "The following persons shall be incompetent to testify . . . A negro or mulatto, bond or free, except in pleas of the State against a negro or mulatto, bond or free, or in civil cases in which negroes or mulattoes alone are parties." Enslaved people could sue for their freedom in certain circumstances but could not testify as sworn witnesses, leaving them dependent on testimony from white witnesses to meet their burden of proof. See *Missouri Revised Statutes* (1845), chapter 69, 531, which relied heavily on "An Act to Enable Persons Held in Slavery, to Sue for Their Freedom," June 27, 1807, in *Laws of the Territory of Louisiana*. See also VanderVelde, *Mrs. Dred Scott*, 234; Ehrlich, *They Have No Rights*, 42–43; Fehrenbacher, *Dred Scott Case*, 251.

62. *DS*, 404; *WGFL*, 578.

63. Stephen H. Smith to George H. Smith, Linn County, February 2, 1863, F-1263, Provost Marshals' File, M343-251.

64. Testimony of T. C. Williams, January 9, 1864, T. C. Williams, Franklin County, to Colonel C. W. Marsh, Provost Marshal General, February 1864, F-1232, Provost Marshals' File, M343-30.

65. C. S. Jeffries, Union, Franklin County, Mo., to Colonel and Provost Marshal H. C. Eitzen, Washington, Franklin County, Mo., May 4, 1863, F-1347, Provost Marshals' File, M345-143.

66. T. C. Williams, [Assistant Provost Marshal?], to [illegible], St. Clair, Franklin County, April [4], 1863, F-1192, Provost Marshals' File, M345-127.

67. T. D. Price, Assistant Provost Marshal, Marion County, Mo., to Lieutenant Colonel and Provost Marshal General James Broadhead, July 27, 1863, F-1245, Provost Marshals' File, M345-65.

68. "Sworn Statement of Harriet Meyers, Slave of James Woods," May 16, 1864, F-1156, Provost Marshals' File, M345-190. Other examples of enslaved women reporting slave owners to provost marshals include "Sworn Statement of Rachel Meyer," May 16, 1864, F-1156, Provost Marshals' File, M345-190; "Sworn Statement of Louisa Jane Florence,"

May 16, 1864, F-1280, Provost Marshals' File, M345-296; "Sworn Statement of Mary Ann Griffith," May 16, 1864, F-1280, Provost Marshals' File, M345-296.

69. "Sworn Statement of Lucinda Turner," June 2, 1864, F-1408, Provost Marshals' File, M345-271.

70. Samuel Glover to Abraham Lincoln, April 13, 1863, quoted in Parrish, *Frank Blair*, 178; Gerteis, *Civil War St. Louis*, 272; John F. Ryland et al. to His Excellency Governor H. R. Gamble, June 4, 1863, R-44 1863, LR 2786, in *DS*, 457.

71. Lucien Eaton to Major General J. M. Schofield, May 30, 1863, E-101 183, LR 2593, in *WGFL*, 571–73.

72. Egbert B. Brown, Commander of the District of Central Missouri, Jefferson City, to Major General J. M. Schofield, Commander of the Department of the Missouri, July 14, 1863, vol. 225/525 DMo, 184–85, Letters Sent, ser. 3372, District of Central Missouri, RG 393, pt. 2, no. 217, in *WGFL*, 576.

73. Greer W. Davis, Slaveholder, Jackson, Mo., to Major General Samuel R. Curtis, Commander of the Department of the Missouri, February 24, 1863, D-83 1863, LR 2593, in *DS*, 449–50.

74. M. P. Cayce, Delegate in the Missouri State Convention, Farmington, Mo., to Major General J. M. Schofield, Commander of the Department of the Missouri, July 31, 1863, C-655 1863, LR 2593, in *DS*, 460.

75. Colonel George H. Hall, Commander of the 4th Subdistrict of the District of Central Missouri, Marshall, Mo., to Major James Rainsford, Headquarters of the District, September 18, 1863, ULR, in *WGFL*, 579.

76. Colonel C. W. Parker, Troy, Mo., to Brigadier General T. J. McKean, March 26, 1863, ULR, in *DS*, 454–55. See also Major John Y. Clopper to Major George Merrill, March 21, 1863, filed with Parker to McKean, February 23, 1863, P-95 1863, LR 2593, in *DS*, 455–56.

77. Colonel C. W. Parker to Brigadier General Thomas J. McKean, March 26, 1863, in *DS*, 455.

78. John H. Estill to General R. C. Vaughan, May 30, 1863, enclosed in John F. Ryland et al. to His Excellency Governor H. R. Gamble, June 4, 1863, R-44 1863, LR 2786, in *DS*, 458; Lucien Eaton to Major General J. M. Schofield, May 30, 1863, E-101 1863, LR 2593, in *WGFL*, 571–73.

79. E. P. Cayce, Farmer, Farmington, Mo., to M. P. Cayce, June 19, 1863, C-17 1863, LR 2593, in *BME*, 227.

80. Elvira Ascenith Weir Scott Diary, August 31, 1863, Folklore Collection, Western Historical Manuscript Collection–Columbia, University of Missouri, Columbia; Burke, *On Slavery's Border*, 306–7.

81. John F. Ryland et al. to His Excellency Governor H. R. Gamble, June 4, 1863, R-44 1863, LR 2786, in *DS*, 457; H. B. Johnson to the Commander of the District of the Border, August 14, 1863, vol. 186 DMo, Letters Received, ser. 3107, District of the Border, RG 393, pt. 2, no. 200, in *WGFL*, 577.

82. Lucien Eaton to Major General J. M. Schofield, May 30, 1863, E-101 1863, LR 2593, in *WGFL*, 573.

83. *George W. McClure v. Pacific Rail Road Company*, 35 Mo. 189 (1864), filed in the Circuit Court of Pettis County, October 3, 1862, Missouri Supreme Court Case Files, Office of the Secretary of State, Missouri State Archives, Jefferson City.

84. G. R. Taylor to Major General J. M. Schofield, June 10, 1863, T-110 1863, LR 2593; Taylor to Schofield, August 5, 1863, enclosing W. N. Grover to Taylor, August 3, 1863, T-163 1863, LR 2593; *DS*, 466.

NOTES TO CHAPTER TWO 145

85. I. H. Sturgeon to Major General J. M. Schofield, September 9, 1863, enclosing Washington Graves et al. to Sturgeon, August 31, 1863, s-706 1863, LR 2593, in *DS*, 465; *Laws of the State of Missouri, Passed* (1865), 128–29, cited in *DS*, 466; Schwalm, *Emancipation's Diaspora*, 68. Major General William S. Rosecrans, commander of the Department of the Missouri from January to December 1864, did not determine a policy for common carriers until April 1864, when he clarified that railroad companies had military authorization to carry "colored persons having free papers, good under the laws of the State, or issued by competent Military authorities." For primary sources referring to Rosecrans's order, see Major H. M. Dunn to Rosecrans, April 13, 1864, Rosecrans, April 19, 1864, endorsement on Sturgeon to Major O. D. Greene, April 7, 1864, s-793 1864, LR 2786, in *DS*, 466.

86. Major General Samuel R. Curtis to Colonel Bernard G. Farrar, May 14, 1863, vol. 13, DMo, 457, Letters Sent, ser. 2571, DM, pt. 1, in *WGFL*, 574; Schwalm, *Emancipation's Diaspora*, 67–68, 77–80.

87. *DS*, 403; Gerteis, *Civil War St. Louis*, 271–72.

88. Major Henry S. Eggleston, 2nd Battalion, 1st Wisconsin Cavalry, report of skirmishes at Jonesborough and L'Anguille Ferry, Ark., August 9, 1862, in *OR*, ser. 1, vol. 13, 203.

89. *DS*, 259; Major General Samuel R. Curtis, Headquarters, Army of the Southwest, Helena, Ark., to Major General H. W. Halleck, Washington, D.C., July 31, 1862, in *OR*, ser. 1, vol. 13, 525; *DS*, 25; Special Orders, no. 1250, August 15, 1862, General J. R. Chalmers Papers, ser. 117, Collections of Officers' Papers, Records of Military Commands, RG 109, in *DS*, 292. Curtis's "free papers" were actually certificates with printed orders to confiscate enslaved individuals and granted them a pass into free territory. The certificates read, "Permitted to pass the pickets of this command northward, and are forever emancipated from a master who permitted them to assist in an attempt to break up the Government and Laws of our Country."

90. Colonel N. P. Chipman, Helena, to General Samuel R. Curtis, Steamer Sunshine, December 30, 1862, in *OR*, ser. 1, vol. 22, part 1, 886; *WGFL*, 574; Gerteis, *Civil War St. Louis*, 218–19; Parsons, *Memoir of Emily Elizabeth Parsons*, 54–55, 61.

91. Samuel Sawyer, Superintendent of Contrabands at Helena, Ark., to General Benjamin M. Prentiss, Commander of the District of Eastern Arkansas, St. Louis, March 16, 1863, s-239 1863, LR 2593, in *WGFL*, 565; Maria R. Mann to Elisa, February 10, 1863, Mann to unknown, undated fragment, quoted in Gerteis, *Civil War St. Louis*, 274.

92. Samuel R. Curtis to Brigadier General Benjamin M. Prentiss, March 9, 1863, in *OR*, ser. 1, vol. 22, pt. 2, 146, quoted in Gerteis, *Civil War St. Louis*, 274.

93. Samuel Sawyer, Superintendent of Contrabands at Helena, Ark., St. Louis, Mo., to Brigadier General Benjamin M. Prentiss, Commander of the District of Eastern Arkansas, March 16, 1863, s-239 1863, LR 2593, in *WGFL*, 565–67; Sawyer to Major General Samuel R. Curtis, April 18, 1863, in *OR*, ser. 1, vol. 22, pt. 2, 293; Gerteis, *Civil War St. Louis*, 274, 276; Schwalm, *Emancipation's Diaspora*, 80.

94. Gerteis, *Civil War St. Louis*, 275–76. Lucien Eaton also wrote about the fifteen hundred contrabands housed in the Missouri Hotel with "a quartermasters,—a surgeon—& some clerks" (Eaton to Schofield, May 30, 1863, E-101 1863, LR 2593, in *WGFL*, 572).

95. Gerteis, *Civil War St. Louis*, 272, 276, 279–82; Schwalm, *Emancipation's Diaspora*, 55, 80.

96. Major General J. M. Schofield, Commander of the Department of the Missouri, St. Louis, to the Honorable E. M. Stanton, Secretary of War, July 17, 1863, M-1499, LR 94, in *DS*, 461–63, quoted in Gerteis, *Civil War St. Louis*, 280.

97. Department of the Missouri, General Orders, no. 64, July 8, 1863, in *OR*, ser. 1, vol. 22, pt. 2, 359–60, quoted in Gerteis, *Civil War St. Louis*, 279–80; Schwalm, *Emancipation's Diaspora*, 80.

98. William A. Eads File, April 15, 1864, F-1309, Provost Marshals' File, M345-82.

99. Testimony of Major D. C. Fitch and Captain M. H. Jewett, Members of the Louisville Contraband Commission, before the American Freedmen's Inquiry Commission, Louisville, Ky., [November 1863], filed with O-328, LR 94, in *DS*, 592; Excerpt from Headquarters, Department of the Missouri, Special Orders, no. 307, November 10, 1863, filed with J-445 1864, Letters Received, RG 107, NARA; Major General J. M. Schofield to Lieutenant Colonel J. O. Broadhead, December 9, 1863, M-927 1864, LR 2786, in *BME*, 189–90; Headquarters, Department of the Missouri, General Orders, no. 35, March 1, 1864, Orders and Circulars, RG 94, ser. 44, NARA, in *DS*, 411–12.

100. Charles Jones to His Excellency Abraham Lincoln, March 24, 1863, in *DS*, 452; Jones to General John Davidson, March 24, 1863, ULR, cited in *DS*, 453; Burke, *On Slavery's Border*, 286.

101. Testimony of Jasper A. Guthridge, Private and Clerk for Col. Robinson, Reg. 23, Missouri Volunteer Infantry, August 8, 1863, in Robinson Court Martial, 49, 50; Testimony of 1st Lieutenant Benjamin F. Wyatt, Co. C, Reg. 23, Missouri Volunteer Infantry, August 8, 1863, in Robinson Court Martial, 37. Captain Crandall was a member of Co. G in the 23rd Missouri Regiment Volunteer.

102. Testimony of Susan Roberts and Julia Jones, October 8, 1878, Testimony of William Coleman, December 8, 1878, both in Samuel Perkins File, Co. K, Reg. 56, USCI, WA 172.706, CWPF.

103. Charles Jones, Missouri Slaveholder, St. Louis, to His Excellency Abraham Lincoln, March 24, 1863, J-198 1863, Letters Received, RG 107, in *DS*, 451–52.

104. Captain Stephen E. Jones, Headquarters, District of Western Kentucky, Louisville, to Colonel F. A. Dick, Provost Marshal General of the Department of the Missouri, April 15, 1863, B-128 1863, Letters Received, ser. 3514, Department of the Ohio, RG 393, pt. 1, in *DS*, 453–54.

105. Ibid., and attached endorsements, in *DS*, 453–54.

106. Testimony of Thomas North, August 5, 1863, John B. Gray, Adjutant General of Missouri, St. Louis, to Major General Samuel R. Curtis, Commander, Department of the Missouri, April 10, 1863, transcribed in Testimony of John B. Gray, August 5, 1863, both in Robinson Court Martial, 15, 8–9. See also *General Orders*, Supplement, no. 87, in Robinson Court Martial, 52–55.

107. Testimony of John B. Gray, Adjutant General of Missouri, August 5, 1863, in Robinson Court Martial, 8, 11.

108. Testimony of Benjamin F. Wyatt, Lieutenant, Co. C, Reg. 23, Missouri Volunteer Infantry, August 8, 1863, Testimony of Thomas North, August 5, 1863, both in ibid., 44, 15.

109. Testimony of Thomas North, August 5, 1863, Testimony of John L. McBride, Constable for the City and County of St. Louis, August 5, 1863, Testimony of Jasper A. Guthridge, Private and Clerk for Colonel Robinson, Reg. 23, Missouri Volunteer Infantry, August 8, 1863, all in ibid., 17–22, 25, 50.

110. Brigadier General Lewis Merrill, Hudson, Mo., to Colonel James Henry Lane, Wellsville, Mo., October 28, 1862, in *OR*, ser. 1, vol. 13, 767.

111. Robinson Court Martial; *Supplement*, pt. 3, vol. 3, ser. 95, 55.

112. Testimony of Thomas North, August 5, 1863, in Robinson Court Martial, 19.

113. *St. Louis Westliche Post* quoted in "Spirit of the German Press," *Missouri Republican*, August 16, 1863, in *OR*, ser. 1, vol. 22, pt. 2, 548; Gerteis, *Civil War St. Louis*, 276–81.

114. Major General H. W. Halleck to Colonel William P. Carlin, January 9, 1862, ULR, in *DS*, 424.

115. Although the Union military had hoped to avoid the issue of fugitive slaves, the actions of the enslaved population demanded that the military address the issue during the war (Berlin, "Who Freed the Slaves?").

CHAPTER 3. "A SOLDIER'S WIFE IS FREE"

1. Ann Valentine to Andrew Valentine, January 19, 1864, enclosed in Brigadier General William A. Pile to Major O. D. Greene, February 11, 1864, P-91 1864, LR 2593, in *BME*, 686–87; Astor, *Rebels on the Border*, 13, 18–23, 30; Hurt, *Agriculture and Slavery*, 301–2; Burke, *On Slavery's Border*, 12, 48, 51, 95.

2. *BME*, 88–189; *DS*, 46; Blassingame, "Recruitment of Negro Troops." For the national implications of the enlistment of African American men, see Cornish, *Sable Arm*; Foner, *Fiery Trial*, 240–49; Louis P. Masur, *Lincoln's Hundred Days*, 219–38. Under Schofield's General Order no. 135, enslaved men could enlist without their masters' permission, but loyal masters could apply for monetary compensation.

3. Burke, *On Slavery's Border*, 292–97; Schwalm, *Emancipation's Diaspora*, 56–57, 80; Blassingame, "Recruitment of Negro Troops," 332, 338; *BME*, 12. For Kansas and some other states, the number of black enlistees credited to the state exceeded the entire population of free black residents in 1860. A total of 440 black men served in Iowa's Civil War regiments; for Illinois, that figure was 1,811, and for Kansas, it was 2,080 (*DS*, 410).

4. Sam Bowmen to "Dear Wife," May 10, 1864, W-497 1864, LR 2593, in *DS*, 483–85, cited in Burke, *On Slavery's Border*, 296.

5. Gerteis, *Civil War St. Louis*, 291–92.

6. Ann Valentine to Andrew Valentine, January 19, 1864, enclosed in Brigadier General William A. Pile to Major O. D. Greene, February 11, 1864, P-91 1864, LR 2593, in *BME*, 686–87.

7. Astor, *Rebels on the Border*, 121–22; Samito, *Becoming American under Fire*, 40–43. On the concept of military citizenship, see Kerber, *No Constitutional Right*, 236–45. After the war, African American suffrage activists linked voting rights with military service, a phenomenon covered in Kate Masur, *Example for All the Land*. The process of conceptually transforming the act of fighting in the war into an act of joining an army of liberation is discussed in Louis P. Masur, *Lincoln's Hundred Days*, 232–33; Gallman, "In Your Hands"; Schwalm, *Hard Fight for We*, 121.

8. Bruce, *New Man*, 99.

9. Statement of Eliza Jimmerson, January 23, 1865, in James M. Martien File, Provost Marshals' File, M345-179.

10. For African American Civil War service as an assertion of masculinity, see Cullen, "I's a Man Now"; Samito, *Becoming American under Fire*, 40–43; Schwalm, *Emancipation's Diaspora*, 107. For the circulation of wartime soldiering images, see Gallman, "Snapshots."

11. Statement of Edy Jimmerson, January 23, 1865, in James M. Martien File, Provost Marshals' File, M345-179.

12. Richard Morton to Martha Morton, November 4, 1864, in Richard Morton File, Co. E, Reg. 65, WA 137.651, WC 1.998.621, CWA 538.641, USCI, CWPF.

13. Mrs. E. Stewart to the President of the U. States (Care of Provost Marshal, St. Louis), [December 1863], s-340 1863, Letters Received, Colored Troops Division, RG 94, ser. 360, NARA, in DS, 476.

14. Bercaw, Gendered Freedoms, 32–33; Frankel, Freedom's Women, 31–35.

15. Testimony of Claiborne Holiday, August 14, 1894, in Thomas Hughes File, Co. G, Reg. 65, USCI, and Co. G, Reg. 67, USCI, IA 487.723, IC 415.777, WA ?74.164, WC 249.568, CWPF.

16. Testimony of Charlotte Hicks, August 16, 1894, in Thomas Hughes File, CWPF.

17. BME, 188–90; DS, 410–11.

18. BME, 188–89; Gerteis, Civil War St. Louis, 283; Blassingame, Slave Testimony, 332; DS, 409–10.

19. J. H. Lathrop, President of University of Missouri, Columbia, Mo., to General Clinton B. Fisk, Commander of the District of North Missouri, March 8, 1865, ULR, in WGFL, 618.

20. G. W. Miller to General Egbert B. Brown, Boonville, Mo., January 6, 1864, Provost Marshals' File, M345-191.

21. Affidavit of Aaron Mitchell, January 4, 1864, ULR, in BME, 237–38. For white conservatives' violent response to African American enlistment in the border states, see Astor, Rebels on the Border, 131–35.

22. Schwalm, Hard Fight for We, 144; Frankel, Freedom's Women, 34.

23. General Affidavit of Sarah Carter, August 14, 1915, General Affidavit of George Carter, August 22, 1913, both in George Carter File, Reg. 65, IA 996.570, IC 984.918, WA 1.051.439, WC 796.541, CWPF; Edith Jane Perkins, Grey's Summit, Mo., to "Sirs," September 9, 1878, in Samuel Perkins File, Co. K, Reg. 56, USCI, WA 172.706, CWPF.

24. Testimony of Frassie Watkins, St. Charles, Mo., [before March 20, 1883], in Francis Watkins File, Co. H, Reg. 56, USCI, WA 281.533, CWPF.

25. Declaration for Widow's Pension, in James Madison Castleman File, Co. H, Reg. 65, USCI, WA 571.535, CWPF; Testimony of Sidney Castleman, St. Louis, Mo., January 13, 1896, in Peter Pitman File, Co. A, Reg. 65, USCI, IA 143.861, IC 92.600, WA 890.407, CWA 1.075.338, CWPF.

26. Susie King Taylor, Black Woman's Civil War Memoirs, 41, 51, 61.

27. Missouri freedpeople, interviewed 1892, published in Blassingame, Slave Testimony, 508.

28. Testimony of Jane Barker, February 10, 1868, in Cain Barker File, Co. A, Reg. 68, USCI, WA 155.596, CWA 310.542, CWPF.

29. Testimony of John Poe, February 10, 1868, Cain Barker File, Co. A, Reg. 68, USCI, WA 155.596, CWA 310.542, CWPF.

30. Testimony of Robert Robinson, April 9, 1901, in Albert Grimes File, Reg. 56, USCI, unassigned (WA 143.549, WC 512.614), CWPF.

31. DS, 48, 411. See also Excerpt from Special Orders, no. 307, Headquarters, Department of the Missouri, November 10, 1863, filed with J-445 1864, Letters Received, RG 107; Major General J. M. Schofield to Lieutenant Colonel J. O. Broadhead, December 9, 1863, M-927 1863, LR 2786, cited in DS, 411; Documents 91–94, BME, 242–49; Documents 222, 223A, DS, 587–93.

32. Schwalm, Hard Fight for We, 138.

33. Bruce, New Man, 107–12.

34. Sarah McBain, Columbia, Mo., to Richard McBain, Co. D, Reg. 62, USCI, Octo-

ber 21, 1865, in Richard McBain (alias) Richard Roberson File, Co. D, Reg. 62, USCI, IA 824.380, IC 677.152, WA 520.995, CWA 723.495, RG 15, NARA.

35. Testimony of Mary Jane Davis, October 25, 1877, in Isaac Davis File, Co. A, Reg. 65, USCI, WA 184.881, WC 179.287, CWPF.

36. Testimony of Major D. C. Fitch and Captain M. H. Jewett before the American Freedmen's Inquiry Commission, November 1863, filed with O-328 1863, LR 94, in DS, 592; Gerteis, *Civil War St. Louis*, 78.

37. Testimony of Mary T. Dyson, September 27, 1922, in Emmanuel Porter (alias) Bradford Pruett File, Co. A, Reg. 62, USCI, IA 447.410, IC 335.643, WA 1.175.845, WC 928.200, CWPF.

38. Testimony of Major D. C. Fitch and Captain M. H. Jewett before the American Freedmen's Inquiry Commission, November 1863, filed with O-328 1863, LR 94, in DS, 592.

39. Herbert P. Fromein to Henry, Co. A, 2nd Missouri Volunteers of African Descent, February 2, 1864, enclosed in Brigadier General William A. Pile to Major O. D. Greene, February 11, 1864, P-91 1864, LR 2593.

40. Frankel, *Freedom's Women*, 19; Schwalm, *Hard Fight for We*, 136; Burke, *On Slavery's Border*, 292, 297.

41. J. F. Benjamin to Provost Marshal, Hannibal, Mo., May 17, 1864, Provost Marshals' File, M345-109.

42. Martha Glover to Richard Glover, December 30, 1863, enclosed in Brigadier General William A. Pile to Major O. D. Greene, February 11, 1864, P-91 1864, LR 2593, in BME, 244.

43. Ibid., 244–45.

44. Brigadier General William A. Pile to Major General W. S. Rosecrans, February 23, 1864, enclosed in Pile to Major O. D. Greene, March 17, 1864, P-197 1864, LR 2593, in BME, 245–46.

45. Brigadier General William A. Pile to the Honorable Henry T. Blow, February 26, 1864, enclosed in Pile to Major O. D. Greene, March 17, 1864, P-197 1864, LR 2593, in BME, 248–49.

46. "The Colored Recruits at Benton Barracks," *DMD*, January 20, 1864.

47. Deposition of Lorenda Williamson, September 27, 1881, in Simon Williamson File, Reg. 65, USCI, CWPF.

48. Captain A. J. Hubard to Brigadier General William A. Pile, February 6, 1864, enclosed in Pile to Major O. D. Greene, February 11, 1864, P-91 1864, LR 2593, in BME, 687–88.

49. 1st Lieutenant William P. Deming to Brigadier General William A. Pile, February 1, 1864, enclosed in Pile to Major O. D. Greene, February 11, 1864, in BME, 242–43.

50. 1st Lieutenant William P. Deming, Co. H, 2nd Missouri Volunteers, of African Descent, Benton Barracks, Mo., February 1, 1864; Colonel G. H. Barrett, 1st Missouri, and R. B. Foster, 1st Lieutenant, Commanding, Co. I, 1st Missouri Volunteers, of African Descent, January 9, 1863, reported that "the wives and children of Priv. Marshall Taylor of Co. 'I' have been abducted away by foul means and taken to Ky." And Herbert P. Frowein, Warrenton, Mo., to Henry, Co. A, 2nd Missouri Volunteers, of African Descent, February 2, 1864, "wife of Henry wishes to get away masters are selling slaves to Ky" (all in alphabetical order in Vol. 746/1911, 1912, 1913 DMo [Entries 2890–92], in "Letters Sent," USCT, 1863–65, ser. 2890, DM, pt. 1).

51. Brigadier General William A. Pile to Major O. D. Greene, February 11, 1864, in *BME*, 242.

52. Lieutenant A. A. Rice, Provost Marshal, Mexico, Mo., to Colonel, Provost Marshal General of the Department of the Missouri, March 31, 1864, LR 2786, in *WGFL*, 600.

53. E. B. Brown, Commander of the District of Central Missouri, to Major O. D. Greene, Headquarters, Department of the Missouri, March 19, 1864, filed with S-264 1864, LR 2593, in *WGFL*, 593.

54. Lieutenant William Argo, Provost Marshal, Sedalia, Mo., to Brigadier General William A. Pile, Superintendent of the Organization of Missouri Black Troops, March 21, 1864, A-111 1864, LR 2593, in *DS*, 481.

55. Major J. Nelson Smith, Commander of the Station at Independence, Mo., to 1st Lieutenant E. L. Burthoud, Headquarters, 4th Subdistrict of Central Missouri, March 15, 1864, Letters Received, ser. 3379, District of Central Missouri, RG 393, pt. 2, no. 217, NARA, in *WGFL*, 589.

56. Lieutenant J. H. Smith, Provost Marshal, 3rd Subdistrict of the District of Central Missouri, Warrensburg, Mo., to General E. B. Brown, Commander of the District of Central Missouri, April 14, 1864, ULR, in *WGFL*, 602.

57. Major A. C. Marsh to Colonel J. P. Sanderson, April 5, 1864, M-454 1864, LR 2786, in *DS*, 482.

58. Lieutenant Franklin Swamp to Brigadier General William A. Pile, March 11, 1864, S-264 1984, LR 2593, in *WGFL*, 595.

59. Missouri slave owners could and did sue steamboat and railroad companies when escaped slaves used common carriers. See *DS*, 465–66, particularly I. H. Sturgeon, Railroad President, to Major General J. M. Schofield, September 9, 1863, LR 2593.

60. Brigadier General Thomas Ewing Jr. to Lieutenant Colonel C. W. Marsh, August 3, 1863, B-604 1863, LR 2593, in *BME*, 228.

61. In response to General Pile's inquiries about the stranded family members, Lieutenant Franklin Swamp, the provost marshal for Tipton, reported that he had orders not to give passes to the enslaved kin of black soldiers. Pile advocated sending family members to the contraband camp at Benton Barracks (Swamp to Pile, March 11, 1864, S-264 1984, LR 2593, in *WGFL*, 595).

62. Brigadier General E. B. Brown to Major O. D. Greene, January 22, 1864, filed as C-85 1864, LR 2593, in *WGFL*, 592.

63. E. B. Brown, Commander of the District of Central Missouri, to Major O. D. Greene, Headquarters, Department of the Missouri, March 19, 1864, filed with S-264 1864, LR 2593, in *WGFL*, 593.

64. A. Kempinsky, Wellsville, Mo., to Acting Provost Marshal General Colonel Marsh (received by S. S. Burdett), St. Louis, February 7, 1864, in *OR*, ser. 1, vol. 34, pt. 2, 268.

65. Lieutenant A. A. Rice, Provost Marshal, Mexico, Mo., to Colonel, Provost Marshal General of the Department of the Missouri, March 31, 1864, LR 2786, in *WGFL*, 600–601.

66. Lieutenant A. A. Rice, Assistant Provost Marshal, Mexico, Mo., to Colonel J. P. Sanderson, Provost Marshal General, March 31, 1864, in *OR*, ser. 1, vol. 34, pt. 2, 799; Sanderson, endorsing and forwarding Rice's letter to the general commander of the Missouri, April 4, 1864, in *OR*, ser. 1, vol. 34, pt. 2, 799–800.

67. Lieutenant Jeff A. Mayhall to Brigadier General William A. Pile, February 4, 1864, P-91 1864, LR 2593, enclosed in Pile to Major O. D. Greene, February 11, 1864, in *BME*, 243.

68. S. S. Burdett, Acting Provost Marshal General, Headquarters, Department of the

Missouri, Office of the Provost Marshal General, St. Louis, February 9, 1864, endorsement on Captain John Gould to the Honorable E. M. Stanton, January 21, 1864, G-71 1864, Letters Received, RG 107, NARA, in *BME*, 247.

69. Captain Hiram Cornell to Colonel J. P. Sanderson, March 28, 1864, C-258 1864, LR 2786, in *BME*, 688.

70. Lieutenant A. A. Rice, Assistant Provost Marshal, Mexico, Mo., to Colonel J. P. Sanderson, Provost Marshal General, March 31, 1864, in *OR*, ser. 1, vol. 34, pt. 2, 799; also published in *WGFL*, 600.

71. Captain John Gould, Army Commissary Officer, to the Honorable E. M. Stanton, January 21, 1864, endorsed by S. S. Burdett, Acting Provost Marshal General, February 9, 1864, and by Major General W. S. Rosecrans, Commanding the Department of the Missouri, February 13, 1864, G-71 1864, Letters Received, RG 107, NARA, in *BME*, 247.

72. Statement of Eviline Cox, Monroe County, Mo., June 6, 1864, Provost Marshals' File, M345-60; Statement of Hannah Carey, Hannibal, Mo., May 5, 1864, Provost Marshals' File, M345-46.

73. Statement of Paulina Jones and Pass, Hannibal, Marion County, Mo., February 22, 1864, Provost Marshals' File, M345-148.

74. Statement of Maria Brown, Hannibal, Mo., May 9, 1864, Provost Marshals' File, M345-38.

75. Statement of Mary Franklin, Hannibal, Mo., April 26, 1864, Provost Marshals' File, M345-96.

76. Lieutenant Jeff A. Mayhall, Assistant Provost Marshal, to Brigadier General William A. Pile, February 4, 1864, P-91, LR 2593, enclosed in Pile to Major O. D. Greene, February 11, 1864, in *BME*, 243.

77. Brigadier General William A. Pile to Major O. D. Greene, March 29, 1864, filed with S-264 1864, LR 2593, in *WGFL*, 593.

78. 1st Lieutenant William P. Deming to Brigadier General William A. Pile, February 1, 1864, enclosed in Pile to Major O. D. Greene, February 11, 1864, P-91 1864, LR 2593, in *BME*, 242–43; Deposition of Almeda Patterson, Kansas City, Mo., November 15, 1918, January 29, 1919, Deposition of Mary Jane Jordan, Mo., January 18, 1919, Deposition of Harriet Estis, Warrensburg, Mo., January 14, 1919, Department of the Interior Questionnaire of Martin Patterson, May 4, 1898, April 13, 1915, all in Martin Patterson File, Co. H, Reg. 65, USCT, CWPF.

79. S. A. Douglas, Agent of St. Louis Transfer Co., St. Louis, to General W. S. Rosecrans, November 17, 1864, Letters Received, A-516 1864, ser. 3285, St. Louis District, RG 393, pt. 2, NARA.

80. *WGFL*, 558; Gerteis, *Civil War St. Louis*, 224, 287, 291; Captain W. H. Corkhill, Superintendent of Contrabands at the Benton Barracks Contraband Camp, Mo., to Acting Assistant Adjutant General J. H. Clendening, Headquarters, Superintendent of the Organization of Missouri Black Troops, March 28, 1864, Miscellaneous Letters and Reports Received, ser. 2595, DM, pt. 1, in *WGFL*, 597–98, cited in Berlin, *Civil War St. Louis*, 291; Captain W. H. Corkhill to Assistant Adjutant General O. D. Greene, April 27, 1864, C-415 1864, LR 2593, in WGFL, 598. For background on the refugees housed at Benton Barracks, see *WGFL*, 558; Schwalm, *Emancipation's Diaspora*, 54, 80, 128–29.

81. "The Colored Recruits at Benton Barracks," *DMD*, January 20, 1864; Downs, *Sick from Freedom*.

82. Bell, "She Loves Army Man," 57; Testimony of Arry Rice (Wife), St. Louis, Septem-

ber 27, 1886, in Spottswood Rice File, Co. A, Reg. 67, USCI, IA 487.999, IC 529.750, WA 880.044, WC 659.775, CWPF.

83. Spotswood Rice to Kitty Digs, [September 3, 1864], F. W. Diggs to General W. S. Rosecrans, September 10, 1864, D-296 1864, LR 2593, in *BME*, 690.

84. Private Spotswood Rice, St. Louis, to "My Children," [September 3, 1864], enclosed in F. W. Diggs to General W. S. Rosecrans, September 10, 1864, D-296 1864, LR 2593, in *BME*, 689–90.

85. Bell, "She Loves Army Man," 59.

86. General William A. Pile endorsement on Lieutenant William Argo to Brigadier General William A. Pile, March 21, 1864, A-111, LR 2593, in *DS*, 481–82; Brigadier General William A. Pile to Major O. D. Greene, March 29, 1864, filed with S-264 1864, LR 2593, in *WGFL*, 594–95.

87. Major L. C. Matlack, St. Louis District Provost Marshal, Headquarters, St. Louis District, St. Louis, to W. M. Marshall, St. Louis, March 20, 1865, LS, entry 1734.

88. Statement of Annie Link, March 25, 1864, F-1481, Provost Marshals' File, M345-167.

89. Statement of Lucinda Farris, June 14, 1865, Provost Marshals' File, M345-89.

90. L. C. Matlack, Provost Marshal, St. Louis District, to Colonel J. H. Baker, Provost Marshal General, June 14, 1865, LS, entry 1735.

91. Major L. C. Matlack, Provost Marshal, Headquarters, St. Louis, to Captain Donaldson, Draft Rendezvous, Benton Barracks, Mo., April 18, 1865, Major Matlack, 17th Illinois Cavalry and District Provost Marshal, Headquarters, St. Louis District, St. Louis, to Major Barker, Paymaster, April 22, 24, 1865, all in ibid., entry 1734.

92. Charles S. Hills, Staff and Assistant Provost Marshal, Headquarters, 1st Subdistrict, St. Louis District, St. Louis, to L. W. Heath, 1st Subdistrict, St. Louis District, St. Louis, May 25, 1864, LS, entry 1733.

93. Captain Charles S. Hills, Assistant Provost Marshal, Headquarters, 1st Subdistrict, St. Louis District, St. Louis, to Colonel J. P. Sanderson, PMG, May 27, 1864, in ibid.

94. Ibid.

95. Captain Charles S. Hills to Whom It May Concern, August 18, 1864, in ibid.

96. Affidavit of Carroll Bergin in the Case of John Magner, January 20, 1865, F-1365, in Provost Marshals' File, M345-173.

97. Major L. C. Matlack, Provost Marshal, Headquarters, St. Louis District, St. Louis, to Isaac Walker, March 31, 1865, LS, entry 1734.

CHAPTER 4. "THE FIRST MORNING OF THEIR FREEDOM"

1. "Testimony of Charlotte Ford," September 13, 1864, in Thomas Farrell File, CMCF, LL-2638.

2. Parrish, *Missouri under Radical Rule*, 115–16; *Revised Statutes* (1856), chapter 168, section 6, 1577, 1579.

3. The apparent exception to this rule, when enslaved people could sue for their freedom, is distinct from testifying as a sworn witness. Under Missouri law, enslaved people had standing to sue for freedom under certain circumstances. They could sue for their freedom, file charges for "trespass and false imprisonment," and give affidavits. But even under these conditions, they could not speak in court but had to find white witnesses to prove their case. See also VanderVelde, *Mrs. Dred Scott*, 234; Ehrlich, *They Have No Rights*, 42–43; Fehrenbacher, *Dred Scott Case*, 251. For African American Union soldiers in the military courts, see Samito, *Becoming American under Fire*, 77–102.

4. Major L. C. Matlack, Provost Marshal, Headquarters, St. Louis District, St. Louis, to *DMD* and *DMR*, April 17, 1865, LS, entry 1734.

5. For an example of complaints about property seized by the military, see Captain Charles S. Hills, Provost Marshal, Headquarters, St. Louis District, St. Louis, to Lieutenant Henry Shadick, Assistant Provost Marshal, Cape Girardeau, Mo., September 22, 1864, Hills to Colonel Joseph Darr Jr., Acting Provost Marshal General, Department of the Missouri, November 13, 1864, both in LS, entry 1733.

6. In 1860, only 2.1 percent of municipal St. Louis's 160,773 residents were African Americans (Joseph C. G. Kennedy, *Population of the United States in 1860*, 297). By 1866, the city's population had increased to 204,327 (Primm, *Lion of the Valley*, 192, 265–66). According to the 1864 Missouri Census, African Americans comprised 3.3 percent of St. Louis's population and included 367 enslaved people and 6,450 free people of color ("Report of the Census Takers," *DMR*, February 22, 1865).

7. On the broad vision of equal rights promoted by the African American community, see Nieman, "Language of Liberation," 67–90. On the expansive claims for equality made by the black community in Washington, D.C., during the Civil War and Reconstruction, see Kate Masur, *Example for All the Land*. The African American community's assertion of equality and positive rights continued after the Civil War. Freedwomen brought gendered claims to the Freedmen's Bureau and petitioned the bureau agents for justice in a variety of arenas, including custody of children, assault, and labor practices. See Farmer-Kaiser, *Freedwomen and the Freedmen's Bureau*. Zipf demonstrates that African Americans in North Carolina promoted the concept of parental rights during the age of slave emancipation and beyond (*Labor of Innocents*, 69–70, 84–105).

8. See Captain Charles S. Hills, Provost Marshal, Headquarters, St. Louis District, St. Louis, to St. Louis Post Commander, July 30, 1864, LS, entry 1733; Major H. H. Williams, Provost Marshal, Headquarters, St. Louis District, St. Louis, to Colonel J. H. Baker, February 15, 1865, Major L. C. Matlack, Provost Marshal, Headquarters, St. Louis District, St. Louis, to Baker, March 18, 1865, both in LS, entry 1734.

9. See Major H. H. Williams, Provost Marshal, Headquarters, St. Louis District, St. Louis, to Colonel J. H. Baker, December 30, 1864, January 3, 1865, L. C. Matlack, St. Louis District Provost Marshal, to Brigadier General Thomas Ewing, Commanding St. Louis District, March 8, 1865, all in LS, entry 1734.

10. Tenants sought injunctions to prevent landlords from taking civil action. Landlords, in turn, petitioned provost marshals to cease interference in civil concerns. See, for example, Captain Charles S. Hills, Provost Marshal, Headquarters, St. Louis District, St. Louis, to August Ernst, June 4, 1864, Hills to Whom It May Concern, August 18, 1864, both in LS, entry 1733.

11. State law passed during the Civil War protected soldiers who were Missouri citizens and their families from civil proceedings, including actions taken for nonpayment of rent. The provost marshals often found themselves enforcing this law through correspondence with tenants, landlords, and justices of the peace. For an example of this application, see Captain Charles S. Hills, Assistant Provost Marshal, Headquarters, 1st Subdistrict, St. Louis District, St. Louis, to T. W. Cruth, Justice of the Peace, St. Louis, May 25, 1864, LS, entry 1733. Hills was concerned that the law did not apply where the soldier was either African American or a citizen of another state; see Charles S. Hills to Colonel J. P. Sanderson, PMG, St. Louis, May 27, 1864, LS, entry 1733.

12. Provost marshals would write an open letter for the complainant to carry warning of the consequences of violating her rights. For an example issued to an African Ameri-

can woman for her use in a rental dispute, see Captain Charles S. Hills, Provost Marshal, Headquarters, St. Louis District, St. Louis, to Whom It May Concern, August 18, 1864, LS, entry 1733.

13. See, for example, Major L. C. Matlack, Provost Marshal, Headquarters, St. Louis District, St. Louis, to Colonel J. H. Baker, Provost Marshal General, District of the Missouri, April 3, 1865, Matlack to Nimrod Snyder, St. Louis, April 18, 1865, both in LS, entry 1734.

14. See Major L. C. Matlack, Provost Marshal, Headquarters, St. Louis District, St. Louis, to Nimrod Snyder, St. Louis, March 18, 1865, H. H. Williams, St. Louis District Provost Marshal, to Mrs. Demas, February 7, 1865, Williams to Mr. Busha, February 13, 1865, Williams to Colonel J. H. Baker, Provost Marshal General, District of the Missouri, January 7, 1865, Matlack to Baker, March 11, 1865, all in LS, entry 1734.

15. Mark E. Neely, *Fate of Liberty*, 35; Gerteis, *Civil War St. Louis*, 132.

16. Astor, *Rebels on the Border*, 113–19; Fellman, *Inside War*; Sutherland, *Savage Conflict*, 18–25, 58–65.

17. Mark E. Neely, *Fate of Liberty*, 46; Gerteis, *Civil War St. Louis*, 128.

18. Mark E. Neely, *Fate of Liberty*, 35; Gerteis, *Civil War St. Louis*, 132.

19. The St. Louis District provost marshal operated as the lowest-level marshal in the city. The Military District of St. Louis encompassed a large swath of territory that included but was not limited to St. Louis City and St. Louis County. The city of St. Louis was designated as the 1st Military Subdistrict. The letter books stored at the National Archives include copies of letters that the marshal or his clerks wrote and sent from the St. Louis District office (LS, entries 1733–35).

20. See Testimony of Charlotte Ford, September 13, 1864, in Thomas Farrell File, CMCF, LL-2638; Testimony of Mary Smith, January 23, 1865, in Charles Frank File, CMCF, NN-3520. African American women made most of their visits to the St. Louis District provost marshal's office between January 1864 and April 1865, by which time the Missouri legislature had rewritten state statutes to permit African Americans to testify in civil courts ("Miscellaneous: African Descent—Persons Of," section 29, *Laws of the State of Missouri, Passed* [1865], 66).

21. "Miscellaneous: African Descent—Persons Of," section 29, *Laws of the State of Missouri, Passed* [1865], 66.

22. Martha Saxton, "City Women," 78–79, 83, 86–89.

23. Table 1 shows the proportions of African American men versus women who petitioned the provost marshal. Edwards has revealed how the legal culture of antebellum southern communities filed complaints while embedded within a community. The informal practices surrounding the legal realm meant that an individual might act as a witness even if not formally placed on a witness list. Furthermore, groups of people could visit a magistrate or a justice of the peace. The line between the specific individual making the complaint and the rest of the community was fluid in the antebellum context (*People and Their Peace*, 87–88). On the history of the practices of coverture in the United States, in particular the interactions of contraband women with the vagrancy laws, see Kerber, *No Constitutional Right*, 47–67. On the colonial-era practice of women appearing before the court as femme sole litigants, see Dayton, *Women before the Bar*, 69–104.

24. For examples of African American women's efforts to use the St. Louis District provost marshal to reclaim enslaved children, see Major L. C. Matlack, District Provost

Marshal, Headquarters, St. Louis District, St. Louis, to Colonel J. H. Baker, PMG, April 3, 1865, Matlack to Nimrod Snyder, April 18, 1865, LS, entry 1734.

25. "Captain Hills Emancipates a Slave," *DMD*, August 1864.

26. *BME*, 183, 187–90.

27. In one instance, we have a "boy" who had been employed on the chartered steamer *Clara Bell*. He claimed that a watchmen had put him ashore at a wood yard "this side of Memphis" rather than pay him his wages. The provost marshal ended up referring the matter to the district quartermaster, with the expectation that the next step would be to take the question to the ship's clerk. See Captain Charles S. Hills, Assistant Provost Marshal, Headquarters, 1st Subdistrict, St. Louis District, St. Louis, to Captain Parson, Assistant Quartermaster, June 20, 1864, LS, entry 1733 [image 1-062].

28. Men also brought labor complaints, although their places of employment and types of labor differed from those of African American women. For examples of men's labor complaints, see Charles S. Hills, St. Louis District Provost Marshal, to William H. Ayers, St. Louis County, Mo., November 29, 1864, H. H. Williams, St. Louis District Provost Marshal, to Johnson, St. Louis County, Mo., January 30, 1865, both in LS, entry 1734. For examples of African American women's labor complaints, see Williams to Mrs. Demas, February 7, 1865, Williams to Mr. Busha, February 13, 1865, both in LS, entry 1734. For examples of men reporting physical assaults, see Williams to Colonel J. H. Baker, Provost Marshal General, District of the Missouri, February 15, 1865, L. C. Matlack, St. Louis District Provost Marshal, to Baker, March 18, 1865, both in LS, entry 1734. For examples of African American women reporting physical assaults, see Williams to Baker, January 7, 1865, Matlack to Baker, March 11, 1865, both in LS, entry 1734. For examples of reports involving the forcible or fraudulent impressments of African American men as substitutes, see Williams to Baker, January 3, 1865, Matlack to Brigadier General Thomas Ewing, Commanding St. Louis District, March 8, 1865, both in LS, entry 1734.

29. U.S. Military Telegraph, Henry and Lee Ashbrook, n.d., F-1219, in Provost Marshals' File, M345-10.

30. Testimony of T. C. Williams, January 9, 1864, T. C. Williams, Franklin County, to Colonel Marsh, Provost Marshal General, February 1864, "Inventory of Boyle Elliot's Slaves," all in F-1232, Provost Marshals' File, M345-30.

31. Brigadier General John McNeil, Rolla, Mo., to Colonel J. P. Sanderson, PMG, September 3, 1864, F-1151, in Provost Marshals' File, M345-174.

32. The Second Confiscation Act was enforced by local provost marshals in Missouri after General Curtis issued Order no. 35. See Gerteis, *Civil War St. Louis*, 270–72; DS, 30, 403–4.

33. Testimony of Mary Catherine, 1862, Snell and Greens Testimony, April 11, 1862, Testimony of the Caldwell Negroes, 1862, all in F-1482, Provost Marshals' File, M345-168.

34. Charges and Specifications, Zaidee J. Bagwell File, CMCF, LL-548.

35. Testimony of William K. Patrick, April 18, 1863, 18, in ibid.

36. "Ordered to Be Tried by Military Commission," March 31, 1863, F-1463, Provost Marshals' File, M345-[].

37. Gerteis, "Friend of the Enemy," 171.

38. Affidavit of Julia Chamberlain, June 30, 1864, F-1409, Provost Marshals' File, M345-272.

39. Statement of Eveline Mericks [*sic*], June 5, 1863, F-1490, Provost Marshals' File, M345-297.

40. Office of the Gratiot Street Military Prison to Lieutenant Colonel F. A. Dick, PMG, January 29, 1863, F-1185, Provost Marshals' File, M345-44.

41. Affidavit of Patrick Rogers, July 26, 1864, F-1309, Provost Marshals' File, M345-82.

42. Affidavit of James W. Ferguson, May 27, 1864, Affidavit of Robert Custer, May 27, 1864, both in F-1237, Provost Marshals' File, M345-51.

43. Captain Charles S. Hills, Assistant Provost Marshal, Headquarters, 1st Subdistrict, St. Louis District, to Office of the Assistant Provost Marshal, St. Louis, May 27, 1864, F-1237, in ibid.

44. Captain P. H. Young, Assistant Provost Marshal, Warrenton, Mo., to Captain Charles S. Hills, Assistant Provost Marshal, 1st Subdistrict, St. Louis District, St. Louis, July 12, 1864, with enclosed endorsement from Lieutenant Colonel J. M. Bassett, Provost Marshal, Headquarters, District of North Missouri, Office of the Provost Marshal, St. Joseph, Mo., June 16, 1864, F-1237, in ibid.

45. Colonel J. P. Sanderson, Office of the Provost Marshal General, St. Louis, "Special Order No. 107," April 25, 1864, Jep Arrot and E. N. Leeds to Sanderson, April 25, 1864, both in F-1189, Provost Marshals' File, M345-100.

46. McCurry has defined the pro-slavery republican culture of the slave South. White yeomen could share in the identity of master and citizen through their governance of wives and children. The construction of the appropriate republican citizen depended on the subordination of all household dependents, which included not just enslaved people but white women and children. Within this context, antebellum feminist movements that attempted to move women outside of their classification of household dependents presented an affront to the construction of the "master" and posed a threat to the cultural construction of pro-slavery ideology. See McCurry, "Two Faces of Republicanism."

47. This claim of loyalty carries with it historical connotations relevant to the gendered construction of citizenship in the early republic. The concept of the *feme covert* implied that married women lacked the obligation to declare loyalty to the state, as they were mere residents of the state whose political relationships were mediated by their husbands. In contrast, the obligation to assert political loyalty positions women as members rather then mere residents of the state. See Kerber, *No Constitutional Right*, 3–34, esp. 26–27; Kerber, "Paradox of Women's Citizenship."

48. Galusha Anderson, *Story of a Border City*, 186–87; Gerteis, "Outrage on Humanity," 304–5.

49. Quoted in Gerteis, "Friend of the Enemy," 167, 175.

50. A new generation of scholarship has articulated the gendered experiences of women under slavery and how the sale of children informed enslaved women's moral judgment of the white slaveholding community. In her 1999 preface to *Ar'n't I a Woman?*, Deborah Gray White underlines the importance of recognizing that the violation of African American women's bodies and the sale of their children were "simultaneous manifestations of racism and sexism" (5–6). Jennifer L. Morgan has demonstrated how racial ideology targeted the bodies of African women to justify theories of racial inferiority and the subjugation of enslaved women. Furthermore, Morgan's analysis of wills in Barbados and South Carolina shows the appropriation of the reproductive capacity of enslaved women was intertwined with legal and social assumptions and played a constitutive role in the construction of slaveholder identity (*Laboring Women*, 69–106; on the complicated experience of reproduction in the lives of enslaved women, see esp. 114–15).

51. Statement of Dr. J. B. Burnett Regarding Negro Named Theodore, September 27, 1861, F-1289, in Provost Marshals' File, M345-41. The outcome of the dispute is unknown.

52. Special Order no. 153, by Order of Brig. Gen. Carr, Gen. Leighton, Major and Provost Marshal General, St. Louis Division, January 20, 1862, F-1583, in Union Provost Marshals' File of Papers Relating to Two or More Civilians, M416-4, RG 109, NARA.

53. Major H. H. Williams, Provost Marshal, Headquarters, St. Louis District, St. Louis, to Mrs. [Haisley?], No. 10 Sixth Street, St. Louis, January 9, 1865, LS, entry 1734.

54. Affidavit of Fannie M. Duvall, November 18, 1863, Betty Stauson File, F-1267, Provost Marshals' File, M345-225.

55. Testimony of Mary Smith, January 23, 1865, in Charles Frank File, CMCF, NN-3520.

56. Testimony of Mary Smith, January 23, 1865, in Charles Frank File, CMCF, NN-3520; "Letter from S. S. Burdett, Provost Marshal General," October 24, 1863, F-1322, Provost Marshals' File, M345-96.

57. Parrish, *Missouri under Radical Rule*, 17–19; Parrish, *Turbulent Partnership*, 200–201.

58. Major L. C. Matlack, Provost Marshal, Headquarters, St. Louis District, St. Louis, to Winrod Snyder, April 18, 1865, LS, entry 1734.

59. Major L. C. Matlack, Provost Marshal, Headquarters, St. Louis District, St. Louis, to Colonel J. H. Baker, Provost Marshal General, April 3, 1865, LS, entry 1734. Several women besides Ellen Carter applied to the St. Louis District provost marshal for assistance in freeing their children from slavery in April 1865. See, for example, Emma M. Williams (Matlack to Snyder, April 18, 1865, Entry 1734), Sarah Kelaw (Matlack to Baker, April 22, 1865, Entry 1734), and Leticia Meyers (Matlack to Baker, April 26, 1865, Entry 1735), all in LS.

60. Parrish, *Missouri under Radical Rule*, 17–19.

61. Testimony of Charlotte Ford, September 13, 1864, in Thomas Farrell File, CMCF, LL-2638.

62. Captain Charles S. Hills, Assistant Provost Marshal, Headquarters, 1st Subdistrict, St. Louis District, St. Louis, to Colonel J. P. Sanderson, PMG, St. Louis, May 30, 1864, LS, entry 1733.

63. Bensel, *Yankee Leviathan*, 139–42.

64. "A Woman Sent to Prison for Stoning Negroes," *DMD*, October 17, 1864.

65. John B. Means, Clerk, St. Louis District Provost Marshal Headquarters, to Mr. Dickson, In Charge of Female Prison, St. Charles Street, St. Louis, October 15, 1864, LS, entry 1734.

66. See, for example, Captain Charles S. Hills to Colonel J. P. Sanderson, May 31, 1864; Hills to Major J. E. D. Cozens, June 3, 1864 (an assault by St. Louis city policeman John Welch on an African American man, James Davis); Hills to Sanderson, July 26, August 17, 1864; all in LS, entry 1733.

67. Charges and Specifications, Testimony of Charlotte Ford, September 13, 1864, in Thomas Farrell File, CMCF, LL-2638.

68. "General Orders, No. 172," Headquarters, Department of the Missouri, September 21, 1864, in Thomas Farrell File, CMCF, LL-2638.

69. Charles S. Hills, Provost Marshal, Headquarters, St. Louis District, St. Louis, to Colonel Joseph Darr, 1st Assistant Provost Marshal General, Department of the Missouri, September 5, 1864, LS, entry 1733.

70. Ibid.

71. Ibid.

72. Lieutenant S. W. Collins, Office Provost Guard, to Captain W. Minten, Commanding, Provost Guard, City, St. Louis District, St. Louis, February 15, 1864, F-1310, Provost Marshals' File, M345-83.

73. H. H. Williams, St. Louis District Provost Marshal, to Colonel J. H. Baker, PMG, January 7, 1865, LS, entry 1734.

74. "City News," *DMD*, January 9, 1865.

75. H. H. Williams, St. Louis District Provost Marshal, to Colonel J. H. Baker, PMG, January 7, 1865, LS, entry 1734.

76. "Gratiot Prison Receipt for John Ferguson," January 7, 1865, "Commitment of John Ferguson," January 7, 1865, "Received from Guard," [signed by] Colonel J. H. Baker, PMG, all in F-1316, Provost Marshals' File, M345-90.

77. J. P. Vastine, Circuit Attorney, St. Louis County, Mo., to Colonel J. H. Baker, Provost Marshal General, January 18, 1865, Baker to Vastine, January 18, 1865, both in F-1316, Provost Marshals' File, M345-90; "Provost Items," *DMD*, January 19, 1865. The outcome of the case is unknown.

78. L. C. Matlack, St. Louis District Provost Marshal, to Colonel J. H. Baker, PMG, March 11, 1865, LS, entry 1734; "Provost Items," *DMR*, 17 March 1865.

79. Affidavit of Margaret Carter, July 8, 1864, F-1265, Provost Marshals' File, M345-253.

80. Statement of Jane Jones, December 14, 1864, Emily Partridge Eaton, President, Freedmen's Relief Society, St. Louis, to Provost Marshal, December 14, 1864, Lieutenant Edward P. Bigelow, Provost Marshal, St. Louis District, St. Louis, to PMG, December 16, 1864, Lieutenant Colonel and Acting Provost Marshal General C. W. Davis, to Bigelow, December 14, 1864, all in F-1351, Provost Marshals' File, M345-147. Jones testified that she received five dresses and $5.50 from Mrs. Gordon, which may have hurt Jones's case.

81. Article IX, sections 29, 36, *Revised Statutes of the State of Missouri* (1856), 1:643.

82. "Crimes and Punishments," chapter 47, article IX, section 27, *Missouri Revised Statutes* (1845), 1:413; "Crimes and Punishments," chapter 50, article IX, section 29, *Revised Statutes of the State of Missouri* (1856), 1:643; "Crimes and Punishments," chapter 50, article III, section 30, *Revised Statutes of the State of Missouri* (1856), 1:577; "Crimes and Punishments," chapter 50, article III, section 31, *Revised Statutes of the State of Missouri* (1856), 1:577.

83. "Recorder's Court," *DMD*, June 18, 1864.

84. "To Receive Five Stripes," *DMR*, February 13, 1865.

85. See article II, section 32, *Revised Statutes of the State of Missouri* (1856), 1:565.

86. Charles S. Hills, Assistant Provost Marshal, Headquarters, 1st Subdistrict, St. Louis District, St. Louis, to Mrs. Robinson, Corner 9th & Wash Streets, St. Louis, June 7, 1864, LS, entry 1733.

87. Richmond, Virginia, was an exception to this trend because of the number of enslaved men employed in tobacco and iron factories (Wade, *Slavery in the Cities*, 23–25, 120–21).

88. Captain Charles S. Hills, Assistant Provost Marshal, Headquarters, 1st Subdistrict, St. Louis District, St. Louis, to Mrs. Leslie, St. Louis, July 12, 1864, LS, entry 1733.

89. Major L. C. Matlack, Provost Marshal, Headquarters, St. Louis District, St. Louis, to John Bennett, St. Louis, March 18, 1865, LS, entry 1734.

90. Affidavit of Jennie Blanton in the Case of Mary Cursley, December 29, 1864, F-1247, Provost Marshals' File, M345-65. See also Affidavit of Mary Wallace v. Alex Busha, February 20, 1865, F-1290, Provost Marshals' File, M345-42; Major H. H. Williams, Provost Marshal, Headquarters, St. Louis District, St. Louis, to Mr. Busha, Carondelet, Mo., February 13, 1865, LS, entry 1734.

91. Major H. H. Williams, Provost Marshal, Headquarters, St. Louis District, St. Louis, to Mrs. Demas, February 7, 1865, LS, entry 1734.

92. Affidavit of Harriet Hampden, January 28, 1865, "Special Order No. 12," January 28, 1865, both in F-1345, Provost Marshals' File, M345-137.

93. Affidavits in the Case of Levi Clark and Wife v. Asa D. Gates, January 24, 1865, Balance Sheets in the Levi Clark Case, January 23, February 3, 1865, all in F-1323, Provost Marshals' File, M345-101.

94. "Law and Order in This Military Department," DMR, February 20, 1865.

95. Gerteis, Civil War St. Louis, 313.

96. Ibid., 307–8.

97. Ibid., 310.

98. "The Missouri Convention," DMD, January 19, 20, 1865; "Missouri State Convention," DMD, January 20, 1865; Parrish, Missouri under Radical Rule, 115–16; "Military Sub-Districts in the Military District of St. Louis," DMD, July 18, 1864.

99. "Negro Witnesses," DMD, January 7, 1865.

100. "City News," DMD, January 9, 1865; "A Point of Difference," Tri-Weekly Missouri Republican, January 9, 1865.

101. "Declaration of Rights," article I, section III, Revised Statutes of the State of Missouri (1866), 21. Four months earlier, on February 20, 1865, the General Assembly of the State of Missouri had anticipated the ratification of the new constitution and passed an act repealing the racial restrictions on testimony. See "Miscellaneous: African Descent—Persons Of," Laws of the State of Missouri, Passed (1865), section 29, 66.

102. Gerteis, Civil War St. Louis, 313, 315.

103. Major L. C. Matlack, 17th Illinois Cavalry and District Provost Marshal, Headquarters, St. Louis District, St. Louis, to Colonel J. H. Baker, Provost Marshal General, St. Louis, May 1, 1865, LS, entry 1735.

104. Major L. C. Matlack, 17th Illinois Cavalry and Provost Marshal, Headquarters, St. Louis District, St. Louis, to the Honorable Francis Rodman, Secretary of State, Jefferson City, Mo., April 7, 1865, Matlack to Major L. Eaton, Judge Advocate General, Headquarters, Department of the Missouri, April 10, 1865, both in LS, entry 1734.

105. L. C. Matlack, Headquarters, St. Louis District, St. Louis, to "the Democrat, Republican and District of St. Louis," April 17, 1865, in ibid. In contrast to Missouri, Kentucky's state courts refused to accept black testimony immediately following the Civil War, prompting the Freedmen's Bureau to establish courts in the state until the military tribunals were declared unconstitutional. Thereafter, the bureau assisted in transferring such cases to federal court. The Kentucky state legislature did not alter state law to confer equal testimony rights until 1872. See Astor, Rebels on the Border, 154–60.

106. "For Rent," DMR, April 14, 1865.

107. Kerber, "Presidential Address," 16–17.

CHAPTER 5. THE LEGACY OF SLAVE MARRIAGE

1. Pension Application of Nancy Richards, March 5, 1872, Testimony of Fort Mason and John Crowson, March 9, 1872, Testimony of Nancy Richards, June 8, 1877, all in James Richards File, Co. E, Reg. 60, USCT, WA 202.213, WC 162.287, Mother's Application no. 408.145, CWPF.

2. For a discussion of how citizenship forms its meanings through social practices and through the testing of the boundaries of rights and obligations, see Canning and Rose, "Gender, Citizenship, and Subjectivity."

3. For the role of marriage in the gendered definition of citizenship, see Kerber, No

Constitutional Right; Basch, *In the Eyes of the Law*. On the gendered aspects of republican political theory, see Pateman, *Sexual Contract*.

4. On the right to marry as part of the process of emancipation, see Frankel, *Freedom's Women*, 79–122; Schwalm, *Hard Fight For We*, 234–48.

5. On the domestic slave trade from the Upper South to Missouri and the sale of Missouri slaves for export to other states, see Burke, *On Slavery's Border*, 38–41, 118–25; Astor, *Rebels on the Border*, 66–67. For background on the slave market's reliance on the Upper South, see Johnson, *River of Dark Dreams*, 403–6. On slave sales from Upper South border cities into the interstate trade, see Johnson, *Soul by Soul*, 6–7.

6. The struggle for the right to marriage was a central goal of African American women. White feminists already had marital recognition and emphasized other goals, such as the right to divorce (Basch, *Framing American Divorce*). On white feminists' criticism of and the reformation of nineteenth-century marital property laws, see Basch, *In the Eyes of the Law*.

7. Frankel, *Freedom's Women*, 30, 39–44, 51–52.

8. *BME*, 187; *WGFL*, 63. Pile's approach differed from that found throughout much of the Union military establishment, which discouraged or outright forbade soldiers' wives and children from joining enlistees at military camps.

9. Testimony of Colonel William A. Pile, [November 29,] 1863, in Testimony Taken in Kentucky, Tennessee, and Missouri, November and December 1863, Final Reports, M-619, Roll 201, LR 94; *DS*, 256; *BME*, 187; Gerteis, *Civil War St. Louis*, 218.

10. Cott, *Public Vows*, 83–87.

11. Testimony of Colonel William A. Pile, [November 29,] 1863, in Testimony Taken in Kentucky, Tennessee, and Missouri, November and December 1863, Final Reports, M-619, Roll 201, LR 94.

12. Schwalm, *Hard Fight for We*, 234–48, 249–54, 257–60; Frankel, *Freedom's Women*, 40–55, 56–78. On the use of marital and gendered relationships in contestations between freedpeople, the Freedmen's Bureau, and planters, see Bercaw, *Gendered Freedoms*, 118–34.

13. Frankel, *Freedom's Women*, 31–38; Schwalm, *Hard Fight For We*, 88–97; *WGFL*, 63.

14. *DS*, 256, 261; Frankel, *Freedom's Women*, 40–44; Franke, "Becoming a Citizen"; Orders, No. 15, March 28, 1864, L. Thomas Letters and Orders, Generals' Papers and Books, RG 94, ser. 159, NARA, in *BME*, 712n1.

15. Frankel, *Freedom's Women*, 44, 44–55.

16. Ibid., 40–44, 79–82.

17. Chaplain A. B. Randall to Brigadier General L. Thomas, February 28, 1865, R-189 1865, LR 94, in *BME*, 712. The history of the family life of enslaved people is heavily influenced by the statistical analysis of Freedmen's Bureau marriage registers in Gutman, *Black Family*, which demonstrates that a large proportion of enslaved people lived in stable, two-parent households. Gutman may have deemphasized the impact of the slave trade and the power of slaveholders to disrupt family relationships, particularly the marital and romantic choices of young people.

18. General Orders, No. 41, Headquarters, 60th USCI, February 3, 1865, Issuances, 60th USCI, Regimental Books and Papers USCT, RG 94, G-221, NARA, in *BME*, 709.

19. Ibid.

20. Deposition of Thomas H. Benton, June 13, 1904, in Chatman Pryor File, Co. A, Reg. 56, USCI, WA 141.199, WC 95.508, CWA 680.381, Father's Application no. 299.233, CWPF.

21. N. E. Ivers, Special Examiner, Galesburg, Ill., to Commissioner of Pensions, July 13, 1908, in Lilburn Jackson alias Jackson Carter File, Co. D, Reg. 65, USCI, IA 602.794, IC 541.159, WA 864.645, WC 653.116, CWA 1.172.274, CWPF.

22. Deposition of John M. Crowder, October 1, 1881, Simon Williamson to Lorenda Williamson, Benton Barracks, St. Louis, March 31, [?], both in Simon Williamson File, Reg. 65, USCI, WA 140.439, WC 113.001, CWA 177.826, Contested Widow's Certificate no. 193.493, CWPF.

23. Deposition of Jane Barker, February 10, 1868, in Cain Barker File, Co. A, Reg. 68, USCI, WA 155.596, CWA 310.542, CWPF.

24. On the massacre at Fort Pillow, see Witt, *Lincoln's Code*, 248–49, 257–58; Cornish, *Sable Arm*, 173–79; McPherson, *Battle Cry of Freedom*, 748, 794–95.

25. *Congressional Globe*, June 25, 1864, 3233, quoted in Basler, "And for His Widow," 293; Franke, "Becoming a Citizen."

26. Scholarship on the creation and regulation of the Civil War widows' pensions includes Holmes, "Such Is the Price"; Skocpol, *Protecting Soldiers and Mothers*; Basler, "And for His Widow," 291–94. On the gendered construction of pension law, see McClintock, "Civil War Pensions." On the claims of African American pensioners as part of the construction of citizenship, see Franke, "Becoming a Citizen"; Regosin, *Freedom's Promise*. For an analysis of the political work performed by Civil War widows who applied for federal pensions, see Brimmer, "All Her Rights and Privileges."

27. On the Pension Bureau's interpretations of slave family formations, see Regosin, *Freedom's Promise*, 101–8. On the state's policy of legally restricting Civil War pensions to recipients classified as "morally worthy," see Skocpol, *Protecting Soldiers and Mothers*, 148–51.

28. James Adams File, Co. A, Reg. 65, USCI, WA 76.716, WC 154.908, CWPF.

29. Statement of Adjutant General's Office, Washington, D.C., January 7, 1865, Testimony of Ester Watkins and Francis Collins, March 14, 1866, Widows' Declaration for Army Pension, February 23, 1867, Testimony of Sallie Smith, June 1, March 4, 1869, Testimony of George Cole and Mollie Burgess, March 4, 1869, Statement of W. H. Corkhill, Hospital Chaplain, U.S.A., November 1, 1864, Retainer of Lawyer, March 3, 1866, Widow's Claim for Pension, November 2, 1864, all in Champ C. Smith File, CWPF.

30. Declaration of Cynthia Buford before Clerk of the St. Louis County Court, May 14, 1866, Deposition of John Crowser, February 13, 1867, Declaration for Pension of Children, May 3, 1901, Claimant's Appeal to the Secretary of the Interior, October 11, 1901, Claim under the General Law, Department of the Interior, April 7, 1903, all in Nathaniel Buford (alias) Craig File, Co. K, Reg. 56, USCI, WA 128.075, WC 91.590, Minor's Application no. 741.153, CWPF; Act of January 25, 1879, 20 Stat. 265 (1879), cited in McClintock, "Civil War Pensions," 464; on the pension claims of children, see 462–63; Regosin, *Freedom's Promise*, 123.

31. Application of Eliza Perkins for a Widow's Pension, October 12, 1868, April 23, 1867, both in Thomas Perkins File, Co. B, Reg. 62, USCT, WA 166.721, WC 123.209, CWPF. For other successful applications by women who lacked official marriages, see Widows' Declaration for Army Pension of Sharady Shelly, May 14, 1866, in Isaac Shelly File, Reg. 56, USCT, WA 126.823, WC 115.524, Application of Louisa Maupin for Widow's Pension, April 23, 1867, in Samuel Maupin File, Co. K, Reg. 56, USCT, WA 306.849, WC 231.068, CWA 146.317, Contested Widow's Certificate no. 120.973, Widow's Application for Pension, January 8, 1868, in Joshua Brooks File, Co. K, Reg. 56, USCI, WA 156.637, WC 155.265, all in CWPF.

32. Widow's Application of Charlotte Washington, October 11, 1866, Statement of George Washington and Anderson Bowles, October 11, 1866, Statement of Gustavus Brown and Melinda Lucas, October 11, 1866, Statement from Adjutant General's Office, Washington, D.C., November 7, 1866, Statement from the Surgeon General's Office, Record and Pension Bureau, Washington, D.C., November 17, 1866, all in Henry Washington File, Co. C, Reg. 56, USCT, WA 135.611, WC 110.085, CWPF.

33. Widow's Application for Army Pension, March 1, 1867, L. C. Black, Special Agent, Washington, D.C., to the Honorable J. W. Baker, Commissioner of Pensions, November 6, 1874, Testimony of Millie Crockett, September 23, 1868, all in Robert Smith (alias) Poindexter (alias) Martin File, Co. D, Reg. 56, USCI, WA 144.189, WC 122.668, Minor's Application no. 712.572, Mother's Application no. 254.954, CWPF.

34. McClintock, "Civil War Pensions," 466, 476–77.

35. Stevenson, *Life in Black and White*, 160–61, 234, 243, 326; Stevenson, "Black Family Structure," 52–53; Schwalm, *Hard Fight for We*, 245–47; Frankel, *Freedom's Women*, 90–92, 97–105, 125. On the definition and analysis of "sweethearting" and "took-up" intimate relationships, see Frankel, *Freedom's Women*, 90–104. Cott demonstrates that marital monogamy in the United States was challenged by other marital and sexual practices (*Public Vows*, 105–11).

36. Testimony of Joseph Poindexter, October 19, 1874, in Robert Smith (alias) Poindexter (alias) Martin File, CWPF.

37. Testimony of Rachel Jackson, George Massey, Umstead Smith, and Martha Smith, May 10, 1873, in ibid.

38. Frankel emphasizes the role of community standards in the determination of legitimate marriages in postwar Mississippi (*Freedom's Women*, xii).

39. For the application process for emancipated widows, special investigators, and Civil War pension claims, see Franke, "Becoming a Citizen"; McClintock, "Civil War Pensions," 474–76; Regosin, *Freedom's Promise*, 82–96.

40. Pension Application of Lorenda Williamson, January 7, 1867, Affidavit of Lorenda Williamson, March 18, 1868, Claim for Widow's Pension of Lorenda Williamson, passed May 4, 1868, Application for Widow's Pension, January 7, 1867, all in Simon Williamson File, USCI, WA 140.439, WC 113.001, CWA 177.826, Contested Widow's Certificate no. 193.493, CWPF.

41. Original Pension Application of Silva Williamson, July 23, 1869, Deposition of John Standly, February 28, 1874, Deposition of David North, February 28, 1874, September 28, 1881, Report by Special Examiner George W. McKean, October 1, 1881, all in ibid.

42. Report by Special Examiner George W. McKean, October 1, 1881, in ibid.

43. For persuasive arguments about the political salience of laws governing marriage, female sexual activity, and family formation, see Bardaglio, *Reconstructing the Household*; Bynum, *Unruly Women*; Cott, *Public Vows*; Edwards, "Marriage Covenant"; Edwards, *Gendered Strife and Confusion*.

44. For the political and personal implications of legal marriage for emancipated slaves, see Frankel, *Freedom's Women*; Edwards, "Marriage Covenant," 81–124; Franke, "Becoming a Citizen."

45. Report by Special Examiner George W. McKean, October 1, 1881, in Simon Williamson File, CWPF.

46. Deposition of Lorenda Williamson, September 27, 1881, in ibid.

47. For freedpeople's informal marriages, pension agents, and the Pension Bureau, see Frankel, *Freedom's Women*, 86–92.

48. On the Pension Bureau's rules for collecting evidence for the pension claim, see Regosin, *Freedom's Promise*, 36–53.

49. Deposition of John Standley, February 28, 1874, Deposition of Jacob Wood, February 28, 1874, Deposition of David North, September 28, 1881, Deposition of Louisa North, September 29, 1881, Deposition of Flavius J. North, September 29, 1881, Deposition of James G. North, September 28, 1881, all in Simon Williamson File, CWPF.

50. Deposition of Lorenda Williamson, September 27, 1881, in ibid.

51. Pension Application of Lorenda Williamson, January 7, 1867, Deposition of John Standley, February 28, 1874, Deposition of Lorenda Williamson, September 27, 1881, all in ibid.

52. Affidavits of Ella Walker and Gustavus Brown, March 18, 1867, Deposition of Lee Jeffries, September 27, 1881, Deposition of Lorenda Williamson, September 27, 1881, all in ibid.

53. Report by Special Examiner George W. McKean, October 1, 1881, in ibid.

54. See Act of June 6, 1866, 14 Stat. 58 (1866) quoted in McClintock, "Civil War Pensions," 474; Regosin, *Freedom's Promise*, 83–84.

55. Act of June 6, 1873, chapter 234, section 11, 17 Stat. 566 (1873) (revising, consolidating, and amending laws relating to pensions), quoted in Franke, "Becoming a Citizen"; see also section 4705 of the Revised Statutes of the United States (1873–74), quoted in Regosin, *Freedom's Promise*, 84.

56. Affidavits of Ella Walker and Gustavus Brown, March 18, 1867, Deposition of Lee Jeffries, September 27, 1881, Deposition of Jacob Wood, February 28, 1874, Deposition of David North, September 28, 1881, Deposition of Louisa North, September 29, 1881, all in Simon Williamson File, CWPF.

57. Deposition of John M. Crowder, October 1, 1881, in ibid.

58. Deposition of Lorenda Williamson, September 27, 1881, Simon Williamson to Lorenda Williamson, Benton Barracks, St. Louis, February 21, March 31, [?], all in ibid.

59. Simon Williamson to Lorenda Williamson, February 21, [?], in ibid.

60. Simon Williamson to Lorenda Williamson, March 31, [?], in ibid.

61. Deposition of Lorenda Williamson, September 27, 1881, in ibid. For primary-source evidence of the abuse of soldiers' wives, see Lieutenant Jeff A. Mayhall to Brigadier General William A. Pile, February 4, 1864, P-91 1864, LR 2593; Martha Glover to Richard Glover, December 30, 1863, enclosed in Pile to Major O. D. Greene, February 11, 1864, P-91 1864, LR 2593, both quoted in *BME*, 243–44, cited in Gerteis, *Civil War St. Louis*, 284. For background on the formation of the USCT in Missouri, see Blassingame, "Recruitment of Negro Troops."

62. Testimony by Henry M. Post, Attorney, May 11, 1870, quoted in report, n.d., in Simon Williamson File, CWPF.

63. Simon Williamson to Lorenda Williamson, Benton Barracks, St. Louis, March 31, [?], Pension Application of Lorenda Williamson, January 7, 1867, both in Simon Williamson File, CWPF.

64. Deposition of Jane Gibson, July 2, 1900, Deposition of Delpha Carrico, November 7, 1901, Deposition of Louis Camp, November 7, 1901, Report from the Department of the Interior, Bureau of Pensions, July 12, 1900, all in Henry Gibson alias Cordon File, Co. A, Reg. 65, USCI, IA 824.111, IC 682.680, WA 686.255, CWPF.

65. Deposition of Lewis Camp, November 7, 1901, in ibid.

66. Camp, *Closer to Freedom*, 64–65; McLaurin, *Celia, a Slave*. For a discussion of how sexual violence was deployed in postemancipation political struggles as a tool to

deny citizenship status to freedwomen, see Rosen, *Terror in the Heart*. On slaveholder terror and the "spectacle of public discipline," see Glymph, *Out of the House of Bondage*, 55–57. Slave owners retained the right to refuse permission and dissolve slave marriages in progress (Frankel, *Freedom's Women*, 9–10). On the consent of slave owners to abroad marriages, see Schwalm, *Hard Fight for We*, 52–53. On the antebellum U.S. slave "geography of containment," slave patrols, and policing, see Camp, *Closer to Freedom*, 16–20, 24–28.

67. Deposition of Samson Edwards, December 17, 1901, in Henry Gibson alias Cordon File, CWPF.

68. Deposition of Benjamin Fields, December 16, 1901, in ibid.

69. Deposition of Lucy Edwards, December 16, 1901, in ibid.

70. Jane Lewis (alias Jane Davis) gave birth to her daughter, Sadie, in 1863 at Brunswick, Mo. Jane Lewis married her first husband, Pampon Lewis, while living as a slave and, in addition to Sadie, bore a daughter named Julia, a son named George, and two other children who died. Pampon Lewis died while serving in the Union Army (Deposition of Sadie Vandenburg, December 18, 1901, in Henry Gibson alias Cordon File, CWPF).

71. Deposition of Samson Edwards, December 17, 1901, in ibid.

72. Deposition of Jane Gibson, December 18, 1901, in ibid.

73. Deposition of George Carrico, November 7, 1901, in ibid.

74. Assistant Secretary to the Commissioner of Pensions, n.d., J. A. Cuddy, Chief of Law Division, Department of the Interior, Bureau of Pensions, Washington, D.C., to Chief of the Southern Division, July 12, 1900, both in ibid.

75. Testimony of Sinai Johnson, 10, in *Johnson v. Johnson*, March Term 1870, Missouri State Supreme Court Case Files, Missouri State Historical Society, Jefferson City; *Johnson v. Johnson*, 45 Mo. 597.

76. "Petition of Sinai D. Johnson by Her Next Friend Charlton H. Tandy, Plaintiff," St. Louis Circuit Court, April Term 1868, filed in *Johnson v. Johnson*, Missouri State Supreme Court Case Files.

77. Testimony of Sinai Johnson, 10, in *Johnson v. Johnson*, Missouri State Supreme Court Case Files.

78. Testimony of Sinai Johnson, 10–11, Testimony of Demas Johnson, 18, Testimony of Rufus Pettiford, 20, all in *Johnson v. Johnson*, Missouri State Supreme Court Case Files.

79. Testimony of Sinai Johnson, 11, Testimony of Charlton H. Tandy, 13–14, Testimony of Cloe Jackson, 15, all in ibid.

80. Testimony of Sinai Johnson, 11; Testimony of Charlton H. Tandy, 13, both in ibid.

81. Testimony of Sinai Johnson, 10, 11–12, in ibid.

82. Testimony of Demas Johnson, 17, in ibid.; *Johnson v. Johnson*, 45 Mo. 597.

83. Frankel, *Freedom's Women*, 80–82; Schwalm, *Hard Fight for We*, 243–44; Berlin, Miller, and Rowlands, "Afro-American Families," 92, 98; Litwack, *Been in the Storm*, 262–63.

84. Stevens, *History of Central Baptist Church*, 9–11, 29–31; *Johnson v. Johnson*, 45 Mo. 597; Testimony of Sinai Johnson, 10, in *Johnson v. Johnson*, Missouri State Supreme Court Case Files.

85. Testimony of Ed. Collins, Testimony of Rufus Pettiford, 21–22, both in in *Johnson v. Johnson*, Missouri State Supreme Court Case Files.

86. Stevens, *History of Central Baptist Church*, 29–30.

87. Testimony of Charlton H. Tandy, 12–13, in *Johnson v. Johnson*, Missouri State Supreme Court Case Files.

88. Biographical Description of Charlton H. Tandy, Charlton H. Tandy Papers, Western Historical Manuscript Collection, University of Missouri–St. Louis; Testimony of Charlton H. Tandy, 13, in *Johnson v. Johnson*, Missouri State Supreme Court Case Files; Wright, *No Crystal Stair*, 36, 37–38; Greene, Kremer, and Holland, *Missouri's Black Heritage*, 105; Jack, "Tandy, Charleton." On Tandy's work in organizing aid to the Exodusters, see Kremer, *James Milton Turner*, 106–7.

89. Stevens, *History of Central Baptist Church*, 13.

90. On the black church's role in regulating marriage, see Schwalm, *Hard Fight for We*, 242, 244; Frankel, *Freedom's Women*, 84–86.

91. Testimony of E. L. Woodson, 16, in *Johnson v. Johnson*, Missouri State Supreme Court Case Files.

92. Testimony of Henry Thomas, 19, Testimony of E. L. Woodson, 16, both in *Johnson v. Johnson*, Missouri State Supreme Court Case Files.

93. Testimony of Sinai Johnson, 24, Testimony of Ed. Collins, 21, both in ibid.

94. Testimony of Charlton Tandy, 13, 23, in ibid.

95. Testimony of Ed. Collins, 21, in ibid.

96. Testimony of Ed. Collins, 21, Testimony of Rufus Pettiford, 20–21, both in *Johnson v. Johnson*, Missouri State Supreme Court Case Files.

97. Testimony of Rufus Pettiford, 20, Testimony of Ed. Collins, 21, Testimony of Henry Thomas, 19, Testimony of Jack Davison, 20, Testimony of Fave Ubanks, 22, Testimony of Sinai Johnson, 12, Testimony of Eliza Davison, 22, all in ibid.

98. Testimony of Sinai Johnson, 11, in ibid.

99. Testimony of Demas Johnson, 19, Defendant's Instructions Refused, 26, Judgment, 9, "Petition of Sinai D. Johnson by Her Next Friend Charlton H. Tandy, Plaintiff," St. Louis Circuit Court, April Term 1868, all in ibid.

100. Motion Filed by Appellant's Attorneys, in ibid.

101. *Johnson v. Johnson*, 45 Mo. 595 (1870).

102. Ibid., 597–601.

103. Regosin has argued that the Civil War pension claims of ex-slave families reveal the citizenship claims that freedpeople made on the U.S. federal government. See Regosin, *Freedom's Promise*.

EPILOGUE

1. Unnamed author, April 21, 1863, enclosed with Colonel Henry Almsteads, 2nd Missouri Artillery Volunteers, Commanding Post Headquarters, Post St. Louis, to Major General S. R. Curtis, Commanding Department of the Missouri, n.d., Letter 98-A, LR 2593; Schwalm, *Emancipation's Diaspora*, 79.

2. Unnamed author, April 21, 1863, enclosed with Colonel Henry Almsteads, 2nd Missouri Artillery Volunteers, Commanding Post Headquarters, Post St. Louis, to Major General S. R. Curtis, Commanding Department of the Missouri, n.d., Letter 98-A, LR 2593.

3. Petition Filed for Plaintiff, April 29, 1869, in *Anderson Davis and Lucy Ann Davis v. the Missouri Rail Road Company*, June 1869, Case no. 12726, St. Louis Circuit Court Case Files, *St. Louis Circuit Court Historical Records Project*.

4. On freedwomen's efforts to expand the substance of emancipation beyond slavery and particularly to reconstruct social relations, see Schwalm, *Hard Fight for We*, 187–233.

5. *Martha Turner v. the People's Railway Company*, June 1866, Case no. 0-2218, St. Louis Circuit Court Case Files.

6. Answer to Amended Petition, January 13, 1868, in *Susan Taylor v. the Missouri Railroad Co.*, October 1867, Case no. 6083, St. Louis Circuit Court Case Files; Answer to Amended Petition, January 13, 1868, in *Abraham Watson and Frances Watson v. the Missouri Railroad Co.*, October 1867, Case no. 6082, St. Louis Circuit Court Case Files.

7. Petition for Damages, June 22, 1867, in *Abraham Watson and Frances Watson v. the Missouri Railroad Company*, Case no. 6082, St. Louis Circuit Court Case Files; "Colored People Not Allowed on Street Cars," *DMD*, June 5, 1867.

8. Nineteenth-century railroads, for example, divided their cars into a "ladies' car" and the "smoker." Single men occupied the smoker, while male family members had the option to ride in the ladies' car with women and children. On African American women who claimed a gender by asserting their right to ride in the ladies' car, see Welke, *Recasting American Liberty*, 280–322, 323–78; Welke, "When All the Women Were White." For common carriers and the postwar legalities of equal access, see Kate Masur, *Example for All the Land*, 89, 100–104.

9. "Railroad Equality," *DMD*, June 4, 1867; "Colored People Not Allowed on Street Cars," *DMD*, June 5, 1867; *Jane Reese v. Missouri Horse Railroad Company* (filed June 18, 1867), October 1867, Case no. 6043, St. Louis Circuit Court Case Files.

10. *Neptune M. and Caroline Williams v. Bellefontaine Railway Company*, October 1867, Case no. 6083, Circuit Court Docket Book, Case Missing from St. Louis Circuit Court Case Files; "Street Cars and Colored People," *DMR*, May 4, 1868; "Lo, the Poor Negro," *St. Louis Times*, May 2, 1868; Parrish, *Missouri under Radical Rule*, 112.

11. McKerley, "'Good Laws' and 'Unfriendly Legislation'"; Low, "Freedmen's Bureau," 258–63.

12. Parrish, *History of Missouri*, 120–28; Parrish, *Turbulent Partnership*, 197–201.

13. McKerley, "'Good Laws' and 'Unfriendly Legislation'"; Low, "Freedmen's Bureau," 258–63; "Introduction," *Records of the Assistant Commissioner for the State of Arkansas, Bureau of Refugees, Freedmen, and Abandoned Lands, 1865–1869*, Letters and Telegrams Received, from Subordinate Officers, vols. 1(5) and 2(6), May 1865–October 1866, Roll 6, M-979, 1974, NARA.

14. McKerley, "'Good Laws' and 'Unfriendly Legislation'"; Greene, Kremer, and Holland, *Missouri's Black Heritage*, 93.

15. Fanny Wilson, Caruthersville, Mo., to Governor Thomas C. Fletcher, Jefferson City, Mo., August 9, 1867, 87:105–6, endorsement by Fletcher to Bureau of Freedmen, Refugees, and Abandoned Lands, St. Louis, August 22, 1867, 87:106, forwarded by R. A. Seeley, Special Agent, Bureau of Freedmen, Refugees, and Abandoned Lands, to Major General O. O. Howard, War Department, Bureau of Freedmen, Refugees, and Abandoned Lands, Washington, D.C. August 26, 1867, 87:106, endorsed to Brevet Major General W. P. Carlin, Assistant Commissioner, Tennessee, Bureau of Freedmen, Refugees, and Abandoned Lands, Nashville, August 30, 1867, 87:106, returned by Lieutenant Colonel Thomas S. Palmer, Acting Assistant Commissioner, Tennessee, Bureau of Freedmen, Refugees, and Abandoned Lands, Nashville, September 4, 1867, 87:107, endorsed to Brevet Brigadier General Sidney Burbank, Assistant Commissioner, Kentucky, Bureau of Freedmen, Refugees, and Abandoned Lands, Louisville, September 9, 1867, 87:107, all in Letters Received, ser. 1138, Superintendent at Columbus, Kentucky, RG 105 [A-4580],

NARA. I am grateful to John W. McKerley for bringing Fannie Wilson's case to my attention and sending me copies of the primary evidence. I also thank the Freedmen and Southern Society Project at the University of Maryland for making this evidence available from their files.

16. "An Address by the Colored People of Missouri to Friends of Equal Rights," October 12, 1865, in *A Speech on "Equality before the Law"* (St. Louis: Democrat Book and Job, 1866), 26.

17. McKerley, "'We Promise to Use the Ballot,'" 205–24; Gerteis, *Civil War St. Louis*, 292–93; Greene, Kremer, and Holland, *Missouri's Black Heritage*, 95–97; Parrish, "Reconstruction Politics in Missouri," 20; Dwight, "Black Suffrage in Missouri," 48–68.

18. "Good News from St. Louis," *CR*, October 21, 1865.

19. *CR*, August 25, 1866; "Book and Paper Notices," *CR*, January 25, 1868; "Important Letter," *CR*, November 19, 1870.

20. W. R. Revels, "St. Louis, Mo., Correspondence," *CR*, July 21, 1866.

21. Delaney, *From the Darkness*, 62–63.

22. *Gould's St. Louis Directory* (St. Louis: Gould, 1873), 1141–42; "Colored Societies," *Gould's St. Louis Directory* (St. Louis: Gould, 1876), 1249.

23. *CR*, April 20, 1872.

Bibliography

ARCHIVAL COLLECTIONS BY REPOSITORY

Missouri History Museum, St. Louis
Bemis Collection, Bemis Family Papers, 1861–65
Civil War Collection
William Carr Lane Collection
Dexter P. Tiffany Civil War Collection
Dexter P. Tiffany Slavery Collection

National Archives and Records Administration, Washington, D.C.
National Archives Microfilm Publication M345: Union Provost Marshal Files Pertaining
    to Individual Citizens, Record Group 109
National Archives Microfilm Publication M416: Union Provost Marshal Files Pertaining
    to Two or More Citizens, Record Group 109
Record Group 15: Records of the Veterans Administration
Record Group 94: Records of the Adjutant General's Office, 1780s–1917
Record Group 107: Records of the Office of the Secretary of War
Record Group 109: War Department Collection of Confederate Records
Record Group 153: Records of the Office of the Judge Advocate General (Army)
Record Group 393: Records of the U.S. Army Continental Commands, 1820–1920

Office of the Secretary of State, Missouri State Archives, Jefferson City
Supreme Court Case Files

St. Louis Circuit Court Historical Records Project, http://www.stlcourtrecords
.wustl.edu/ (accessed September 5, 2014)
Circuit Court Case Files, 1804–75
Criminal Court Record Books, 1831–76
Freedom Suits Case Files, 1814–60
St. Louis County Court Records

Western Historical Manuscript Collection—Columbia, Columbia, Mo.
Folklore Collection

William R. Perkins Library, Duke University, Durham, N.C.
Missouri Militia Papers, 1860–65

PUBLISHED PRIMARY SOURCES

Statutes and Government Reports

"Before Dred Scott: Freedom Suits in Antebellum Missouri." *Missouri State Archives,* http://www.sos.mo.gov/archives/education/aahi/beforedredscott/1824MissouriLaw .asp. Accessed September 1, 2014.

Guy, V. E. "Synoptical Biography of Our Grand Matrons." In *Official Proceedings of the Twenty-Fifth Annual Communication of the Grand Court, Heroines of Jericho for the State of Missouri and Its Jurisdiction.* Sedalia, Mo.: Hodges, 1899.

Jenkins, Ebony. "Freedom Licenses in St. Louis City and County, 1835–1865." N.d. *Jefferson National Expansion Memorial—Freedom Licenses (U.S. National Park Service),* http://www.nps.gov/jeff/historyculture/upload/Freedom%20License%20Report.pdf. Accessed September 1, 2014.

Kennedy, Joseph C. G. *Population of the United States in 1860.* Washington, D.C.: U.S. Government Printing Office, 1864.

Laws of the State of Missouri. "Freedom," sections 1–5, 1824. *Missouri Digital Heritage: Before Dred Scott: Freedom Suits in Antebellum Missouri.* http://www.sos.mo.gov /archives/education/aahi/beforedredscott/1824MissouriLaw.asp. Accessed August 26, 2013.

Laws of the State of Missouri, Fourteenth General Assembly, First Session. Jefferson City: Lusk, 1847.

Laws of the State of Missouri, Passed at the Regular Session of the Twenty-Third General Assembly. Jefferson City: Curry, 1866.

Laws of the State of Missouri, Twelfth General Assembly, First Session. Jefferson City: Lusk, 1843.

Laws of the Territory of Louisiana. Chapter 35, "Freedom," sections 1–5, 1807. *St. Louis Circuit Court Historical Records Project,* http://www.stlcourtrecords.wustl.edu/about -1807-statute.php. Accessed December 16, 2008.

Missouri Revised Statutes. Vol. 1. St. Louis: Dougherty, 1845.

"Police Commissioners' Report." In *Mayor's Message with Accompanying Documents Submitted to the Common Council of the City of Saint Louis, at the Opening of the First Stated Session, May 12, 1862.* St. Louis: Knapp, 1862.

Revised Statutes of the State of Missouri. St. Louis: Argus, 1835.

Revised Statutes of the State of Missouri. Jefferson City: Lusk, 1856.

Revised Statutes of the State of Missouri. Jefferson City: Foster, 1866.

U.S. Bureau of the Census. *Seventh Census of the United States, 1850.* Washington D.C.: National Archives and Records Administration, 1850.

U.S. Congress. *Statutes at Large, Treaties, and Proclamations of the United States of America, from December 5, 1859, to March 3, 1863.* Vol. 12. Boston: Little, Brown, 1863.

Books and Articles

Anderson, Galusha. *The Story of a Border City during the Civil War.* Boston: Little, Brown, 1908.

Bell, Mary A. "She Loves Army Man." In *"Ain't But a Place": An Anthology of African American Writings about St. Louis,* edited by Gerald L. Earley. St. Louis: Missouri Historical Society Press, 1998.

Boernstein, Henry. *Memoirs of a Nobody: The Missouri Years of an Austrian Radical, 1849–1866.* Translated by Steven Rowan. St. Louis: Missouri Historical Society Press, 1987.

Brown, William Wells. *Clotel; or, The President's Daughter*. 1853. Armonk, N.Y.: Sharpe, 1996.

———. *Narrative of William W. Brown, an American Slave, Written by Himself*. Boston: Anti-Slavery Office, 1847. http://docsouth.unc.edu/neh/brown47/menu.html. Accessed August 26, 2013.

Bruce, Henry C. *The New Man: Twenty-Nine Years a Slave, Twenty-Nine Years a Free Man*. 1895. Miami, Fla.: Mnemosyne, 1969.

"Churches." *Kennedy's St. Louis Directory*. St. Louis: Kennedy, 1860.

Clamorgan, Cyprian. *The Colored Aristocracy of St. Louis*. Edited by Julie Winch. 1858. Columbia: University of Missouri Press, 1999.

Delaney, Lucy A. *From the Darkness Cometh the Light; or, Struggles for Freedom*. St. Louis: Smith, 189?. http://docsouth.unc.edu/neh/delaney/menu.html. Accessed August 26, 2013.

Doerschuk, Albert N. "Extracts from War-Time letters, 1861–1864." *Missouri Historical Review* 23, no. 1 (October 1928): 100–101.

Duke, Basil W. *Reminiscences of General Basil W. Duke, C.S.A.* 1911. New York: Cooper Square, 2001.

Earley, Gerald L., ed. *"Ain't but a Place": An Anthology of African American Writings about St. Louis*. St. Louis: Missouri Historical Society Press, 1998.

Forman, Jacob G. *The Western Sanitary Commission: A Sketch*. St. Louis: Studley, 1864.

Frémont, Jessie Benton. *The Letters of Jessie Benton Frémont*. Edited by Pamela Herr and Mary Lee Spence. Urbana: University of Illinois Press, 1993.

———. *The Story of the Guard: A Chronicle of the War*. Boston: Ticknor and Fields, 1863.

"Interview with Betty Abernathy (Ex-Slave)." In *The American Slave: A Composite Autobiography: Arkansas Narratives, Part 7, and Missouri Narratives*, vol. 11, edited by George P. Rawick. Westport, Conn.: Greenwood, 1972.

Keckley, Elizabeth. *Behind the Scenes; or, Thirty Years a Slave, and Four Years in the White House*. 1868. New York: Oxford University Press, 1988.

McKowen, Bethiah P. "Civil War Letters of Bethiah Pyatt McKowen, Part I." Edited by James W. Goodrich. *Missouri Historical Review* 62, no. 2 (January 1973): 227–52.

Mendenhall, Willard Hall. *Missouri Ordeal, 1862–1864: Diaries of Willard Hall Mendenhall*. Edited by Margaret Mendenhall Frazier. Newhall, Calif.: Boyer, 1985.

Napton, William B. *The Union on Trial: The Political Journals of Judge William Barclay Napton, 1829–1882*. Edited by Christopher Phillips and Jason L. Pendleton. Columbia: University of Missouri Press, 2005.

Parsons, Emily. *Memoir of Emily Elizabeth Parsons*. Edited by Theophilus Parsons. Boston: Little, Brown, 1880.

Snead, Thomas L. *The Fight for Missouri: From the Election of Lincoln to the Death of Lyon*. New York: Scribner's, 1886.

Supplement to the Official Records of the Union and Confederate Armies. Wilmington, N.C.: Broadfoot, 1999.

Taylor, Susie King. *A Black Woman's Civil War Memoirs: Reminiscences of My Life in Camp with the 33rd U.S. Colored Troops, Late 1st South Carolina Volunteers*. Edited by Patricia W. Romero. New York: Wiener, 1995.

Thomas, James. *From Tennessee Slave to St. Louis Entrepreneur: The Autobiography of James Thomas*. Edited by Loren Schweninger. Columbia: University of Missouri Press, 1984.

Thompson, L. S. *The Story of Mattie Jackson: Her Parentage, Experience of Eighteen*

Years in Slavery, Incidents during the War, Her Escape from Slavery, a True Story, . . . as Given by Mattie. Lawrence, Mass.: Sentinel, 1866. http://docsouth.unc.edu/neh /jacksonm/menu.html. Accessed August 26, 2013.

U.S. War Department. *The War of the Rebellion: A Compilation of Official Records of the Union and Confederate Armies.* 128 vols. Washington, D.C., 1880–1901.

The Western Sanitary Commission: A Sketch of Its Origin, History, Labors for the Sick and Wounded of the Western Armies, and Aid Given to Freedmen and Union Refugees, with Incidents of Hospital Life. St. Louis: Studley, 1864.

Williams, Andrew. "Narrative of Andrew Williams." In "Civil War on the Kansas-Missouri Border: The Narrative of Former Slave Andrew Williams." Edited by William A. Dobak. *Kansas History* 6, no. 4 (Winter 1983–84), 237–42.

Winter, William C., ed. "'Like Sheep in a Slaughter Pen': A St. Louisan Remembers the Camp Jackson Massacre, May 10, 1861." *Gateway Heritage* 15, no. 4 (Spring 1995): 56–71.

Newspapers

Christian Recorder (Philadelphia)
Colored American (New York)
Daily Missouri Democrat (St. Louis)
Daily Missouri Republican (St. Louis)
Frank Leslie's Illustrated Weekly (New York)
Harper's Weekly (New York)
North Star (Rochester, New York)
St. Louis Daily Evening News
Tri-Weekly Missouri Republican (St. Louis)

SECONDARY SOURCES

Adler, Jeffrey S. *Yankee Merchants and the Making of the Urban West: The Rise and Fall of Antebellum St. Louis.* Cambridge: Cambridge University Press, 1991.

Alexander, Leslie M. *African or American?: Black Identity and Political Activism in New York City, 1784–1861.* Urbana: University of Illinois Press, 2008.

Anderson, Kristen. "German Americans, African Americans, and the Republican Party in St. Louis, 1865–1872." *Journal of American Ethnic History* 28, no. 1 (Fall 2008): 34–51.

Arenson, Adam. *The Great Heart of the Republic: St. Louis and the Cultural Civil War.* Cambridge: Harvard University Press, 2011.

Asen, Robert. "A Discourse Theory of Citizenship." *Quarterly Journal of Speech* 90, no. 2 (2004): 189–211.

Astor, Aaron. *Rebels on the Border: Civil War, Emancipation, and the Reconstruction of Kentucky and Missouri.* Baton Rouge: Louisiana State University Press, 2012.

Bardaglio, Peter W. *Reconstructing the Household: Families, Sex, and the Law in the Nineteenth-Century South.* Chapel Hill: University of North Carolina Press, 1995.

Basch, Norma. *Framing American Divorce: From the Revolutionary Generation to the Victorians.* Berkeley: University of California Press, 1999.

———. *In the Eyes of the Law: Women, Marriage, and Property in Nineteenth-Century New York.* Ithaca: Cornell University Press, 1982.

Basler, Roy P. "And for His Widow and His Orphan." *Quarterly Journal of the Library of Congress* 27, no. 4 (October 1970): 291–94.

Bellamy, Donnie D. "Free Blacks in Antebellum Missouri, 1820–1860." *Missouri Historical Review* 67, no. 2 (January 1973): 198–226.

Benedict, Bryce D. *Jayhawkers: The Civil War Brigade of James Henry Lane.* Norman: University of Oklahoma Press, 2009.

Bennett, Jeffrey A. *Banning Queer Blood: Rhetorics of Citizenship, Contagion, and Resistance.* Tuscaloosa: University of Alabama Press, 2009.

Bensel, Richard Franklin. *Yankee Leviathan: The Origins of Central State Authority in America, 1859–1877.* Cambridge: Cambridge University Press, 1990.

Bentley, George R. *A History of the Freedmen's Bureau.* Philadelphia: University of Pennsylvania, 1955.

Bercaw, Nancy. *Gendered Freedoms: Race, Rights, and the Politics of Household in the Delta, 1861–1875.* Gainesville: University Press of Florida, 2003.

Berlin, Ira. "Who Freed the Slaves?" In *Union and Emancipation: Essays on Politics and Race in the Civil War Era,* edited by David W. Blight and Brooks D. Simpson. Kent, Ohio: Kent State University Press, 1997.

Berlin, Ira, Barbara J. Fields, Thavolia Glymph, Joseph P. Reidy, and Leslie S. Rowland, eds. *The Destruction of Slavery.* Ser. 1, vol. 1 of *Freedom: A Documentary History of Emancipation, 1861–1867.* New York: Cambridge University Press, 1985.

Berlin, Ira, Steven F. Miller, Joseph P. Reidy, and Leslie S. Rowland, eds. *The Wartime Genesis of Free Labor: The Upper South.* Ser. 1, vol. 2, of *Freedom: A Documentary History of Emancipation, 1861–1867.* New York: Cambridge University Press, 1993.

Berlin, Ira, Steven F. Miller, and Leslie S. Rowlands. "Afro-American Families in the Transition from Slavery to Freedom." *Radical History Review* 1988, no. 42 (September 1988): 89–121.

Berlin, Ira, Joseph P. Reidy, and Leslie S. Rowland, eds. *The Black Military Experience.* Ser. 2 of *Freedom: A Documentary History of Emancipation, 1861–1867.* New York: Cambridge University Press, 1982.

Blassingame, John W. "The Recruitment of Negro Troops in Missouri during the Civil War." *Missouri Historical Review* 58, no. 3 (April 1964): 326–38.

———, ed. *Slave Testimony: Two Centuries of Letters, Speeches, Interviews, and Autobiographies.* Baton Rouge: Louisiana State University Press, 1977.

Blight, David W. "No Desperate Hero: Manhood and Freedom in a Union Soldier's Experience." In *Divided Houses: Gender and the Civil War,* edited by Catherine Clinton and Nina Silver. New York: Oxford University Press, 1992.

———. *Race and Reunion: The Civil War in American Memory.* Cambridge: Harvard University Press, 2001.

———. *Slave No More: Two Men Who Escaped to Freedom, Including Their Own Narratives of Emancipation.* Orlando, Fla.: Harcourt, 2007.

Boman, Dennis K. *Lincoln's Resolute Unionist: Hamilton Gamble, Dred Scott Dissenter and Missouri's Civil War Governor.* Baton Rouge: Louisiana State University Press, 2006.

Boris, Eileen. "Citizenship Embodied: Racialized Gender and the Construction of Nationhood in the United States." In *Identity and Intolerance: Nationalism, Racism, and Xenophobia in Germany and the United States,* edited by Norbert Finzsch and Dietmar Schirmer. Washington, D.C.: German Historical Institute; Cambridge: Cambridge University Press, 1998.

Boydston, Jeanne. *Home and Work: Housework, Wages, and the Ideology of Labor in the Early Republic.* New York: Oxford University Press, 1990.

Brimmer, Brandi Clay. "All Her Rights and Privileges: African-American Women and the Politics of Civil War Widows' Pensions." Ph.D. diss., University of California at Los Angeles, 2006.

Briscom, Richard. "Francis Johnson: Philadelphia Bandmaster and Composer." *University of Pennsylvania Almanac* 58, no. 22 (February 14, 2012). http://www.upenn.edu/almanac/volumes/v58/n22/bandmaster.html. Accessed August 28, 2013.

Brockett, L. P. *Woman's Work in the Civil War: A Record of Heroism, Patriotism, and Patience.* Philadelphia: Ziegler, McCurdy, 1867.

Brown, Elsa Barkley. "Negotiating and Transforming the Public Sphere: African American Political Life in the Transition from Slavery to Freedom." *Public Culture* 7, no. 1 (Winter 1994): 107–46.

———. "To Catch the Vision of Freedom: Reconstructing Southern Black Women's Political History, 1865–1880." In *African American Women and the Vote, 1837–1965*, edited by Ann D. Gordon with Bettye Collier-Thomas et al. Amherst: University of Massachusetts Press, 1997.

Buchanan, Thomas C. *Black Life on the Mississippi: Slaves, Free Blacks, and the Western Steamboat World.* Chapel Hill: University of North Carolina Press, 2004.

Bynum, Victoria. *Unruly Women: The Politics of Social and Sexual Control in the Old South.* Chapel Hill: University of North Carolina Press, 1992.

Camp, Stephanie M. H. *Closer to Freedom: Enslaved Women and Everyday Resistance in the Plantation South.* Chapel Hill: University of North Carolina Press, 2004.

———. "The Pleasures of Resistance: Enslaved Women and Body Politics in the Plantation South, 1830–1861." *Journal of Southern History* 68, no. 3 (August 2002): 533–72.

Canning, Kathleen. "The Body as Method?: Reflections on the Place of the Body in Gender History." *Gender and History* 11, no. 3 (November 1999): 499–513.

Canning, Kathleen, and Sonya O. Rose. "Gender, Citizenship, and Subjectivity: Some Historical and Theoretical Considerations." *Gender and History* 13, no. 3 (November 2001): 427–43.

"'Cathy Williams' Story,' as Published in the January 2, 1876 *St. Louis Daily Times*." In Phillip Thomas Tucker. *Cathay Williams: From Slave to Female Buffalo Soldier.* Mechanicsburg, Pa.: Stackpole, 2002.

Catterall, Helen Tunnicliff, and James J. Hayden. *Judicial Cases Concerning American Slavery and the Negro.* Vol. 5, *Cases from the Courts of States North of the Ohio and West of the Mississippi Rivers, Canada, and Jamaica.* Washington, D.C.: Carnegie Institution of Washington, 1937.

Christensen, Lawrence O. "Black St. Louis: A Study in Race Relations, 1865–1916." PhD diss., University of Missouri, 1972.

———. "Race Relations in St. Louis, 1865–1916." *Missouri Historical Review* 78, no. 2 (January 1984): 123–36.

Cimbala, Paul A. *Under the Guardianship of the Nation: The Freedmen's Bureau and the Reconstruction of Georgia, 1865–1870.* Athens: University of Georgia Press, 1997.

Cimprich, John. *Slavery's End in Tennessee, 1861–1865.* Tuscaloosa: University of Alabama Press, 1985.

The Civil War. Directed by Ken Burns. Public Broadcasting Service, 1990.

Clark, Elizabeth B. "'The Sacred Rights of the Weak': Pain, Sympathy, and the Culture of Individual Rights in Antebellum America." *Journal of American History* 82, no. 2 (September 1995): 463–93.

Clinton, Catherine. "Reconstructing Freedwomen." In *Divided Houses: Gender and the Civil War*, edited by Catherine Clinton and Nina Silver. New York: Oxford University Press, 1992.

Coalier, Paula. "Beyond Sympathy: The St. Louis Ladies' Union Aid Society and the Civil War." *Gateway Heritage* 11, no. 1 (Summer 1990): 38–51.

Cohen, William. *At Freedom's Edge: Black Mobility and the Southern White Quest for Racial Control, 1861–1915*. Baton Rouge: Louisiana State University Press, 1991.

Coleman, Willi. "Architects of a Vision: Black Women and Their Antebellum Quest for Political and Social Equality." In *African American Women and the Vote, 1837–1965*, edited by Ann D. Gordon with Bettye Collier-Thomas et al. Amherst: University of Massachusetts Press, 1997.

Corbett, Katharine. "Missouri's Black History: From Colonial Times to 1970." *Gateway Heritage* 4, no. 1 (1983): 16–25.

———. "Refugees of War." In *In Her Place: A Guide to St. Louis Women's History*. St. Louis: Missouri Historical Society Press, 1999.

Cornish, Dudley Taylor. *The Sable Arm: Black Troops in the Union Army, 1861–1865*. 1956. Lawrence: University Press of Kansas, 1987.

Cott, Nancy F. *Public Vows: A History of Marriage and the Nation*. Cambridge: Harvard University Press, 2000.

Cottrol, Robert J. *The Long, Lingering Shadow: Slavery, Race, and Law in the American Hemisphere*. Athens: University of Georgia Press, 2013.

Cullen, Jim. "'I's a Man Now': Gender and African American Men." In *Divided Houses: Gender and the Civil War*, edited by Catherine Clinton and Nina Silver. New York: Oxford University Press, 1992.

Curry, Leonard P. *The Free Black in Urban America, 1800–1850: The Shadow of the Dream*. Chicago: University of Chicago Press, 1981.

Dailey, Jane. *Before Jim Crow: The Politics of Race in Postemancipation Virginia*. Chapel Hill: University of North Carolina Press, 2000.

Day, Judy, and M. James Kedro. "Free Blacks in St. Louis: Antebellum Conditions, Emancipation, and the Postwar Era." *Bulletin of the Missouri Historical Society* 30, no. 2 (January 1974): 117–35.

Dayton, Cornelia Hughes. *Women before the Bar: Gender, Law, and Society in Connecticut, 1639–1789*. Chapel Hill: University of North Carolina Press for the Institute of Early American History and Culture, 1995.

Downs, Jim. "The Other Side of Freedom: Destitution, Disease, and Dependency among Freedwomen and Their Children during and after the Civil War." In *Battle Scars: Gender and Sexuality in the American Civil War*, edited by Catherine Clinton and Nina Silber. Oxford: Oxford University Press, 2006.

———. *Sick from Freedom: African-American Illness and Suffering during the Civil War and Reconstruction*. Oxford: Oxford University Press, 2012.

Du Bois, W. E. B. *Black Reconstruction in America: An Essay toward the Part Which Black Folk Played in the Attempt to Reconstruct Democracy in America, 1860–1880*. New York: Russell and Russell, 1936.

Dunbar, Erica Armstrong. *A Fragile Freedom: African American Women and Emancipation in the Antebellum City*. New Haven: Yale University Press, 2008.

Dwight, Margaret L. "Black Suffrage in Missouri, 1865–1877." PhD diss., University of Missouri, 1978.

Earle, Jonathan, and Diane Mutti Burke, eds. *Bleeding Kansas, Bleeding Missouri: The Long Civil War on the Border.* Lawrence: University Press of Kansas, 2013.

Edwards, Laura F. *Gendered Strife and Confusion: The Political Culture of Reconstruction.* Urbana: University of Illinois Press, 1997.

———. "'The Marriage Covenant Is at the Foundation of All Our Rights': The Politics of Slave Marriages in North Carolina after Emancipation." *Law and History Review* 14, no. 1 (Spring 1996): 81–124.

———. *The People and Their Peace: Legal Culture and the Transformation of Inequality in the Post-Revolutionary South.* Chapel Hill: University of North Carolina Press, 2009.

———. "Status without Rights: African Americans and the Tangled History of Law and Governance in the Nineteenth-Century U.S. South." *American Historical Review* 112, no. 2 (April 2007): 365–93.

Efford, Alison Clark. *German Immigrants: Race, and Citizenship in the Civil War Era.* Cambridge: Cambridge University Press, 2013.

Ehrlich, Walter. *They Have No Rights: Dred Scott's Struggle for Freedom.* Westport, Conn.: Greenwood, 1979.

Eliot, William G. *The Story of Archer Alexander: From Slavery to Freedom, March 30, 1863.* Westport, Conn.: Negro Universities Press, 1970.

Emberton, Carole. "'Only Murder Makes Men': Reconsidering the Black Military Experience." *Journal of the Civil War Era* 2, no. 3 (2012): 369–93.

Farmer-Kaiser, Mary. "'Because They Are Women': Gender and the Virginia Freedmen's Bureau's War on Dependency." In *The Freedmen's Bureau and Reconstruction: Reconsiderations,* edited by Paul A. Cimbala and Randall M. Miller. New York: Fordham University Press, 1999.

———. *Freedwomen and the Freedmen's Bureau: Race, Gender, and Public Policy in the Age of Emancipation.* New York: Fordham University Press, 2010.

Faulkner, Carol. *Women's Radical Reconstruction.* Philadelphia: University of Pennsylvania Press, 2004.

Fede, Andrew. *People without Rights: An Interpretation of the Fundamentals of the Law of Slavery in the U.S. South.* New York: Garland, 1992.

———. *Roadblocks to Freedom: Slavery and Manumission in the United States South.* New Orleans: Quid Pro, 2011.

Fehrenbacher, Don E. *The Dred Scott Case: Its Significance in American Law and Politics.* New York: Oxford University Press, 1978.

Feimster, Crystal N. "General Benjamin Butler and the Threat of Sexual Violence during the American Civil War." *Daedalus* 138 (Spring 2009): 126–34.

———. "Rape and Justice in the Civil War." *New York Times,* April 25, 2013.

Fellman, Michael. "Emancipation in Missouri." *Missouri Historical Review* 83, no. 1 (October 1988): 36–56.

———. *Inside War: The Guerrilla Conflict in Missouri during the American Civil War.* New York: Oxford University Press, 1989.

Fields, Barbara Jeanne. *Slavery and Freedom on the Middle Ground: Maryland during the Nineteenth Century.* New Haven: Yale University Press, 1985.

Finkelman, Paul. *An Imperfect Union: Slavery, Federalism, and Comity.* Chapel Hill: University of North Carolina Press, 1981.

———. "Rehearsal for Reconstruction: Antebellum Origins of the Fourteenth Amendment." In *The Facts of Reconstruction: Essays in Honor of John Hope Franklin,* edited by Eric Anderson and Alfred A. Moss Jr. Baton Rouge: Louisiana State University Press, 1991.

Finkelman, Paul, and Stephen E. Gottlieb. "Introduction: State Constitutions and American Liberties." In *Towards a Usable Past: Liberty under State Constitutions*, edited by Paul Finkelman and Stephen E. Gottlieb. Athens: University of Georgia Press, 2009.

Fisher, H. D. *The Gun and the Gospel: Early Kansas and Chaplain Fisher*. Chicago: Medical Century, 1897.

Fitzgerald, Michael W. "Emancipation and Military Pacification: The Freedmen's Bureau and Social Control in Alabama." In *The Freedmen's Bureau and Reconstruction: Reconsiderations*, edited by Paul A. Cimbala and Randall M. Miller. New York: Fordham University Press, 1999.

———. *Urban Emancipation: Popular Politics in Reconstruction Mobile, 1860–1890*. Baton Rouge: Louisiana State University Press, 2002.

Flores, William V., and Rina Benmayor. "Constructing Cultural Citizenship." In *Latino Cultural Citizenship: Claiming Identity, Space, and Rights*, edited by William V. Flores and Rina Benmayor. Boston: Beacon, 1997.

———. *Latino Cultural Citizenship: Claiming Identity, Space, and Rights*. Boston: Beacon, 1997.

Foner, Eric. *The Fiery Trial: Abraham Lincoln and American Slavery*. New York: Norton, 2010.

———. *Reconstruction: America's Unfinished Revolution, 1863–1877*. New York: Harper and Row, 1988.

Franke, Katherine M. "Becoming a Citizen: Reconstruction Era Regulation of African American Marriage." *Yale Journal of Law and the Humanities* 11 (1999). http://digital commons.law.yale.edu/yjlh/vol11/iss2/2. Accessed September 7, 2014.

Frankel, Noralee. *Freedom's Women: Black Women and Families in Civil War Era Mississippi*. Bloomington: Indiana University Press, 1999.

Fraser, Nancy. "Rethinking the Public Sphere: A Contribution to the Critique of Actually Existing Democracy." In *Habermas and the Public Sphere*, edited by Craig Calhoun, 109–42. Cambridge: MIT Press, 1992.

———. "What's Critical about Critical Theory?: The Case of Habermas and Gender." In *Unruly Practices: Power, Discourse, and Gender in Contemporary Social Theory*. Minneapolis: University of Minnesota Press, 1989.

"Free Men and Women of Color in St. Louis City Directories, 1821–1860." *St. Louis Public Library: Premier Library Sources*, http://previous.slpl.org/libsrc/freemen.htm. Accessed May 30, 2009.

Gallagher, Gary W. *The Union War*. Cambridge: Harvard University Press, 2011.

Gallman, J. Matthew. "'In Your Hands That Musket Means Liberty': African American Soldiers and the Battle of Olustee." In *Wars within a War: Controversy and Conflict over the American Civil War*, edited by Joan Waugh and Gary W. Gallagher. Chapel Hill: University of North Carolina Press, 2009.

———. "Snapshots: Images of Men in the United States Colored Troops." *American Nineteenth Century History* 13, no. 2 (June 2012): 127–51.

Gerteis, Louis S. *The Civil War in Missouri: A Military History*. Columbia: University of Missouri Press, 2012.

———. *Civil War St. Louis*. Lawrence: University Press of Kansas, 2001.

———. "'A Friend of the Enemy': Federal Efforts to Suppress Disloyalty in St. Louis during the Civil War." *Missouri Historical Review* 96, no. 3 (April 2002): 165–87.

———. *From Contraband to Freedman: Federal Policy toward Southern Blacks, 1861–1865.* Westport, Conn.: Greenwood, 1973.

———. "'An Outrage on Humanity': Martial Law and Military Prisons in St. Louis during the Civil War." *Missouri Historical Review* 96, no. 4 (July 2002): 302–22.

Glymph, Thavolia. *Out of the House of Bondage: The Transformation of the Plantation Household.* Cambridge: Cambridge University Press, 2008.

———. "Rose's War and the Gendered Politics of a Slave Insurgency in the Civil War." *Journal of the Civil War Era* 3, no. 4 (December 2013): 501–32.

———. "'This Species of Property': Female Slave Contrabands in the Civil War." In *A Woman's War: Southern Women, Civil War, and the Confederate Legacy*, edited by Edward Campbell and Kym Rice. Charlottesville: University Press of Virginia, 1997.

Goldfield, David R. "Pursuing the American Urban Dream: Cities in the Old South." In *The City in Southern History: The Growth of Urban Civilization in the South*, edited by Blaine A. Brownell and David R. Goldfield. Port Washington, N.Y.: National University Publications, 1977.

Goldin, Claudia Dale. *Urban Slavery in the American South, 1820–1860: A Quantitative History.* Chicago: University of Chicago Press, 1976.

Greene, Lorenzo J., Gary R. Kremer, and Antonio F. Holland. "Slaves without Masters: Free Blacks before the Civil War." In *Missouri's Black Heritage*, rev. ed., edited by Gary R. Kremer and Antonio F. Holland. Columbia: University of Missouri Press, 1993.

———. *Missouri's Black Heritage.* Rev. ed. Edited by Gary R. Kremer and Antonio F. Holland. Columbia: University of Missouri Press, 1993.

Grimsley, Mark. *The Hard Hand of War: Union Military Policy toward Southern Civilians, 1861–1865.* Cambridge: Cambridge University Press, 1995.

Gross, Ariela J. "Beyond Black and White: Cultural Approaches to Race and Slavery." *Columbia Law Review* 101, no. 3 (April 2001): 640–90.

———. *Double Character: Slavery and Master in the Antebellum Southern Courtroom.* Princeton: Princeton University Press, 2000.

Gutman, Herbert G. *The Black Family in Slavery and Freedom, 1750–1925.* New York: Vintage, 1976.

Hadden, Sally E. *Slave Patrols: Law and Violence in Virginia and the Carolinas.* Cambridge: Harvard University Press, 2001.

Hager, Ruth Ann (Abels). *Dred and Harriet Scott: Their Family Story.* St. Louis: St. Louis County Library, 2010.

Hahn, Steven. *A Nation under Our Feet: Black Political Struggles in the Rural South from Slavery to the Great Migration.* Cambridge: Belknap Press of Harvard University Press, 2003.

Harris, Leslie M. *In the Shadow of Slavery: African Americans in New York City, 1626–1863.* Chicago: University of Chicago Press, 2003.

Hartman, Saidiya V. *Scenes of Subjection: Terror, Slavery, and Self-Making in Nineteenth-Century America.* New York: Oxford University Press, 1997.

Hartog, Hendrik. "The Constitution of Aspiration and 'The Rights That Belong to Us All.'" *Journal of American History* 74, no. 3 (December 1987): 1013–34.

Holmes, Amy E. "'Such Is the Price We Pay': American Widows and the Civil War Pension System." In *Toward a Social History of the American Civil War*, edited by Maris A. Vinovskis. Cambridge: Cambridge University Press, 1990.

Huebner, Timothy S. "Roger B. Taney and the Slavery Issue: Looking beyond—and before—Dred Scott." *Journal of American History* 97, no. 1 (June 2010): 17–38.

———. *The Southern Judicial Tradition: State Judges and Sectional Distinctiveness, 1790–1890.* Athens: University of Georgia Press, 1999.

Hunter, Tera W. *To 'Joy My Freedom: Southern Black Women's Lives and Labors after the Civil War.* Cambridge: Harvard University Press, 1993.

Hurt, R. Douglas. *Agriculture and Slavery in Missouri's Little Dixie.* Columbia: University of Missouri Press, 1992.

Hyman, Harold M., and William M. Wiecek. *Equal Justice under Law: Constitutional Development, 1835–1875.* New York: Harper and Row, 1982.

Jack, Bryan M. "Tandy, Charleton (1836–1919)." *BlackPast.org: Remembered and Reclaimed.* http://www.blackpast.org/?q=aah/tandy-charleton-1836-1919. Accessed May 17, 2009.

Johnson, Walter. *River of Dark Dreams: Slavery and Empire in the Cotton Kingdom.* Cambridge: Belknap Press of Harvard University Press, 2013.

———. *Soul by Soul: Life inside the Antebellum Slave Market.* Cambridge: Harvard University Press, 1999.

Jones, Jacqueline. *Labor of Love, Labor of Sorrow: Black Women, Work, and the Family, from Slavery to the Present.* New York: Basic Books, 1985.

———. *Saving Savannah: The City and the Civil War.* New York: Knopf, 2008.

Jones, Martha S. *All Bound Up Together: The Woman Question in African American Public Culture, 1830–1900.* Chapel Hill: University of North Carolina Press, 2007.

———. "Leave of Court: African American Claims-Making in the Era *Dred Scott v. Sanford*." In *Contested Democracy: Freedom, Race and Power in American History,* edited by Manisha Sinha and Penny Von Eschen. New York: Columbia University Press, 2007.

Kantrowitz, Stephen. *More Than Freedom: Fighting for Black Citizenship in a White Republic, 1829–1889.* New York: Penguin, 2012.

Kaufman, Kenneth C. *Dred Scott's Advocate: A Biography of Roswell M. Field.* Columbia: University of Missouri Press, 1996.

Kelley, Robin D. G. *Race Rebels: Culture, Politics, and the Black Working Class.* New York: Free Press, 1994.

Kennedy, Cynthia M. *Braided Relations, Entwined Lives: The Women of Charleston's Urban Slave Society.* Bloomington: Indiana University Press, 2005.

Kennington, Kelly Marie. "River of Injustice: St. Louis Freedom Suits and the Changing Nature of Legal Slavery in Antebellum America." PhD diss., Duke University, 2009.

Kerber, Linda K. "'I Have Don . . . Much to Carrey on the Warr': Women and the Shaping of Republican Ideology after the American Revolution." In *Toward an Intellectual History of Women: Essays by Linda K. Kerber.* Chapel Hill: University of North Carolina Press, 1997.

———. "The Meanings of Citizenship." *Journal of American History* 84, no. 3 (December 1997): 833–54.

———. *No Constitutional Right to Be Ladies: Women and the Obligations of Citizenship.* New York: Hill and Wang, 1998.

———. "The Paradox of Women's Citizenship in the Early Republic: The Case of *Martin vs. Massachusetts*, 1805." *American Historical Review* 97, no. 2 (April 1992): 349–78.

———. "Presidential Address: The Stateless as the Citizen's Other: A View from the United States." *American Historical Review* 112, no. 1 (February 2007): 1–34.

———. "Separate Spheres, Female Worlds, Woman's Place: The Rhetoric of Women's History." *Journal of American History* 75, no. 1 (June 1988): 9–39.

Kettner, James H. *The Development of American Citizenship, 1608–1870.* Chapel Hill: University of North Carolina Press, 1978.

Keyssar, Alexander. *The Right to Vote: The Contested History of Democracy in the United States.* New York: Basic Books, 2000.

Komisaruk, Catherine. *Labor and Love in Guatemala: The Eve of Independence.* Stanford, Calif.: Stanford University Press, 2013.

Kopelson, Heather Miyano. *Faithful Bodies: Performing Religion and Race in the Puritan Atlantic.* New York: New York University Press, 2014.

Kremer, Gary R. *James Milton Turner and the Promise of America: The Public Life of a Post–Civil War Black Leader.* Columbia: University of Missouri Press, 1991.

Levine, Bruce. *The Spirit of 1848: German Immigrants, Labor Conflict, and the Coming of the Civil War.* Urbana: University of Illinois Press, 1992.

Lipsitz, George. *The Sidewalks of St. Louis: Places, People, and Politics in an American City.* Columbia: University of Missouri Press, 1991.

Litwack, Leon F. *Been in the Storm So Long: The Aftermath of Slavery.* New York: Knopf, 1979.

———. *North of Slavery: The Negro in the Free States, 1790–1860.* Chicago: University of Chicago Press, 1961.

Low, W. A. "The Freedmen's Bureau in the Border States." In *Radicalism, Racism, and Party Realignment: The Border States during Reconstruction*, edited by Richard O. Curry. Baltimore: Johns Hopkins Press, 1969.

Masur, Kate. *An Example for All the Land: Emancipation and the Struggle over Equality in Washington D.C.* Chapel Hill: University of North Carolina Press, 2010.

———. "'A Rare Phenomenon of Philological Vegetation': The Word 'Contraband' and the Meanings of Emancipation in the United States." *Journal of American History* 93, no. 4 (March 2007): 1050–84.

Masur, Louis P. *Lincoln's Hundred Days: The Emancipation Proclamation and the War for the Union.* Cambridge: Belknap Press of Harvard University Press, 2012.

McClintock, Megan J. "Civil War Pensions and the Reconstruction of Union Families." *Journal of American History* 83, no. 2 (September 1996): 456–80.

McCurry, Stephanie. "The Two Faces of Republicanism: Gender and Proslavery Politics in Antebellum South Carolina." *Journal of American History* 78 (March 1992): 1245–64.

McFeely, William S. *Yankee Stepfather: General O. O. Howard and the Freedmen.* New Haven: Yale University Press, 1968.

McKerley, John W. "Citizens and Strangers: The Politics of Race in Missouri from Slavery to the Era of Jim Crow." PhD diss., University of Iowa, 2008.

———. "'Good Laws' and 'Unfriendly Legislation': Race and the Limits of the Law in Postemancipation Missouri." Paper presented at the Society of Civil War Historians Conference, Richmond, Virginia, June 19, 2010.

———. "The Heroines of Jericho: Women's Voluntary Associations and Social Reform in Gilded Age Missouri." Paper presented at Southern Association of Women Historians Conference, Ft. Worth, June 9, 2012.

———. "'We Promise to Use the Ballot as We Did the Bayonet': Black Suffrage Activism and the Limits of Loyalty in Reconstruction Missouri." In *Bleeding Kansas, Bleeding Missouri: The Long Civil War on the Border*, edited by Jonathan Earle and Diane Mutti Burke. Lawrence: University Press of Kansas, 2013.

McLaurin, Melton A. *Celia, a Slave.* Athens: University of Georgia Press, 1991.

Mezey, Naomi. "Law as Culture." In *Cultural Analysis, Cultural Studies, and the Law:*

Moving Beyond Legal Realism, edited by Austin Sarat and Jonathan Simon. Durham, N.C.: Duke University Press, 2003.

Moore, Robert, Jr. "A Ray of Hope Extinguished: St. Louis Slave Suits for Freedom." *Gateway Heritage* 14, no. 3 (Winter 1993–94): 4–15.

Morgan, Jennifer L. *Laboring Women: Reproduction and Gender in New World Slavery.* Philadelphia: University of Pennsylvania Press, 2004.

Morris, Thomas D. "Equality, 'Extraordinary Law,' and Criminal Justice: The South Carolina Experience." *South Carolina Historical Magazine* 83 (January 1982): 15–33.

———. *Free Men All: The Personal Liberty Laws of the North, 1780–1861.* Baltimore: Johns Hopkins University Press, 1974.

———. *Southern Slavery and the Law, 1619–1860.* Chapel Hill: University of North Carolina Press, 1996.

Mutti Burke, Diane. *On Slavery's Border: Missouri's Small-Slaveholding Households, 1815–1865.* Athens: University of Georgia Press, 2010.

———. "'Slavery Dies Hard': Enslaved Missourians' Struggle for Freedom." In *Bleeding Kansas, Bleeding Missouri: The Long Civil War on the Border*, edited by Jonathan Earle and Diane Mutti Burke. Lawrence: University Press of Kansas, 2013.

Myers, Amrita Chakrabarti. *Forging Freedom: Black Women and the Pursuit of Liberty in Antebellum Charleston.* Chapel Hill: University of North Carolina Press, 2011.

Neely, Jeremy. *The Border between Them: Violence and Reconciliation on the Kansas-Missouri Line.* Columbia: University of Missouri Press, 2007.

Neely, Mark E., Jr. *The Fate of Liberty: Abraham Lincoln and Civil Liberties.* New York: Oxford University Press, 1991.

Nieman, Donald G. "The Language of Liberation: African Americans and Equalitarian Constitutionalism." In *The Constitution, Law, and American Life: Critical Aspects of the Nineteenth-Century*, edited by Donald G. Nieman. Athens: University of Georgia Press, 1992.

———. *To Set the Law in Motion: The Freedmen's Bureau and the Legal Rights of Blacks, 1865–1868.* Millwood, N.Y.: KTO, 1979.

Novak, William J. "The Legal Transformation of Citizenship in Nineteenth-Century America." In *The Democratic Experiment: New Directions in American Political History*, edited by Meg Jacobs, William J. Novak, and Julian E. Zelizer. Princeton: Princeton University Press, 2003.

Nystrom, Justin A. *New Orleans after the Civil War: Race, Politics, and a New Birth of Freedom.* Baltimore: Johns Hopkins University Press, 2010.

Oakes, James. *Freedom National: The Destruction of Slavery in the United States, 1861–1865.* New York: Norton, 2013.

O'Donovan, Susan Eva. *Becoming Free in the Cotton South.* Cambridge: Harvard University Press, 2007.

Parrish, William E. *Frank Blair: Lincoln's Conservative.* Columbia: University of Missouri Press, 1998.

———. *A History of Missouri, 1860–1875.* Vol. 3. Columbia: University of Missouri Press, 1973.

———. *Missouri under Radical Rule, 1865–1870.* Columbia: University of Missouri Press, 1965.

———. "Reconstruction Politics in Missouri, 1865–1870." In *Radicalism, Racism, and Party Realignment: The Border States during Reconstruction*, edited by Richard O. Curry. Baltimore: Johns Hopkins Press, 1969.

———. *Turbulent Partnership: Missouri and the Union, 1861–1865.* Columbia: University of Missouri Press, 1963.

——. "The Western Sanitary Commission." *Civil War History* 36, no. 1 (March 1990): 17–35.

Pateman, Carole. *The Sexual Contract*. Stanford: Stanford University Press, 1988.

Penningroth, Dylan C. *The Claims of Kinfolk: African American Property and Community in the Nineteenth-Century South*. Chapel Hill: University of North Carolina Press, 2003.

Phillips, Christopher. *Damned Yankee: The Life of General Nathaniel Lyon*. Columbia: University of Missouri Press, 1990.

——. *Missouri's Confederate: Claiborne Fox Jackson and the Creation of Southern Identity in the Border West*. Columbia: University of Missouri Press, 2000.

——. "'A Question of Power Not One of Law': Federal Occupation and the Politics of Loyalty in the Western Border Slave States during the American Civil War." In *Bleeding Kansas, Bleeding Missouri: The Long Civil War on the Border*, edited by Jonathan Earle and Diane Mutti Burke. Lawrence: University Press of Kansas, 2013.

Pitts, Yvonne. *Family, Law, and Inheritance in America: A Social and Legal History of Nineteenth-Century Kentucky*. Cambridge: Cambridge University Press, 2013.

Primm, James Neal. *Lion of the Valley: St. Louis, Missouri*. Boulder, Colo.: Pruett, 1981.

Rabinowitz, Howard N. "Continuity and Change: Southern Urban Development, 1860–1900." In *The City in Southern History: The Growth of Urban Civilization in the South*, edited by Blaine A. Brownell and David R. Goldfield. Port Washington, N.Y.: National University Publications, 1977.

Randall, James G. *Constitutional Problems under Lincoln*. Rev. ed. Urbana: University of Illinois Press, 1964.

Regosin, Elizabeth. *Freedom's Promise: Ex-Slave Families and Citizenship in the Age of Emancipation*. Charlottesville: University Press of Virginia, 2002.

Reid, Richard. *Freedom for Themselves: Black North Carolina Soldiers and Their Families in the Civil War*. Chapel Hill: University of North Carolina Press, 2008.

Richardson, Joe M. "The American Missionary Association and Black Education in Civil War Missouri." *Missouri Historical Review* 69, no. 4 (July 1975): 433–48.

Roach, Joseph. *Cities of the Dead: Circum-Atlantic Performance*. New York: Columbia University Press, 1996.

Rockman, Seth. *Scraping By: Wage Labor, Slavery, and Survival in Early Baltimore*. Baltimore: Johns Hopkins University Press, 2009.

Rombauer, Robert J. *The Union Cause in St. Louis in 1861: An Historical Sketch*. St. Louis: Nixon-Jones, 1909.

Rosaldo, Renato. "Cultural Citizenship, Inequality, and Multiculturalism." In *Latino Cultural Citizenship: Claiming Identity, Space, and Rights*, edited by William V. Flores and Rina Benmayor. Boston: Beacon, 1997.

Rose, Willie Lee. *Rehearsal for Reconstruction: The Port Royal Experiment*. London: Oxford University Press, 1964.

Rosen, Hannah. "The Rhetoric of Miscegenation and the Reconstruction of Race: Debating Marriage, Sex, and Citizenship in Postemancipation Arkansas." In *Gender and Slave Emancipation in the Atlantic World*, edited by Pamela Scully and Diana Paton. Durham, N.C.: Duke University Press, 2005.

——. *Terror in the Heart of Freedom: Citizenship, Sexual Violence, and the Meaning of Race in the Postemancipation South*. Chapel Hill: University of North Carolina Press, 2009.

Rowan, Steven, ed. *Germans for a Free Missouri: Translations from the St. Louis Radical Press, 1857–1862*. Columbia: University of Missouri Press, 1983.

Ryan, Mary P. *Civil Wars: Democracy and Public Life in the American City during the Nineteenth Century.* Berkeley: University of California Press, 1997.

———. *Women in Public: Between Banners and Ballots, 1825–1880.* Baltimore: Johns Hopkins University Press, 1990.

Saldívar, José David. *Border Matters: Remapping American Cultural Studies.* Berkeley: University of California Press, 1997.

Samito, Christian G. *Becoming American under Fire: Irish Americans, African Americans, and the Politics of Citizenship during the Civil War Era.* Ithaca: Cornell University Press, 2009.

Saville, Julie. *The Work of Reconstruction: From Slave to Wage Laborer in South Carolina, 1860–1870.* Cambridge: Cambridge University Press, 1994.

Saxton, Martha. "City Women: Slavery and Resistance in Antebellum St. Louis." In *Contested Democracy: Freedom, Race, and Power in American History*, edited by Manisha Sinha and Penny Von Eschen. New York: Columbia University Press, 2007.

Schafer, Judith Kelleher. *Becoming Free, Remaining Free: Manumission and Enslavement in New Orleans, 1846–1862.* Baton Rouge: Louisiana State University Press, 2003.

Scharf, J. Thomas. *History of Saint Louis City and County, from the Earliest Periods to the Present Day: Including Biographical Sketches of Representative Men.* Vol. 1. Philadelphia: Everts, 1883.

Schreck, Kimberly. "Her Will against Theirs: Eda Hickam and the Ambiguity of Freedom in Postbellum Missouri." In *Beyond Image and Convention: Explorations in Southern Women's History*, edited by Janet L. Coryell, Martha H. Swain, Sandra Gioia Treadway, and Elizabeth Hayes Turner. Columbia: University of Missouri Press, 1998.

Schultz, Jane E. *Women at the Front: Hospital Workers in Civil War America.* Chapel Hill: University of North Carolina Press, 2004.

Schwalm, Leslie A. *Emancipation's Diaspora: Race and Reconstruction in the Upper Midwest.* Chapel Hill: University of North Carolina Press, 2009.

———. *A Hard Fight for We: Women's Transition from Slavery to Freedom in South Carolina.* Urbana: University of Illinois Press, 1997.

———. "'Overrun with Free Negroes': Emancipation and Wartime Migration in the Upper Midwest." *Civil War History* 50, no. 2 (June 2004): 145–74.

———. "Surviving Wartime Emancipation: African Americans and the Cost of Civil War." *Journal of Law, Medicine, and Ethics* 39, no. 1 (Spring 2011): 21–27.

Scott, Rebecca J. *Degrees of Freedom: Louisiana and Cuba after Slavery.* Cambridge: Belknap Press of Harvard University Press, 2005.

Scott, Rebecca J., and Jean M. Hébrard. *Freedom Papers: An Atlantic Odyssey in the Age of Emancipation.* Cambridge: Harvard University Press, 2012.

Seematter, Mary E. "Trials and Confessions: Race and Justice in Antebellum St. Louis." *Gateway Heritage* 12, no. 2 (Fall 1991): 36–47.

Siddali, Silvana R. *From Property to Person: Slavery and the Confiscation Acts, 1861–1862.* Baton Rouge: Louisiana State University Press, 2005.

Skocpol, Theda. *Protecting Soldiers and Mothers: The Political Origins of Social Policy in the United States.* Cambridge: Harvard University Press, 1992.

Slap, Andrew L. *The Doom of Reconstruction: The Liberal Republican Movement in the Civil War Era.* New York: Fordham University Press, 2006.

Smith-Rosenberg, Carroll. "Dis-Covering the Subject of thse 'Great Constitutional Discussion,' 1786–1789." *Journal of American History* 79, no. 3 (December 1992): 841–73.

Somers, Margaret R. "Citizenship and the Place of the Public Sphere, Law, Community and Popular Culture in the Transition to Democracy." *American Sociological Review* 58, no. 5 (October 1993): 589, 610–11.

Stanley, Amy Dru. "Conjugal Bonds and Wage Labor: Rights of Contract in the Age of Emancipation." *Journal of American History* 75, no. 2 (September 1988): 471–500.

————. *From Bondage to Contract: Wage Labor, Marriage, and the Market in the Age of Slave Emancipation.* Cambridge: Cambridge University Press, 1998.

Steedman, Marek. "Gender and the Politics of the Household in Reconstruction Louisiana, 1865–1878." In *Gender and Slave Emancipation in the Atlantic World,* edited by Pamela Scully and Diana Paton. Durham, N.C.: Duke University Press, 2005.

Steinfeld, Robert J. *Coercion, Contract, and Free Labor in the Nineteenth Century.* Cambridge: Cambridge University Press, 2001.

Stevens, George E. *A History of Central Baptist Church.* St. Louis: King, 1927.

Stevenson, Brenda E. "Black Family Structure in Colonial and Antebellum Virginia: Amending the Revisionist Perspective." In *The Decline in Marriage among African Americans: Causes, Consequences, and Policy Implications,* edited by M. Belinda Tucker and Claudia Mitchell-Kernan. New York: Sage, 1995.

————. *Life in Black and White: Family and Community in the Slave South.* New York: Oxford University Press, 1996.

Stryker, Susan. *Transgender History.* Berkeley, Calif.: Seal, 2008.

Sumler-Edmond, Janice. "The Quest for Justice: African American Women Litigants, 1867–1890." In *African American Women and the Vote, 1837–1965,* edited by Ann D. Gordon with Bettye Collier-Thomas et al. Amherst: University of Massachusetts Press, 1997.

Sutherland, Daniel E. *A Savage Conflict: The Decisive Role of Guerrillas in the American Civil War.* Chapel Hill: University of North Carolina Press, 2009.

Tanner, Henry. *The Martyrdom of Lovejoy . . .* Chicago: Fergus, 1881.

Taylor, Diana. *The Archive and the Repertoire: Performing Cultural Memory in the Americas.* Durham, N.C.: Duke University Press, 2003.

Terborg-Penn, Rosalyn. *African American Women in the Struggle for the Vote, 1850–1920.* Bloomington: Indiana University Press, 1998.

Tomlins, Christopher. *Freedom Bound: Law, Labor, and Civic Identity in Colonizing English America, 1580–1865.* Cambridge: Cambridge University Press, 2010.

Towers, Frank. *The Urban South and the Coming of the Civil War.* Charlottesville: University of Virginia Press, 2004.

Trabscott, Robert W. "Elijah Parish Lovejoy: Portrait of a Radical, the St. Louis Years, 1827–1835." *Gateway Heritage* 8, no. 3 (Winter 1987–88): 32–39.

Trexler, Harrison Anthony. *Slavery in Missouri, 1804–1865.* 1914. In *Slavery in the States: Selected Essays.* New York: Negro Universities Press, 1969.

Tucker, Phillip Thomas. *Cathay Williams: From Slave to Female Buffalo Soldier.* Mechanicsburg, Pa.: Stackpole, 2002.

Tushnet, Mark V. *The American Law of Slavery, 1810–1860.* Princeton: Princeton University Press, 1981.

Vagts, Detlev F. "Military Commissions: The Forgotten Reconstruction Chapter." *American University International Law Review* 23, no. 2 (2008): 231–74.

Valerio-Jiménez, Omar S. *River of Hope: Forging Identity and Nation in the Rio Grande Borderlands.* Durham, N.C.: Duke University Press, 2013.

VanderVelde, Lea. *Mrs. Dred Scott: A Life on Slavery's Frontier.* New York: Oxford University Press, 2010.

VanderVelde, Lea, and Sandhya Subramanian. "Mrs. Dred Scott." *Yale Law Journal* 106, no. 4 (January 1997): 1033–1122.

Voegeli, V. Jacque, *Free but Not Equal: The Midwest and the Negro during the Civil War.* Chicago: University of Chicago Press, 1967.

Volpe, Vernon L. "The Frémonts and Emancipation in Missouri." *Historian* 56, no. 2 (Winter 1994): 330–54.

Vorenberg, Michael. "Citizenship and the Thirteenth Amendment: Understanding the Deafening Silence." In *The Promises of Liberty: The History and Contemporary Relevance of the Thirteenth Amendment,* edited by Alexander Tsesis. New York: Columbia University Press, 2010.

———. *Final Freedom: The Civil War, the Abolition of Slavery, and the Thirteenth Amendment.* Cambridge: Cambridge University Press, 2001.

———. "Reconstruction as a Constitutional Crisis." In *Reconstructions: New Perspectives on the Postbellum United States,* edited by Thomas J. Brown. Oxford: Oxford University Press, 2006.

Wade, Richard C. *Slavery in the Cities: The South, 1820–1860.* New York: Oxford University Press, 1967.

Wagner, Allen E. *Good Order and Safety: A History of the St. Louis Metropolitan Police Department 1861–1906.* St. Louis: Missouri History Museum, 2008.

Webb, W. L. *Battles and Biographies of Missourians; or, The Civil War Period of Our State.* Kansas City: Hudson-Kimberley, 1900.

Welke, Barbara Y. *Recasting American Liberty: Gender, Race, Law, and the Railroad Revolution, 1865–1920.* Cambridge: Cambridge University Press, 2001.

———. "When All the Women Were White and All the Blacks Were Men: Gender, Class, Race, and the Road to Plessy, 1855–1914." *Law and History Review* 13, no. 2 (Fall 1995): 261–316.

West, Isaac. *Transforming Citizenships: Transgender Articulations of the Law.* New York: New York University Press, 2014.

White, Deborah Gray. *Ar'n't I a Woman?: Female Slaves in the Plantation South.* Rev. ed. New York: Norton, 1999.

Whites, LeeAnn. *Gender Matters: Civil War, Reconstruction, and the Making of the New South.* New York: Palgrave Macmillan, 2005.

Winch, Julie. Introduction to Cyprian Clamorgan, *The Colored Aristocracy of St. Louis.* Edited by Julie Winch. Columbia: University of Missouri Press, 1999.

Winter, William C. *The Civil War in St. Louis: A Guided Tour.* St. Louis: Missouri Historical Society Press, 1994.

Witt, John Fabian. *Lincoln's Code: The Laws of War in American History.* New York: Free Press, 2012.

Wright, John A., Sr. *No Crystal Stair: The Story of Thirteen Afro-Americans Who Once Called St. Louis Home.* Florissant, Mo.: Ferguson-Florissant School District, 1988.

Zipf, Karen L. *Labor of Innocents: Forced Apprenticeship in North Carolina, 1715–1919.* Baton Rouge: Louisiana State University Press, 2005.

Zucker, A. E., ed. *The Forty-Eighters: Political Refugees of the German Revolution of 1848.* New York: Columbia University Press, 1950.

Index